Earth to Tables Legacies

Earth to Tables Legacies

Multimedia Food Conversations across Generations and Cultures

Deborah Barndt, Lauren E. Baker, and Alexandra Gelis

with the Earth to Tables Legacies Collaborators

Foreword by Robin Wall Kimmerer

ROWMAN & LITTLEFIELD

Lanham • Boulder • New York • London

Published by Rowman & Littlefield
An imprint of The Rowman & Littlefield Publishing Group, Inc.
4501 Forbes Boulevard, Suite 200, Lanham, Maryland 20706
www.rowman.com

86-90 Paul Street, London EC2A 4NE

www.earthtotables.org

British Library Cataloguing in Publication Information Available

Library of Congress Cataloging-in-Publication Data
Names: Barndt, Deborah, author. | Baker, Lauren E., author. | Gelis, Alexandra, 1975– author.
Title: Earth to tables legacies : multimedia food conversations across generations and cultures /
    Deborah Barndt, Lauren E. Baker, Alexandra Gelis.
Other titles: Multimedia food conversations across generations and cultures
Description: Lanham, Maryland: Rowman & Littlefield [2022] | Includes bibliographical references and index.
Identifiers: LCCN 2021062448 (print) | LCCN 2021062449 (ebook) | ISBN 9781538123485 (cloth) |
    ISBN 9781538123492 (paperback) | ISBN 9781538123508 (epub)
Subjects: LCSH: Food sovereignty. | Food security. | Food supply. | Human-plant relationships.
Classification: LCC HD9000.5 .B3234 2022 (print) | LCC HD9000.5 (ebook) | DDC 338.1/9—dc23/eng/20220112
LC record available at https://lccn.loc.gov/2021062448
LC ebook record available at https://lccn.loc.gov/2021062449

Printed in China

CONTENTS

In memory of
Gustavo Esteva, Cristina Lombana Ochoa,
Travis A. Hill, Brianna Sarita Lozano, and Wayne Roberts

FOREWORD

Robin Wall Kimmerer

On this sleety morning, in the short days of the second pandemic winter I sit by the woodstove shelling beans, feeling as gray as the day. My mental diet has been too high in news of melting glaciers, eroding soils and climate catastrophe which has left me feeling depleted. So , in keeping with our ancestors' reminder that Food is Medicine, I'm going to stir up a remedy, *manoomin mbop*, from the medicine cabinet aka my pantry. In our Potawatomi language we refer to the plants, the ones who take care of us as *Mshkikin*, or Medicine. All of the plants—trees, berries, grasses, herbs, mosses—are understood as medicines. And when that word is opened up, we see that *Mshkikin* means "the strength of the earth." To speak of medicine, we are actually saying that he/she is being healed by the strength of the earth. When we fill our plates, and close our eyes for a minute, breathing in the aroma of goodness we know that our plate is filled by all those who make the strength of the Earth . . . the growers, the swimmers, the pollinators,

the birds who carried the seeds, the endless microbes of the living soil, the pure water, the sweet air, all of these combine to create the contents of our bowl. We are nourished and healed by the strength of the earth for which our first response is gratitude. I offer up my great thanks for the creators of this book and all of the beings whose stories can be found there. The power of gratitude to celebrate earthly gifts and acknowledge one another suffuses the book from Chandra Maracle and Ryan DeCaire's teachings of the Thanksgiving Address to a photo essay of altars decked with cherished cultural foods.

I imagine that you too need nourishment, and you hold it here in your hands. This wonderful book is as restorative as simmering soup, be it green chile posole, moose stew, or Haudenosaunee corn soup. To call this a book is not accurate, as it is so much more, a multimedia conversation around food, carefully crafted with respect for a cross-cultural and intergenerational collaboration. Lovingly co-created by

a team of growers, gatherers, activists, teachers and cooks, this diverse collection of video, lessons, portraits and practices spreads out like a welcoming feast. You will have fine company with whom to share the table; elders and knowledge holders, teachers, farmers, medicine makers, and most of all good storytellers. The wealth of resources provided here is a treasure for listeners and learners at all stages of the journey toward restoring relationship with the land, through the food on our plates.

Dipping into the offerings, feels a bit like gathering around a well-provisioned table to share food and stories. I'm reminded of the opening to Joy Harjo's poem "Perhaps the World Ends Here":

The world begins at a kitchen table. No matter what, we must eat to live.
The gifts of earth are brought and prepared, set on the table.
So, it has been since creation, and it will go on.

As I rinse the *manoomin*, I can smell the marsh and the rice-camp fires and almost hear the laughter between canoes. I feel better already remembering the love my Ojibwe friends put into knocking, parching and dancing this rice that ends up in my bowl. It is savory with garlic and onions and a hefty handful of powdered leeks that I gathered last spring. *G'chi megwech mshkikinek*, great thanks to the medicines.

Good soup takes care, with the richness of the broth and the diversity of the ingredients, and this collection emulates that same attentiveness. I was especially moved by the care and compassion, the mutual respect that underpins the collaboration, with respectful dialogues across ways of knowing, language and the political landscape of food sovereignty. It is multilayered, so that users of the rich materials can just taste or dig deeper. The depth of thought about process as well as product is extraordinary and serves as a model for cross-cultural collaboration and mutual learning.

A bowl of soup may seem like a simple thing, but it steams at the center of a whole web of relationships that are celebrated in these pages. Food is the connecting place for the material strands of our lives, nutrition, health, economics, ecology as well as the intangible emotional and spiritual nourishment it provides. Food links us intimately to our families, to our culture, our history, our language, to the plants, the animals—indeed, food is one of our primary connections to Shkaakmikwe, our Mother Earth, who provides us with all that we need to live: with good food, with medicines, with teachers, with beauty. What are termed "natural resources" or "food commodities" in western society are understood here in a traditional sense as gifts, the gifts from Mother Earth. Every time we fill our plates we are beneficiaries of the gifts of the earth. And the choices we make have consequences that connect to every thread in the web of food relationships.

And as humans, we know how to respond to gifts: we say thank you and then we are called to reciprocity, to give back our gifts in return. This collection is infused with responsibility for reciprocity, addressing how we care for the ones who feed us, by tending to soil, to seeds, to water, to communities and to the sources of knowledge that enable food cultures to thrive. This reciprocity can take the form of restoration—of bringing back the soil, the seeds, the knowledge and the ethics as well as by restoring right relationship between land and peoples.

As I stir my pot, I think about how my language thrives in a bowl of wild rice soup, as I invoke *jiman the canoe, mbes* the lake, and the winnowing tray, *boshkangen*. Stories season the broth. With this soup I thank my ancestors for passing on this knowledge, recall the ducks who taught us how to cook it, and give honor to the prophets who led our people to "the place where the food grows on the water." All of this is held in a bowl of soup. The intersection of food, language, and culture is at the heart of this project. Among the collaborators we hear stories in six different languages—Mohawk, P'urepecha, Mayan, French, Spanish, and English—weaving together. Language sings through this collection. One teacher, Mohawk professor Ryan DeCaire, reminds us that food and language are inseparable, that "People revitalize a language but really a language revitalizes a people. And food revitalizes a people."

Whether the focus is an urban garden in Oaxaca, white corn in Mohawk farms or beets in Ontario soils, all of the stories are permeated with gratitude, with love and respect for the land and the lives who care for us. Each storyteller conveys in their own way the surety that the land loves and cares for us, through the generosity of the plants.

When I finally sit down to my bowl of *manoomin mbop* and taste that first spoonful, there is a kind of relief in my body and mind, that says, "Yes, this is what I needed." It is medicine. I feel nourished by the strength of the earth, in every way. I am fed in a way that a can of soup from the store could never rival, because this soup, like every food described here, is alive. As the stories in this collection attest, we make our food, and our food makes us.

Ancestral food from our homeplaces also strengthens identity. We are fed by the presence of our ancestors; their struggles and triumphs flow from the food into us, making us remember who we are, where and who we stand for. A strong identity is a powerful inoculation against the forces of homogenization that threaten food systems and cultures alike. One of the joys of this book is to visit with folks whose identity shines through in their commitments. I feel stronger for knowing of their presence in the world. A hallmark of the food sovereignty movement is the sharing of food. Righteous food strengthens our relationship to land, helps us love it more and defend it more fiercely.

Harjo's poem goes on to remind us that a lot of hard things happen at the kitchen table, too, with the line,

"Wars have begun and ended at this table." This book does not shy away from the forces that can divide us and devotes thoughtful sections to seeing and exploring those tensions across language, ways of knowing, colonial history, economics, class and culture. The conversation and shared experience of hands in the soil between settler and Indigenous farmers is medicine, too.

These stories of nurture are also stories of resistance and resilience, restoring foodways against all odds. In total, the collection challenges the colonial industrial system of food production and shares the teachings that enable us to imagine and implement a new/ancient relationship with the land, one of mutual nourishing, of reciprocity. A delight for me of the project is that, through facilitator's guides, it invites us all to the table, to be part of a conversation, of mutual unlearning and learning across difference that takes attention, intention, and participation, so that we remember that we know much more together than we do apart.

The care in creation of this story collection is also visible in the framework which is created by its thoughtful title. We often encounter the phrase "Farm to Table" as an emblem of the local food movement, which has been

transforming public awareness and appreciation of where our food comes from. But this title, *Earth to Tables Legacies*, asks us to expand our view, beyond the farm to Mother Earth as the ultimate source of nourishment, from food, to water, air and the music of birdsong and frogs, which is also medicine. It reminds us that Earth is home to more than just humans, that we are all connected and that all flourishing is mutual. We cannot be well if the soil is unhealthy, if the bees disappear and the rain goes away. It is an invitation to consider our role in tending to the Earth with the same loving care for the future that is given to a garden. And the addition of a single letter, from Table to Tables, opens up the mind to the great plurality of tables that are provisioned by the Earth. This book allows us to sit for a moment, savoring the tastes and stories at other tables, which are different than ours and yet deeply the same.

The presence of those plural tables conjures the image of the Great Dish with One Spoon, a teaching shared here by collaborator Rick Hill. This symbol of the Earth feeding us all from the same bowl is the foundation of ancient treaty agreements, including a treaty between my Haudenosaunee neighbors and my Anishinaabe ancestors, wherein the

I hold my bowl of soup in gratitude and think of the haunting last lines of Harjo's powerful poem:

At this table we sing with joy, with sorrow.
    We pray of suffering and remorse. We
    give thanks.
Perhaps the world will end at the kitchen
    table, while we are laughing and crying,
    eating of the last sweet bite.

My hope is that the teachings shared in this collection will be a dose of *Mshkikin*, that helps to keep the Dish full, the Spoon shared and the world whole and green.

Robin Wall Kimmerer is a mother, scientist, decorated professor, and enrolled member of the Citizen Potawatomi Nation. She is the author of Braiding Sweetgrass: Indigenous Wisdom, Scientific Knowledge and the Teachings of Plants *and* Gathering Moss: A Natural and Cultural History of Mosses. *She lives in Syracuse, New York, where she is a SUNY Distinguished Teaching Professor of Environmental Biology and the founder and director of the Center for Native Peoples and the Environment.*

people acknowledge that the gifts of the Earth are to be shared. There is only one Dish and only one Spoon, the same size for everyone. It is a statement about making justice. It also recognizes, that like every bowl, it is finite. When it's empty, it's empty. The people agree to keep that bowl full, to share its gifts and to keep it clean. This also embodies an even larger agreement, not only among people, but between people and the Earth, an agreement that as the Earth cares for us, we will care for her, in the covenant of reciprocity.

But don't say in the years to come that you would have lived your life differently if only you had heard this story. You've heard it now.

—Cherokee writer Thomas King,
The Truth About Stories[1]

Naming the Moment

At the time of this writing, early 2022, we are grappling with a global pandemic and its impacts. COVID-19 has simultaneously locked us down and woken us up. Perhaps the only certainty is that we live with perpetual uncertainty. We do not know what our lives will look like when this book is released, or three or five years in the future.

Food provides a lens for reflecting on the rapidly shifting state of the Earth and all our relations—ecological, political, economic, cultural, spiritual. Most of us, the collaborators involved in the Earth to Tables Legacies project, have been engaged for decades in challenging the global food system and in creating alternatives that are more sustainable, healthy, and just. We know, as Antonio Gramsci suggested a century ago, that we need to regularly assess the forces, or "name the moment,"[2] as both constraints and possibilities for food system transformation constantly change.

The Moment Exposes an Unsustainable and Unjust Food System

The global health crisis lays bare the corporate-controlled industrial food system and sheds new light on the ways that Indigenous peoples sustainably fed themselves over millennia.[3] In the midst of COVID-19, eaters facing food scarcity understood in their bellies our dependence on a global supply chain built on intense fossil fuel use, toxic agrochemicals, the migrant labor of Black and Brown bodies and the consumption of heavily processed foods.[4] It became clear that market-driven global agriculture bears heavy responsibility for the climate crisis, from deforestation and water-intensive monoculture production to factory-farmed meat and depleted soil.[5] Deeply rooted inequities have been sharpened,[6] as racialized essential workers, poor neighborhoods with food insecurity and inadequate housing, and multigenerational households in both the Global North and the Global South suffered the most deaths from the coronavirus and received fewer vaccines.[7] Women bore major responsibility for managing the quarantined household, feeding the family, and homeschooling their children, often losing their place in the official labor market. The deep impacts of the pandemic, combined with increasing awareness of deep structural inequities, meant that the terms "patriarchy," "white supremacy," "cultural genocide," "land back," "Black Lives Matter," and "systemic racism" became normalized in mainstream discourse.

The Moment Offers a Portal to Food Justice

As we grieve the horrific loss of life and rage at the deepening inequities, we also see the pandemic as a "portal to food justice."[8] As food educators and activists, we experienced and encouraged both individual and collective changes: promoting backyard and community gardens as well as local procurement and virtual farmers markets.[9] We joined webinars and rallies (online and in the streets) to protest anti-Black racism,[10] pipelines that infringe upon Indigenous territories and sacred burial sites, police violence against communities of Indigenous, Black, and people of color; we signed online petitions for government responses to the recommendations of the Truth and Reconciliation Commission and of the Missing and Murdered Indigenous Women and Girls Commission, and grieved the discoveries of the unmarked graves of more than one thousand Indigenous children near residential schools; we pushed for institutional changes in our universities' hiring policies and for more inclusive curricula, for municipal food policies that support local procurement, for health policies that redress inequities in urban hot spots and in Indigenous communities. We sought ways to "grab the moment" to nurture the widening public consciousness by promoting conversations and actions for regenerative agriculture, food justice, and food sovereignty.

The Moment for Online Multimedia Education

Another convergence of forces fueled by the pandemic has been the expansion, intensification, and normalization of online educational and cultural activities.[11] We have become intense users of online education as well as its subjects, critics, and promoters. Our Indigenous and Black partners have been inundated with invitations to speak on global webinars that are amplifying the struggles against racism and environmental injustice as well as for Black and Indigenous food sovereignty. Those of us who are settlers and white allies have feasted on a cornucopia of online panels and conferences that have brought the voices of Black and Indigenous food leaders around the world into our homes, accessing wisdom we would never have been exposed to in pre-pandemic times. It's been a yearlong intense seminar like none we could access in a university.

This publication is a bold experiment in multimedia education, intimately connected to the Earth to Tables Legacies website (ettl.ca). Most of the text also appears online, creatively designed and accompanied by video and stunning visuals. We invite you to explore this book in a nonlinear way. The full impact of this multimedia

package can only be fully realized when the reader opens the videos (ettl.ca/v) as well as a short URL with hyperlinks for each of the photo essays (ettl.ca/pe), and when teachers download the ever-evolving online Facilitator Guides (ettl.ca/fg). We provide links to this exciting material throughout the book. The content is constantly evolving, so there will always be more material on the website than in the book.

The pandemic deepened the dialogue among the seventeen collaborators in our Earth to Tables Legacies project, through monthly online zoom gatherings. We reported on the impact of and responses to COVID-19 in very diverse contexts. Our Mexican partners used the time and space imposed by the lockdowns to further food sovereignty resulting in a Mayan milpa and *semillero de aprendizaje* (sowing seeds of learning) in the Yucatán, more family food production in a P'urépecha community in Michoacán, and innovative processing of organic vegetables in Jalisco. In the Canadian context, our Ontario-based farmers worked toward their dream of establishing an agroecology school, our Québec-based farmers/teachers took lessons in growing food into the classroom, our Toronto urban farm director has been a key leader in the Black Food

Chandra Maracle welcomes Legacies collaborators to the table of the Everlasting Tree School in July 2019.

Justice movement; she took a leave of absence to explore and film stories of her ancestral roots in Ghana and started a new job as executive director of SeedChange, an international NGO. Our Haudenosaunee partners at Six Nations influenced both university and local school programs while envisioning a local corn-processing project. We will continue to update our website by adding these and other stories through coproductions of bilingual, or even multilingual, videos. We are constantly sharing these evolving projects and strategizing how we can support each other's initiatives. Within our own small community, we witness a broader trend: expanding alliances of Indigenous, Black, and people of color, along with white allies or accomplices who recognize common experiences of colonization and resistance as well as the urgent need for global solidarity.

As we went into lockdown with the pandemic, we scrambled to complete our earthtotables.org website (ettl.ca/wt) with the videos, photo essays, and accompanying Facilitator Guides. We were able to launch it just as classes and workshops were becoming virtual, and innovative online resources were sought by teachers and community organizers alike. Collectively we organized two global online launches (ettl.ca/wl) of our website, with virtual ceremonial openings, guest resource people from Africa, Asia, and Latin America, and dynamic breakout groups discussing our videos and photo essays. We are not alone in creating new books and online resources that amplify voices aiming to contribute to an anticolonial and decolonial education process. We are constantly updating the Facilitator Guides with new resources we find.

Naming the Project: Earth to Tables Legacies

The Earth to Tables Legacies project promotes dialogue across differences. From its inception, it has been an intergenerational and intercultural exchange of knowledges and practices around food sovereignty: we consciously brought together youth and elders, rural and urban food activists, Indigenous and settler, people of color and white, Canadian and Mexican. We promote dialogue across these differences while recognizing the importance of privileging the voices of those most marginalized through centuries of colonization. We embrace their leadership in creating and expanding a vision of food justice and food sovereignty.

The title of our project—Earth to Tables—emerged through this organic process. The main protagonist in this story is the Earth, but who will speak for her? If she *is* speaking, how can we understand her language? The media report floods and fires, droughts and hurricanes, global heating, health pandemics, and the climate crisis. And yet, even in the midst of a global pandemic, the generous Earth keeps giving. Our project focuses on the loving ways that the Earth speaks to us, if we learn to listen and take time to observe. She shows us how to collaborate with all the relations that support diverse life, from microscopic soil communities to forest, grassland, and wetland landscapes.

The "to" in "Earth to Tables" represents the process of securing (growing, gathering, hunting, fishing) and preparing the food that ends up on our tables. The "to" is about the *relationship* humans have with all the elements of life that sustain us. We relate to these elements in many ways, some that are Life-destroying and some that are Life-giving.

"Tables" represent the human in all our relations. Humans have developed diverse cultures and food practices, so there are many different kinds of tables. The Haudenosaunee ate seated on the ground around a fire in the longhouse. European colonizers introduced tables to the Americas, and to this day, settler-Indigenous negotiations take place around a table, often representing colonial laws and ways of thinking and acting. But we also gather around tables to reconcile our differences and to reclaim community with healthy and culturally appropriate foods.

When the Earth to Tables Legacies project was born in 2015, it became a process of reconnecting the relationships that have been lost through industrial agriculture and a corporate global food system that treats food as any other commodity. Rather, it affirmed food as a life-sustaining medicine, with deep cultural and spiritual meaning.

GLOBAL
ONLINE
LAUNCH
earthtotables.org

LEGACIES EARTH
—TO—
TABLES

A Day of Gratitude for the Sustenance the Earth Provides

CELEBRATING OUR NEW MULTIMEDIA EDUCATIONAL PACKAGE

OCTOBER 12
2020
11:00 – 12:00 EDT

Register at Eventbrite
link above

**Recognizing Thanksgiving Day (Canada),
Indigenous Peoples Day (U.S.),
Día de la Resistencia Indígena (Mexico)**

This one hour program will include the Haudenosaunee
Thanksgiving Address, an introduction to the Earth to Tables
Legacies project, symbolic planting seeds of hope by Legacies
collaborators, and reflections from food leaders around the world.

environmental &
urban change | YORK U

3 Legacies films selected

2020
OFFICIAL SELECTION
PLANET·FOCUS
INTERNATIONAL ENVIRONMENTAL
FILM FESTIVAL

Social Sciences and Humanities
Research Council of Canada
Conseil de recherches en
sciences humaines du Canada

Canada

We started with family and friends, and with our own bioregion. The idea was "to dig where we stand." After the first year of visits and conversations, we stumbled upon the Earth to Tables framework for our exchange through two of our women collaborators. Ontario-based settler farmer Dianne Kretschmar loves to get her hands in the earth, while Mohawk Chandra Maracle starts with the kitchen table as the site for her food activism. Dianne and Chandra represent two ends of food sovereignty, from promoting local organic production to sharing good food with family and friends around the table.

The word "Legacies" has multiple meanings. Legacies can refer to what we carry from the past, and how our ancestors, their experiences and knowledges remain within us. Legacies can also refer to the future, to what we are offering now as a legacy for the next seven generations. Some legacies are heavy and traumatic, leave deep wounds, and require healing. Others are to be cherished, recovered, and shared.

While Dianne faces the legacies of overcultivation and a plethora of forces in agriculture and international migration that make it difficult for her to hire and keep farm labor, Chandra confronts legacies of food practices in Indigenous communities that reflect the intergenerational trauma of residential schools and colonization and leads in recovering Indigenous wisdom in her place and time.

We are all living with the legacy of a destructive, unjust, and unsustainable food system that has "stuffed and starved" populations, and has threatened both human health and the health of the planet.

The stories we focus on here are narrated by food activists who are motivated by a vision of a way of growing, exchanging, and eating food that is healthy—physically, culturally, ecologically, spiritually. From Earth to Tables.

Cherokee writer Thomas King writes, "The truth about stories is that's all we are."[12] But he also cautioned: "So you have to be careful about the stories you tell."[13] We acknowledge that we are sharing only certain stories, told with our specific perspectives. We invite readers to listen and read critically, challenging the ideas within this package, sharing your own stories, and developing your own perspectives.

In the accompanying video, you can follow the evolution of the project (ettl.ca/sp) during its first two years, and meet most of the collaborators as they name some of the themes that emerged from our dialogue.

Naming Our Process: Cocreating with All Our Relations

On the book cover we celebrate its collective authorship, growing out of a process with seventeen Legacies collaborators. Perhaps as important as the content of our book and conversations, is the process—the ways in which we have connected since 2015, and even earlier. Based on personal relationships over time, we have been connecting across big differences: youth/elders, rural/urban, Indigenous/settler, BIPOC/white, Canadian/Mexican (with U.S.-based commentators).

We call our methodology "Pollinating Relationships," which describes the Legacies exchange well as a cross-pollination of people, knowledges, and practices. Since 2015, the Earth to Tables Legacies exchange has been pollinating relationships: across species, across generations, across borders, across ecologies, across cultures, across historical moments.

For us, the collaborative process is as important as our product, the book and website. Perhaps the process of developing relationships is, in fact, our main message. At the root of the environmental crisis is our disconnection from and inability to care for all other living beings. The only way to a sustainable and just food system is through honoring "all our relations."

The thirteen storytellers (ettl.ca/c) form the heart of this multimedia package—men and women, settler and Indigenous food activists, ranging in age from twenty-five to seventy-five, working on farms, in urban agriculture gardens, or on Indigenous food projects in Canada and Mexico. They introduce themselves in chapter 5. Although we wanted to make the process as participatory as possible, we acknowledge some limits of collaboration. The storytellers were intensely involved in the food work that fed the stories they shared. So, there was a role for our production team (ettl.ca/pt)—Deborah Barndt, Lauren Baker, and Alex Gellis—as researchers and writers, photographers and filmmakers, codirectors and coeditors to set the table for the collective conversations. In chapter 5, we share more of our stories to reveal how our relationships shaped the history of the project. We acknowledge that our team of three women represents primarily settler experiences of two white Canadians of European descent and a mixed-race Colombian-Canadian. We recognize that we risk reproducing colonial perspectives in editing the raw material; we deeply appreciate when our Indigenous and Black collaborators correct us. We also invite critical readers of this book to challenge us. This is an ongoing process, and difficult conversations are still to be had. Decolonization is a lifelong commitment.

Naming the Chapters: An Overview and Synthesis

Although these first pages offer a conventional book introduction, we see part I, "Greetings and Gratitude," as the most appropriate protocol for entering the heart of the book and its companion website. Every Indigenous group has its own form of ceremony for the start of an encounter and engagement. Although three different Indigenous communities are participating in the Earth to Tables Legacies exchange (including the Mayan and the P'urépecha in Mexico), we are honoring the practice of the Haudenosaunee (known as the Iroquois Confederacy in French or as Six Nations in English). These original nations straddle the border between the so-called United States and Canada, and their territory includes the bioregion of the production team and our institutional base, York University in Toronto.

When Mohawk professor and food activist Ryan DeCaire first introduced us to the Thanksgiving Address, we were moved by how it created a space for us to enter into an open and respectful dialogue. The protocol of greeting and thanking all the elements of life that sustain us embodies a holistic framework for thinking about food in relationship to all living beings. Chapter 1 includes the link to a ten-minute illustrated video of Ryan and Chandra introducing the Thanksgiving Address as well as the written text of the address in both Mohawk and English, embellished with original drawings by Legacies collaborator and Tuscarora artist Rick Hill.

We have invited food scholars and activists to continue the conversation initiated by Legacies collaborators featured in the videos and photo essays. In the first commentary, Molly Anderson, William R. Kenan Jr. Professor of Food Studies at Middlebury College in Vermont, considers the Thanksgiving Address as a more meaningful alternative to a rote land acknowledgment as it helps us "both to remember whose land we stand upon and also the meaning to these people of that land—and all of their relations in the waters, birds, animals, and other living and nonliving beings connected with it."

Part II, "Setting the Table" (chapters 2, 3, and 4), offers theoretical frameworks for our discussions of food sovereignty, delineates our collaborative methodology, and elaborates on the popular education approach we encourage in the use of the book and website.

The Earth to Tables Legacies exchange grapples with the tensions, struggles, and legacies of broken treaties, systemic racism, and western imperialism. In chapter 2, "Navigating Dynamic Tensions on Common Waters," we identify four interrelated dynamic tensions that represent the broader political, ecological, and cultural context within which we live and work. They correspond to the categories framing the videos and photo essays in the Conversations sections; ways of knowing, earth, justice, and tables. The photographs that open each section are drawn from the climate justice strike in Toronto in 2019, revealing how activists are representing these tensions in the streets.

In "Knowledge Tensions," we explore the roots of the tensions between Eurocentric and Indigenous knowledges through an ongoing colonial process. Although western science has been historically entwined with colonialism, recognition of the symbiotic connections of all living things is growing. Mvskoke

Joy Harjo, U.S. poet laureate, powerfully represents this worldview through her poem "Bless This Land."

Our Legacies exchange is a response to a crisis (environmental, political, cultural, epistemological, and spiritual) perpetuated by the capitalist model of industrial agriculture and a global food system shaped by corporate concentration and environmental destruction. Rather than dwell on what we are up against, we focus on the more healthy and just food system we are trying to recover or create, epitomized by the term food sovereignty. In "Food Tensions: Corporate Food Regime versus Food Sovereignty Movement," we draw on the diverse understandings of all Legacies project collaborators, each defining food sovereignty from her own specific vantage point and role in a more sustainable food system.

"Equity Tensions: Intersectional Identities and Power" acknowledges the intersectional power dynamics at play through all relationships. This section highlights the racism and classism embedded in the industrial food system, showing how Indigenous, Black, and people of color have been most impacted by chemically intensive agriculture, confined animal feedlots, deregulated supply chains, and highly processed food. A Just Transition includes racialized and undocumented workers who grow, process, cook, and distribute food.

The fourth section, "Political Tensions: Capitalism, Colonization, and Reconciliation," locates our multifaceted initiatives for healthy, sustainable, and culturally appropriate food within broader political struggles. Neoliberal capitalism, and its history through European colonization and globalization, is now being challenged by a resurgence and reconciliation process led by Indigenous peoples defending their land and culture, along with a growing number of non-Indigenous allies, including other racialized peoples. Reconciliation needs to be two-pronged, recognizing our interdependence with the Earth and with Indigenous peoples.

Pollination is a process that honors interspecies relations and describes the Legacies exchange well—a cross-pollination of people, knowledges, and practices. Chapter 3, "Pollinating Relationships: Our Collaborative Methodology," emphasizes the centrality of our process, a way of working that is as important as the content. Since 2015, the Earth to Tables Legacies exchange has been pollinating relationships: across generations, borders, languages, histories, rituals, methodologies, mediums, and organizations. We review our collective experience through the lens of these different dimensions of our exchange.

In "Walking the Talk" in chapter 4, we provide a theoretical and practical introduction to the popular education approach that makes this book and website unique. You have in your hands one element of a multimedia educational package that is meant to be used in classes or groups, with the videos and photo essays acting as catalysts for readers and viewers to connect the ideas to their own contexts, to rethink their own perspectives, and to consider their own individual and collective actions. We have created Facilitator Guides for all videos and photo essays as well as the "Dynamics Tensions" and "Pollinating Relationships" chapters precisely to encourage critical, collective, and creative engagement with the stories and issues they raise.

The guides are pdfs that can be downloaded from the online site (ettl.ca/fg). There are two sections: "Digging In" and "Digging Deeper."

"Digging In" offers key terms from each text, photo essay, or video to be explored. A list of generic questions (based on the problem-posing method of Brazilian educator Paulo Freire) leads a group through a process of connecting personally and then collectively, from description to analysis to action. Specific questions dig into the content of the piece, while hands-on activities suggest opportunities for experiential learning. Sections of questions promote intergenerational and intercultural dialogue as well as individual and collective action, both central to the intent of the Earth to Tables Legacies exchange.

In the second half, "Digging Deeper," we offer ever-evolving resources for further research and action, ranging from books and articles to websites, podcasts, and organizations. We see our stories as mere springboards for deeper investigation, with groups seeking out their own interests and resources that are relevant to their own contexts and purposes. This list requires

constant updating, and we welcome additions that users might offer that we could include in the guide.

Part III, "Storytellers," highlights all seventeen collaborators, the thirteen who share their stories as well as the production team members who help bring those stories to life. Most collaborators joined the Earth to Tables Legacies project based on personal

WAYS OF KNOWING
Honouring all relations that sustain life

EARTH
Food sovereignty challenges the corporate food regime

LEGACIES EARTH TO TABLES

JUSTICE
Fighting all systemic inequities

TABLES
Promoting decolonization and reconciliation

friendships, many of them with deep histories. This has been both a strength and a limitation, as we recognize that many groups are not represented. Nonetheless, building on relationships of trust made it possible to share the stories that are the heart of this book, in the "Conversations" chapters. Among the Legacies project storytellers is still a great diversity in age, gender, race, Indigeneity, citizenship, and role in the food system.

Chapter 5 unpacks even more complexity in these identities through four sections. "Meet the Storytellers" offers short bios of the thirteen core collaborators as well as one quote from each, excerpted from their stories within the videos and photo essays. Readers can find more detailed profiles with a photo of all collaborators on the website (ettl.ca/c). Everyone wrote a profile that speaks to four dimensions of their identity: the place where they live and work, their particular passion for food, their perspective on food sovereignty, and their participation in the Legacies project.

"Meet the Production Team" offers an inside view from the codirectors and coeditors of how the project evolved, building on personal relationships and previous projects.

For a more playful way to identify ourselves, we asked every collaborator to choose a food-related icon (e.g., plant, animal, insect, or container) that they identify with. We humanize our identities in this section, "Our Food Icons," revealing personal passions, histories, and personalities. These icons also highlight the interrelation between humans and our food sources: how people shape food and food shapes people.

Our personal histories have also been influenced by movement from one place to another. When we gathered at Six Nations in July 2019, we shared our diverse histories of migration along with the food icons. Although we all live in a narrow latitude of North America (or Turtle Island), all of us have migrated at some point in our lives and have learned from diverse continents, cultures, and culinary practices. "Our Migration Stories" connect us to the broader political, economic, and cultural process of global migration and raise important questions about our relationship to the land we live on now.

Part IV, "Conversations," is the core of our multimedia package and consists of videos and photo essays featuring the voices, practices, and challenges of our collaborators. Although the photo essays appear in print here, you will need to

access the videos and their accompanying Facilitator Guides online.

The enticing menu of videos and photo essays on the table above is organized around four interrelated themes (ways of knowing, earth, justice, and tables), which also coincide with the four dynamic tensions framing the Earth to Tables Legacies project (Knowledge, Food, Equity, and Political Tensions). The underlying "Ways of Knowing" are at the epistemological core of food sovereignty, grounded in the "Earth" as a living organism of all our relations. Food sovereignty promotes social and environmental "Justice" based on equitable rather than hierarchical relations of power. "Tables" represents the site of struggles between neoliberal capitalism and a process of decolonization and reconciliation. Below we introduce each one with its rich array of multimedia stories.

Chapter 6, "Ways of Knowing," introduces four photo essays that highlight the worldviews of the Indigenous peoples represented in our exchange. Along with the Thanksgiving Address video opening the book, in "Haudenosaunee Gifts: Contributions to Our Past and Common Future," Chandra Maracle, Rick Hill, and Ryan DeCaire share their history, the Dish with One Spoon treaty, and the role that the

Haudenosaunee played in the formation of both the so-called United States and Canada. In "Language and Food: A Worldview in Verbs," Mohawk professor Ryan illustrates how Indigenous languages reflect processes and relationships rather than objects. A commentary by Dr. Lorna Wanosts'a7 Williams, member of the Lil'wat Nation and Canada Research Chair in Education and Linguistics at the University of Victoria, reaffirms how crucial the current process of language revitalization is to the survival of Indigenous peoples and their ways of knowing, being, and acting.

We then move to Mexico for two more photo essays by collaborators sharing the cosmovisions of the P'urépecha and Mayan peoples. Fulvio Gioanetto and María Blas, Legacies collaborators living in Michoacán, share their knowledge as an ethnobotanist and a healer, respectively, in "Medicinal Plants in the Purépecha Cosmovision." In her commentary, Haudenosaunee scholar Amber Meadow Adams from Six Nations deepens the conversation by showing how one of the colonial plants Fulvio names contributed to women's illnesses and the destruction of childbirth practices.

Mayans Ángel Kú and Valiana Aguilar, in "Mutual Nurturing: Reweaving Community with Our Elders,"

Legacies collaborators gather at Six Nations in July 2019

emphasize the importance of youth recovering deeper understandings of *comida* from their *abuelos* (grandparents), rebraiding ropes in a weave of community that has been broken. Toronto-based Guna-Rappahannock Monique Mojica brings her land-based embodied understanding as an actor/playwright to her commentary on the essay, comparing her dramaturgy to a process of reweaving the self and community learned from her Guna elders.

Chapter 7, "Earth," offers stories that ground our discussions of food in both human and animal bodies as well as in the soil. The photo essay "Mother's Milk: The Original Food" gathers the stories of five women in the Legacies project (Chandra Maracle, Anna Murtaugh, Hilda Villaseñor, María Blas, and Serena Gioanetto) recounting their very different cultural experiences with breast-feeding. Mexican-Canadian midwife Laura Solis resonates with descriptions of mother's milk as "spiritual food" and "liquid gold" while recounting how formula companies changed breast-feeding for generations. York University professor emerita and nutritional anthropologist Penny Van Esterik connects the Legacies women's stories to both her personal experience and academic research on breast-feeding in Southeast Asia.

The video "The Soil Is Alive" is a dialogue between Mexican organic farmer Fernando Garcia and his Canadian mentor, Dianne Kretschmar, as they share their deepening understanding of the rich life (microorganisms and fungal networks) in the soil and the urgency to change their agricultural practices. Commentator Gilberto Aboites, peasant rights researcher and professor at the Autonomous University of Coahuila in Saltillo, Mexico, reminds us that pre-contact Indigenous peoples always understood the soil as alive.

Fulvio Gioanetto, Legacies collaborator and Italian-Mexican ethnobotanist, shares his practice of transforming weeds into organic fertilizers, herbicides, and pesticides in both Ontario and Michocán, Mexico, in the video "The Alchemy of Agroecology." University of Toronto professor emerita and global food scholar Harriet Friedmann comments on how Fulvio weds his scientific training to Indigenous knowledge, reestablishing place-based agroecological practices that were disrupted by colonization and ignored by global markets.

In the photo essay, "The Animal Food Cycle: We Feed Them, and They Feed Us," Québec-based farmers/teachers Anna Murtaugh and Adam Royal continue the closed-loop farming they learned from their mentor, Dianne Kretschmar, integrating animals into their family, diets, and vegetable gardens. In his commentary, Fred Metallic, director of natural resources for the Listuguj Mi'gmaq Government in Québec, contrasts the colonial hierarchy of humans over animals with the Mi'gmaq hunting protocol of respect for the animal and human obligations to that connection.

"Justice" is a principle that runs through all chapters. However, in chapter 8, we pay particular attention to the power dynamics that are inevitable in any attempt to transform the current global food system into a more sustainable and just process of feeding ourselves.

In the photo essay "Promoting Organic Agriculture in Mexico: From Urban Gardens to Multinational Companies," Fernando Garcia shares the challenges of training suburbanites in Guadalajara, Mexico, to grow their own food and the different challenges he faces as an organic farming consultant for a multinational company producing value-added vegetables. As director of a Washington, D.C., urban farm, commentator Samantha Trumbull empathizes with Fernando's story, reflecting on her experiences of promoting community gardens with poor racialized communities in the U.S. capital.

Markets are key to making healthy food accessible, and the video "Why Farmers Markets?" considers the efforts of Anna Murtaugh and Adam Royal to cofound a farmers market in their rural Québec community, honoring the ways it connects people to their food and to each other. Anna also notes the critical question of costs and accessibility, a conversation that is continued by commentators and key leaders in the Black Food Sovereignty movement—Anan Lololi, Guyanese-born founder of the AfriCan Food Basket in Toronto; and Selam Teclu, Eritrean-born nutritionist, gardener, and bread maker. We also include comments by four Mexican collaborators (Ángel Kú, Valiana Aguilar, Fulvio Gioanetto, and María Blas), who reflect back on the traditional markets in their Indigenous communities.

Legacies collaborator and Black Food Justice leader Leticia Deawuo is featured in the next two companion pieces. In the photo essay, "Food Justice and Urban Agriculture in Action," Lauren Baker interviews Leticia about her history with Black Creek Community Farm and her evolving commitment to food justice by addressing the interrelated systemic barriers such as racism, poverty, housing, and transport. In the video "Black Creek Community

Farm: Healing Our Community," Leticia shows us the many ways that racialized and low-income residents in Toronto's Jane-Finch neighborhood are controlling their own food production, growing culturally appropriate foods, creating safe spaces, and building community.

In her commentary, Karen Washington, cofounder of Black Urban Growers in the United States, and who first named the injustice as "food apartheid," applauds the initiative taken by racialized residents in this Toronto neighborhood to put power and ownership back into the hands of its people, redressing the history of enslaved people in colonial agriculture, and ensuring a future of food security and food justice.

The final video in the "Justice" chapter speaks to a wide range of equity issues: climate justice, agroecology versus multinational production, migrant labor, and the sharing of knowledge between elders and youth. "Who Will Feed Us? The Farm Labour Crisis Meets the Climate Crisis" brings together Ontario-based Dianne Kretschmar and Michoacán-based Fulvio Gioanetto to share views on the precarious future of farming and their desire to pass on sustainable practices to their offspring; Dianne's son, Dan, dreams of an agroecology school, while Fulvio's daughter

Serena and her husband, Miguel, see temporary migration north as one way to support their dreams of an organic rancho in Mexico. In his commentary on the video, Gilberto Aboites, Mexican food researcher and advocate for the Global Rights of Peasants, is inspired to revalue the work of farmers—in particular, migrant labor—so poignantly revealed during the pandemic.

The collection of photo essays and videos in chapter 9, "Tables," draws on literal, metaphorical, and political connotations of its title. The stories take us to the tables where we eat and focus more on that end of the food chain, but with a broader conception of food that incorporates not only the nutritional, but also the social, cultural, and spiritual meanings of food. The table is also a symbol for the political struggles around food rooted in historical inequities provoked by colonization and slavery; food is deeply imbedded in the stories and treaties discussed in the Haudenosaunee Primer, so we are gifted with a vision of other ways to meet around the table.

First, this era of reckoning demands that we learn about the brutal impacts of colonization on Indigenous communities, their health, their families, their relationship to land, and their cultural and spiritual practices. The

photo essay "From the Mush Hole to the Everlasting Tree School: Colonial Food Legacies among the Haudenosaunee" is narrated by Mohawk Chandra Maracle in dialogue with settler historian Ian Mosby as they excavate the role of food in residential schools. They move from Ian's research on how underfed Indigenous children were used for government experiments on malnutrition to Chandra's effort to cofound a Mohawk-centered school that recovers healthier Haudenosaunee traditional food practices.

To continue the conversation, native plant expert, community food activist, and writer Lorraine Johnson notes how this dialogue shows that although food has been a weapon to sever bonds, it can also be used to rebuild relationships with the land as body, body as land, and the act of eating as profound cultivation of a circle that includes the ancestors and future generations. Fulvio Gioanetto compares the Canadian experience of genocide with the struggles of autonomous P'urépecha communities in his home state of Michoacán, Mexico.

A broader notion of food is elaborated in the photo essay "La Comida: The Core of Food Sovereignty" by Gustavo Esteva, Zapotec-Mexican food scholar and founder of UniTierra, University of the Land, in Oaxaca, Mexico. For Gustavo, "comida" does not translate narrowly to "food" but includes all the social activity in growing, preparing, eating, and sharing it, always in a broader context of struggles for Indigenous food sovereignty against the life-destroying food systems promoted by patriarchal and neoliberal capitalism. P'urépecha culinary anthropologist, chef, and food justice activist scholar Claudia Serrato deepens that conversation by highlighting *la comida* as a carrier of ancestral knowledge that recenters *la mujer* (women) and honors *la ceremonia de la comida*, the rituals associated with growing, harvesting, and eating.

Legacies collaborator and Tuscarora historian Rick Hill narrates a trilogy of three PowerPoint presentations that introduce different aspects of Haudenosaunee history, culture, and food practices. In the video "Getting to Know Us," Rick playfully uses the device of the dating game to introduce himself, his culture, and their core values to us. Mashkiiziibii Patty Loew, journalism professor and director of the Center for Native American and Indigenous Research at Northwestern University, highlights Rick's use of narrative and circular storytelling that integrates history, agriculture, spirituality, and

environmental activism, always with both reverence and humor.

In Rick's second video "Living with Your Mother," highly illustrated with his own powerful artwork, we learn about the Haudenosaunee creation story, the original instructions, the Thanksgiving Address, and the Dish with One Spoon Treaty, which could serve as a manifesto for an Indigenous environmental movement. For commentator Tim Leduc, professor at Wilfrid Laurier University, researcher and ally of Indigenous peoples, this Dish goes beyond the political treaties, serving as a spiritual contract between human nations, the beings of creation, and the land's spirit.

"Life in the Longhouse," the third video in the trilogy, focuses on the sustainable food practices of the Haudenosaunee, whose traditional economy was based on hunting, gathering, and cultivating through mound agriculture (corn, beans, and squash) with everyone contributing food and skills to cooperative living in the longhouse. For commentator Mohawk food scholar Kiera (Kaia'tanó:ron) Brant-Birioukov, professor at York University's Faculty of Education, the entire process of growing, harvesting, and lying the grain to make corn soup can be likened to the Haudenosaunee ways

of knowing and learning—a transformational process.

We conclude the "Tables" section with a photo essay, "Cooking and Eating Together: From the Kitchen Table to the Community Meal," which takes the reader on a journey from Six Nations in Ontario to the Gaspé in Quebec, from Jalisco to Michoacán to the Yucatán in Mexico—visiting the tables of Legacies collaborators as they gather with family and friends to prepare and share and celebrate food.

We close the book with the same spirit that opened it. The "Thanksgiving Address" set the tone for the stories and conversations that followed, by offering greetings and gratitude. In a similar spirit, in the "Acknowledgments" (ettl.ca/a), we end by greeting and thanking the hundreds of people who have contributed to this collective process. In truth, it takes a community with diverse histories and skills but a common commitment for food justice and food sovereignty to create a multimedia publication. Honor their names.

All of the Facilitator Guides include written, visual, online, and organizational resources, but we also include a bibliography with key references as an appendix.

PART I
GREETINGS AND GRATITUDE

The Indigenous collaborators in the Earth to Tables Legacies exchange have taught us the importance of cultural protocols or ceremonies to create a mental and emotional space for deep learning and dialogue. Although Legacies collaborators also include Mayan and P'urépecha food activists in Mexico, we are adapting the practice of the Haudenosaunee peoples in the so-called United States and Canada by opening with the Thanksgiving Address in chapter 1. It encourages the readers of this book to enter into these conversations with respect and gratitude for all the interconnections that sustain life, so central to food justice and food sovereignty.

We invite you to read and listen to the voices of Mohawk language professor Ryan DeCaire and Mohawk food leader Chandra Maracle as they offer the *Ohen:ton Karihwatehkwen*, or Thanksgiving Address, in both Mohawk and English.

CHAPTER 1

The Thanksgiving Address

Greetings and Thanks

The Haudenosaunee (known as the Iroquois Confederacy in French or as Six Nations in English) begin every gathering by offering greetings and thanks to all the elements of life that sustain us. This ritual brings everyone into the space with a good mind, ready to listen and learn.

Why begin a book about food sovereignty with a Mohawk greeting? As Chandra explains,

> I love to start any meeting with these words of thanksgiving to all the beings in the natural world. It shows that food is a great universalizer, something that we all need as human beings. In the context of talking about things like decolonization, truth and reconciliation, there are so many things that divide us. But food is a very approachable way of bringing us together, it helps us remember the universality of it all. It's a way to bring people together, not to separate us.

First watch the Thanksgiving Address video (ettl.ca/1), focusing on the images while Ryan speaks in the Mohawk language. Then Chandra offers a further explanation in English. Below you can follow the text in both Mohawk and English, illustrated by drawings by Tuscarora artist Rick Hill. Download the Facilitator Guide (ettl.ca/fg) for the video, which includes a participatory activity with the drawings that Chandra has developed to make the connections between food and all of the elements.

Ohen:ton Karihwatehkwen (in Mohawk)

Karihwahnhotónkwen
Tewatatè:ken, né: wáhi thia'tewenhniserá:ke táhnon nó:nen othé:nen iorihowá:nen tewaterihwahtentià:tha, kanonhweratónhsera entitewáhtka'we. Teniethinonhweratónnion tsi naho'tèn:shon rokwatákwen táhnon roweiennentà:'on kèn:thon tsi ionhontsá:te táhnon tsi tkaronhiatátie.

Né: nen' nè:'e tewana'tónhkhwa ne Ohén:ton Karihwatéhkwen. Eh káti naiohtónhake nonkwa'nikòn:ra.

Onkwe'shòn:'a
Akwé:kon énskat entitewahwe'nón:ni nonkwa'nikòn:ra táhnon teiethinonhwerá:ton ne onkwe'shòn:'a ienákere tsi ionhontsá:te tsi shé:kon rotiio'tátie tsi nahò:ten shakoríhonte ne Shonkwaia'tíson naiá:wen'ne skén:nen aonhtén:ti' tsi ionhontsá:te. Eh káti naiohtónhake nonkwa'nikòn:ra.

Iethi'nisténha Onhóntsa

Akwé:kon énskat entitewahwe'nón:ni nonkwa'nikòn:ra táhnon taiethinonhwerá:ton ne Iethi'nisténha Onhóntsa. Iakorihwató:ken tsi shé:kon taiakohtka'wenhátie ne ako'shatsténhsera. Nè:'e kwi' thí:ken teionkwatonhontsó:ni ne aetiónhnheke táhnon skén:nen taetewatawén:rie ieronhkwe'nà:ke. Eh káti naiohtónhake nonkwa'nikòn:ra.

Kahnekahrónnion

Akwé:kon énskat entitewahwe'nón:ni nonkwa'nikòn:ra táhnon teiethinonhwerá:ton ne kahnekahrónnion tsi shé:kon iotirihwató:ken tsi ionathnekahtentionhátie naiá:wen'ne aionkwania'taná:wen nó:nen ionkwania'táthens táhnon naonsakará:kewe tsi nahò:ten wahétken's ká:ien onhontsà:ke. Eh káti naiohtónhake nonkwa'nikòn:ra.

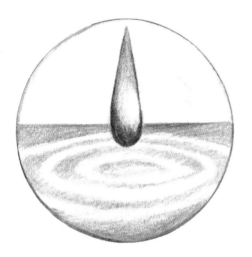

Kentson'shòn:'a

Ó:nen káti akwé:kon énskat entitewahwe'nón:ni nonkwa'nikòn:ra táhnon teiethinonhwerá:ton ne nia'tekéntsake awèn:ke tkontì:teron tsi shé:kon iotinoharenionhátie tsi kahnekahrónnion táhnon taionahtka'wenhátie ne aoti'wà:ron naiá:wen'ne tionhnhéhkwen aionkwá:ton'se. Eh káti naiohtónhake nonkwa'nikòn:ra.

Iothontón:ni

Né: káti akwé:kon énskat entitewahwe'nón:ni nonkwa'nikòn:ra táhnon taiethinnonhwerá:ton ne iothontón:ni shonkwaienthó:wi. Nia'tekahón:take, nia'tekahtè:rake, táhnon nia'tekakwí:rake kwi' wáhi tewanahè:sen ne aétewake nó:nen entewatonhkária'ke táhnon aionkhítsen'te nó:nen enionkwanonhwákten. Eh káti naiohtónhake nonkwa'nikòn:ra.

Otsi'nonwa'shòn:'a

Ó:nen káti akwé:kon énskat entitewahwe'nón:ni nonkwa'nikòn:ra táhnon taiethinonhwerá:ton ne otsi'nonwa'shòn:'a. Nia'tekatsi'nón:wake kwi' shakó'teron onhontsà:ke ne taiotirihwaienawa'kónhake táhnon aiotiianerahstonhátieke ne tsi ionhontsá:te naiá:wen'ne akwé:kon skén:nen aonhtén:ti. Eh káti naiohtónhake nonkwa'nikòn:ra.

Tionhnhéhkwen

Ó:nen akwé:kon énskat entitewahwe'nón:ni nonkwa'nikòn:ra táhnon taiethinonhwerá:ton ne tionhnhéhkwen. Nia'té:kon ase'shòn:'a ionkwá:ien kahehtakónhshon tsi nón:we ionkwaienthóhseron. Né: kwi' ò:ni teiethinonhwerá:ton ne Áhsen Nikontate'kèn:'a - ó:nenhste, onon'ónsera, táhnon osahè:ta. Eh káti naiohtónhake nonkwa'nikòn:ra.

Kahi'shòn:'a

Né: káti akwé:kon énskat entitewahwe'nón:ni nonkwa'nikòn:ra táhnon teiethinonhwerá:ton ne wahianiióntha. Nia'tewà:iake ká:ien onhontsà:ke ne aétewake, aetewahnekónnia'te, táhnon taetewá:iehste ne tionhnhéhkwen. Teiethinonhwerá:ton ò:ni ne niiohontésha; nè:'e kwi' ohén:ton tehshakotáhston ne Shonkwaia'tíson akanèn:rine ne kahihshòn:'a. Eh káti naiohtónhake nonkwa'nikòn:ra.

Kahrhahrónnion
Akwé:kon énskat entitewahwe'nón:ni nonkwa'nikòn:ra táhnon teiethinonhwerá:ton ne kahrhahrónnion táhnon karontakwe'ní:io ne tsi ní:kon karontó:ton onhontsà:ke, Wáhta niiohsennò:ten. Shé:kon tewaniahé:sen ne aétewatste aetewatenonhsónnia'te, aetewatatia'tataríha'te nó:nen enwathó:rate, táhnon tionhnhéhkwen aionkwa':ton'se. Eh káti naiohtónhake nonkwa'nikòn:ra.

Otsi'ten'okòn:'a
Akwé:kon énskat entitewahwe'nón:ni nonkwanikòn:ra táhnon taiethinonhwerá:ton ne otsi'ten'okòn:'a kontinákere tsi ionhontsá:te táhnon ne kwah tkonwatikowá:nen, Á:kweks

niiohsennò:ten, tsi shé:kon taiaonatka'wenhátie ne aoti'shatsténhsera. Eh káti naiohtónhake nonkwa'nikòn:ra.

Kontírio
Akwé:kon énskat entitewahwe'nón:ni nonkwanikòn:ra táhnon taiethinonhwerá:ton ne nia'tekariò:take teionatawénrie tsi kahrhahrónnion tsi shé:kon iethí:kens tsi kontitakhenóntie's kahrhakónhshon táhnon taionatka'wenhátie ne aoti'wà:ron táhnon aotinéhon. Eh káti naiohtónhake nonkwa'nikòn:ra.

Kaié:ri Nikawerá:ke
Akwé:kon énskat entitewahwe'nón:ni nonkwanikòn:ra táhnon teiethinonhwerá:ton ne kaié:ri niiokwèn:rare, othorè:ke, entiè:ke, na'kòn:ke, táhnon ne e'nekèn:ke nonkwá:ti nitionatewerí:non. Shé:kon rotiio'tátie tsi nahò:ten ronaterihón:ton naiá:wen'ne aetewatón:rie. Eh káti naiohtónhake nonkwa'nikòn:ra.

Ionkhihsothó:kon Ratiwè:ras
Akwé:kon énskat entitewahwe'nón:ni nonkwanikòn:ra táhnon taiethinonhwerá:ton ne Ionkhihsothó:kon Ratiwè:ras tsi shé:kon ratiwennotáties táhnon á:se shonnón:nis tsi kahnekahrónnion tsi ionhontsá:te. Eh káti naiohtónhake nonkwa'nikòn:ra.

Ionkhihsótha Ahsonthenhnéhkha Karáhkwa
Akwé:kon énskat entitewahwe'nón:ni nonkwanikòn:ra táhnon teiethinonhwerá:ton ne Ionkhihsótha Ahsonthenhnéhkha Wenhni'tarátie's tsi shé:kon tiekonhsarátie's tsi teionkhihswathe'tén:ni tsi niwahsonté:son's naiá:wen'ne skén:nen aontén:ti tsi ionhontsá:te. Eh káti naiohtónhake nonkwa'nikòn:ra.

Ehtshitewahtsì:'a Entiehkehnékha Karáhkwa
Akwé:kon énskat entitewahwe'nón:ni nonkwanikòn:ra táhnon tehtshitewanonhwerá:ton ne Ehtshitewahtsì:'a Entiehkehnékha Karáhkwa tsi shé:kon thotenniehtonhátie ne rao'shatsténhsera. Eh káti naiohtónhake nonkwa'nikòn:ra.

Iotsistohkwarónnion

Ó:nen akwé:kon énskat entitewahwe'nón:ni nonkwa'nikòn:ra táhnon
teiethinonhwerá:ton ne iotsistohkwarónnion teiotihswathè:ton tsi tkaronhiatátie's tsi shé:kon ionkhina'tón:nis tsi
niiotierá:ton entewatié:ra'te nó:nen ionk-
watia'tahtòn:'on. Eh káti naiohtónhake
nonkwa'nikòn:ra.

Shonkwaia'tíson

Ó:nen káti nón:wa eh nón:we
ia'tentewawennaníhara'ne ne tsi nón:we
thotatenaktarakwén:ni ne Shonkwaia'tíson. Entewehià:rake tsi rohsa'ánion,
rokwatákwen táhnon roweiennentà:'on
akwé:kon nahò:ten tewaniahè:sen
aetiónhnheke. Né: káti akwé:kon énskat
entitewahwe'nón:ni nonkwanikòn:ra
táhnon tetshitewanonhwerá:ton ne
Shonkwaia'tíson. Eh káti naiohtónhake
nonkwa'nikòn:ra.

Karihwahnhó:ton

Ó:nen ká:ti eh niió:re wa'katerihwatk-
wé:ni akewennóhetste' ne kanon-
hsweratónhsera. Tóka' othé:nen
sonke'nikóhrhen, í:se kwi' nen' nè:'e
tsisewaia'tátshon ientsisewatahsón-
teren tsi entisewahtka'we ne kanonhweratónhsera. Ó:nen nón:wa eh
nón:we iahetéwawe ne ioióhe aetew-
arihwahnhotón:ko táhnon enwá:ton
entewaterihwahténtia'te tsi nahò:ten
ionkwaterì:wate. É'tho káti nika-
wén:nake táhnon ó:nen é'tho.

Thanksgiving Address (in English)

Each day, when there is an important
matter at hand, we must give thanks.
We will give thanks for all he has created and prepared for us here on the
earth and in the sky. This is called the
matters before all else. So it be in our
minds.

We bring our minds together as one
and give thanks to the people on the
earth, that they are still tending to their
responsibilities to that peace can be possible on earth. So let it be in our minds.

We bring our minds together as
one and give thanks to the earth, that
in her kindness she still continues to
provide us with her strength for this
is what we need to continue to live

peacefully upon her body. So let it be in
our minds.

We bring our minds together as one
and give thanks to the water, that we still
have waters to cool our bodies, quench
our thirst, and wash away pollutants in
the earth. So let it be in our minds.

We bring our minds together as one
and give thanks to the many kinds of
fish that live in the water, that they still
clean the waters, that we are still able to
use their meat to sustain us. So let it be
in our minds.

We bring our minds together as
one and give thanks to the many kinds
of plants growing on the planet; the
grasses, roots, and shrubbery, that we
depend on when we are in hunger, and
that heal us when we are ill. So let it be
in our minds.

We bring our minds together as one and give thanks to the many kinds of insects. He has created many different types of insects on the earth, they are connected to the beautification of the earth, so that things may come along peacefully. So let it be in our minds.

We bring our minds together as one and give thanks to the many kinds of sustainers, to the many kinds of fresh foods that grow in the gardens we plant. We also give thanks to the three sisters; corn, beans, and squash. So let it be in our minds.

We bring our minds together as one and give thanks to the many kinds of berries (hanging fruits) of the earth in which we eat, that we use to make juice, and that we use to sustain ourselves.

We also give thanks to the strawberry, who was chosen by the Creator to be the leader of the berries/fruit. So let it be in our minds.

We bring our minds together as one and give thanks to the many forests, and the leader of the trees, the maple. That we are still able to use it to make our homes, to keep us warm when it is cold, and that we are still able to use it to sustain ourselves. So let it be in our minds.

We bring our minds together as one and give thanks to the many kinds of birds on the earth, and the leader, the eagle. That we are still provided with their strength. So let it be in our minds.

We bring our minds together as one and give thanks to the many kinds of animals that wander the forests. That we

still see them running about the forests, that they are still us with their skin, and their meat to sustain ourselves. So let it be in our minds.

We bring our minds together as one and give thanks to the four winds: north, south, east and west. That they are still working together so that we can breathe. So let it be in our minds.

We bring our minds together as one and give thanks to our grandmother the moon, that her face still illuminates the night making sure so that it will be peaceful here on earth. So let it be in our minds.

We bring our minds together as one and give thanks to the stars that shine in the sky, that they still show us the way we should go when we are lost. So let it be in our minds.

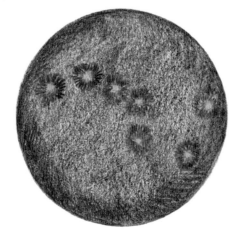

We bring our minds together as one and give thanks to the Creator. We remember that he is the one that he has created, and prepared everything we depend on to live. This is why we bring our minds together to thank him. So let it be in our minds.

Now that I have put the words of thanksgiving through.

If I have forgotten anything, it falls to each of you here to continue to complete it. Now it is time for us to open up the matter, and start the matter at hand.

We bring our minds together as one and give thanks to our elder brother sun, that he is still providing us with his strength. So let it be in our minds.

Continuing the Conversation
"The Thanksgiving Address: Greetings and Thanks" Video

Molly Anderson

Many people in the United States are questioning the value of the brief and nearly obligatory "land acknowledgment" at the beginning of an event or ceremony. For some, it is an empty gesture that changes nothing for the reality of Indigenous people whose land has been stolen, and at most elicits a little twinge of white or settler guilt that, once acknowledged, can be ignored.

The Thanksgiving Address is a more meaningful alternative that might help both to remember whose land we stand upon and also the meaning to these people of that land—and all of their relations in the waters, birds, animals, and other living and nonliving beings connected with it. Rethinking and remembering our interdependence with the natural world is a crucial teaching from Indigenous people for settler people who have lost our way in the world.

By losing our sense of relationship, we have lost the path that Indigenous people followed to be in the world with reverence and respect. And along with that loss of reverence and respect has come the callous ability to treat the living world, on which we depend for our lives, as nothing but a source of wealth to be extracted, a playground, or a waste dump.

The traditional use and ubiquity of the Thanksgiving Address are important to remember as well: this wasn't comparable to a U.S. Thanksgiving Day prayer before dinner but an everyday practice of spirituality. Until reverence and respect infuse every day of settler existence, we will remain painfully separated from our relations and threatened with self-inflicted destruction.

Molly Anderson is the William R. Kenan Jr. Professor of Food Studies at Middlebury College, Vermont. She teaches, writes about, and analyzes food insecurity and the right to food, resilience of food systems, food democracy, and pathways to transformation.

PART II
SETTING THE TABLE

This book and its accompanying website offer a delectable array of food for thought and action. Part I acknowledged the spirit with which we approach our exchange, by greeting and thanking all the elements, human and more than human, that sustain life. This gratitude and sense of interconnection help prepare us to sit down at the human table to reflect on the relationship of Earth to Tables. Before meeting the story-tellers (part III) and entering into conversations about food justice and food sovereignty (part IV), we must first set the table. What is the broader context within which we have these conversations? How do we build relationships to nourish conversations that are open and honest? How do we have these conversations in our own communities? And how do we move to action, to walk the talk?

The three sections of part II speak to these questions. In chapter 2, "Navigating Dynamic Tensions on Common Waters," we acknowledge the complex structural power dynamics that shape the current indus-trial capitalist food system and the countermovements for food justice and food sovereignty. We frame these dialectically as knowledge tensions, food tensions, equity tensions, and political tensions, though they are intersecting and more nuanced in the way they play out in our interactions.

In chapter 3, "Pollinating Relationships: Our Collaborative Methodology," we reflect on our own process of building relationships in the Earth to Tables Legacies project. Pollinating refers to the healthy functioning of a sustainable food system as well as the nurturing of our relations as Legacies partners—across generations, borders, histories, methodologies, mediums, and organizations. As we define our evolving collaborative methodology, we share key moments of learning on our journey since 2015.

The final chapter in part II, chapter 4, "Digging In and Digging Deeper: Facilitating Dialogue and Action," articulates our popular educational approach. It introduces you, the reader, to the unique peda-gogical tools we've created to invite critical, collective, and creative engagement with the stories shared here. We delineate the sections of the Facilitator Guides embedded in each photo essay and video, to encourage individuals and groups to digest this material thoughtfully, to connect it to their own context and experiences, and to use it as a springboard for actions for change.

These ideas, processes, and tools help set the table for a richer dialogue among the diverse collabora-tors and their stories, told in the form of photo essays and videos. They invite you to join us at this table, to continue the conversation.

CHAPTER 2
NAVIGATING DYNAMIC TENSIONS ON COMMON WATERS
The Broader Context of Our Legacies Conversations

In the Legacies exchange, our Haudenosaunee partners Chandra and Rick reminded us of the Two Row Wampum, or *Teioháte Kaswén:ta*, an agreement that dates back to a 1613 treaty between the Haudenosaunee and Dutch. Woven into the beaded wampum are two parallel paths, one representing the Indigenous canoe and the other the European mast ship. This original agreement was based on notions of peace and friendship; each nation would follow its own path while respecting and not intervening in the path of the other. And it was always in relation to all other living beings. As Tuscarora historian Rick clarifies, the agreement was to last "as long as the Sun always makes it bright on earth, the Waters flow in a certain direction, and the Wild Grasses grow at a certain time of year."

The two-row wampum can be seen as a framework for the kind of relationship between Indigenous people and settlers that we desperately need to recover. But we first have to acknowledge the many ways that this treaty has been broken and its impact on our nation-to-nation relationship, as well as our relationship with the common waters that we share.

The Earth to Tables Legacies exchange grapples with the tensions, struggles, and legacies of broken treaties and western imperialism. We have identified four interrelated dynamic tensions that represent the broader political, ecological, and cultural context within which we live and work. They shape our relationships and the conversations that you will find within our videos and photo essays. These tensions represent the ongoing struggle between the Indigenous peoples and settlers,[1] the canoe and the ship. Our colonial histories are complicated by the fact that there are also deep differences among the so-called settlers, as the ships were

Chandra explaining the two-row wampum to Legacies collaborators at Six Nations

controlled by wealthy white Europeans who brutally stuffed Africans into the galleys as part of the Atlantic slave trade, compounding a legacy of white supremacy. And these African "settlers" had deep roots in Indigenous cultures, as did racialized immigrants and exiles from other colonized continents.

We identify these interrelated tensions around the notions of knowledge, food, politics, and equity. They correspond with the way we have framed the videos and photo essays in the Conversations section: as ways of knowing, earth, justice, and tables. The photographs that open each section are drawn from the climate justice strike in Toronto in 2019, revealing how activists are naming these tensions in the streets.

We need to be attentive to how asymmetrical power relationships have enabled conventional Western knowledge to produce hierarchies of knowledge that too often mute modes of understanding in the world as deeply connected and interconnected.[2]

—Gina Starblanket and Heidi Kiiwetinepinesiik Stark

Download the Facilitator Guide (ettl.ca/fg) for this section.

To consider the tensions between Eurocentric and Indigenous knowledges, we have to revisit the history of five hundred years of European colonization and global imperialism, and how it coevolved with western science. For the European colonizers of the Americas, land was seen as *terra nullis* or empty, its wilderness to be tamed, its possession as property to be expanded, its resources to be exploited for human use. This perspective was reinforced by European natural and human sciences, based on philosophies such as Cartesian dualism, separating body and mind, matter and spirit. It was coupled with a view of history as linear, moving toward a higher state of universal progress, epitomized by more recent notions of modernity, development, and globalization.

At a recent Canadian gathering of Indigenous and non-Indigenous scholars reflecting on the contemporary resurgence of Indigenous peoples and efforts toward reconciliation, settler and political scientist James Tully synthesized the impact of this view of knowledge:

Western sciences often dismiss Indigenous knowledges and life ways as primitive, superstitious, soon to die off, lower, or less-developed relative to the superior knowledge and processes of civilization, modernization, and globalization spread around the world by Western peoples. And these two imperious attitudes to the living earth and Indigenous peoples are closely related historically and conceptually.[3]

Climate scientists and environmental activists are recognizing that the current crisis is rooted in this worldview of separation from and possession of land for human use, and greed.

"Dispossession from the living earth is thus not only a monumental ongoing social injustice to Indigenous peoples. It is also a monumental ongoing ecological, epistemological and social injustice to one and all."[4]

In contrast, Indigenous cyclical ways of being and participatory ways of knowing are central to understanding the interdependence of humans with "all our relations" (as acknowledged in the Haudenosaunee Thanksgiving Address). For Indigenous peoples, knowledge is a process and not a product, and is cocreated in relationship with other living entities on the earth. As Leanne Betasamosake Simpson, Michi Saagiig Nishnaabeg scholar, writer, and artist, asserts, "The land, *aki*, is both context and process."[5]

This different way of knowing is reflected in Indigenous languages, as Mohawk professor Ryan Decaire reflects in the photo essay "Language and Food." The word *Tyonnhekhwen* refers

not only to the vegetables and fruits we eat (as objects), but how they sustain us and provide us with life (a relational process).

Although the contrast is stark between some forms of Eurocentric thought and Indigenous ways of knowing, in recent decades there has been a convergence of earth and human sciences, quantum physics, and integral ecology, with Indigenous and traditional ecological knowledges. James Lovelock dug even deeper into ancient European philosophies in formulating his Gaia hypothesis, which was built on the Greeks' belief in the animacy (breath, spirit, energy) of the living earth. This theory has been endorsed by many scientists who are part of the Intergovernmental Panel on Climate Change.

American evolutionary theorist and biologist Lynn Margulis interpreted the Gaia hypothesis as symbiosis, "the immensely complex webs or networks that link all forms of life in relationships of reciprocal interdependence. Temporally, these networks are cyclical."[6]

Robin Wall Kimmerer, plant ecologist and Potawatomi knowledge keeper, was trained in western science: "The questions scientists raised were not 'Who are you?' but "What is it?'. No one asked plants 'What can you tell us?'

The primary question was 'How does it work?' The botany I was taught was reductionist, mechanistic, and strictly objective."[7]

Kimmerer has created spaces for conversations between the western science she was trained in and Indigenous traditional ecological knowledges: "Reciprocity—returning the gift—is not just good manners; it is how the biophysical world works."[8]

Simply put, Kimmerer concludes, "Plants can tell us her story. We just need to learn to listen."[9]

James Tully, settler ally with Indigenous peoples, has come to the same conclusion: "The way people come to know what ways of life co-sustain their interdependent neighbours, human and more-than-human, is to enter into dialogues of mutual learning with them."[10] Tully sees this shift in thinking as representing two epistemic revolutions among non-Indigenous people: recognizing our interdependence with the living earth and with Indigenous peoples.

Mohawk food leader and Legacies collaborator Chandra Maracle draws from both western science and Indigenous knowledge: "I love science as a way to explain things but I'm also deeply soulful and spiritual and looking

Bless This Land[11]

Joy Harjo

Bless this land from the top of its head to the bottom of its feet

. . . From the arctic old white head to the brown feet of tropical rain

Bless the eyes of this land, for they witness cruelty and kindness in this land

. . . From sunrise light upright to falling down on your knees night

Bless the ears of this land, for they hear cries of heartbreak and shouts of celebration in this land

. . . Once we heard no gunshot on these lands; the trees and stones can be heard singing

Bless the mouth, lips and speech of this land, for the land is a speaker, a singer, a keeper of all that happens here, on this land

. . . Luminous forests, oceans, and rock cliff sold for the trash glut
. . . of gold, uranium, or oil bust rush yet there are new stories to be
. . . made, little ones coming up over the horizon

Bless the arms and hands of this land, for they remake and restore beauty in this land

. . . We were held in the circle around these lands by song, and
. . . reminded by the knowers that not one is over the other, no
. . . human above the bird, no bird above the insect, no wind above the grass

Bless the heart of this land on its knees planting food beneath the eternal circle of breathing, swimming and walking this land

. . . The heart is a poetry maker. There is one heart, said the poetry
. . . maker, one body and all poems make one poem and we do not
. . . use words to make war on this land

Bless the gut labyrinth of this land, for it is the center of unknowing in this land

Bless the femaleness and maleness of this land, for each holds the fluent power of becoming in this land

. . . When it was decided to be in this manner here in this place, this
. . . land, all the birds made a birdly racket from indigo sky holds

Bless the two legs and two feet of this land, for the sacred always walks beside the profane in this land

. . . These words walk the backbone of this land, massaging the tissue
. . . around the cord of life, which is the tree of life, upon which this
. . . land stands

Bless the destruction of this land, for new shoots will rise up from fire, floods, earthquakes and fierce winds to make new this land

. . . We are land on turtle's back—when the weight of greed overturns
. . . us, who will recall the upright song of this land

Bless the creation of new land, for out of chaos we will be compelled to remember to bless this land

. . . The smallest one remembered, the most humble one, the one
. . . whose voice you'd have to lean in a thousand years to hear—we
. . . will begin there

Bless us, these lands, said the rememberer. These lands aren't our lands. These lands aren't your lands. We are this land.

. . . And the blessing began a graceful moving through the grasses
. . . of time, from the beginning, to the circling around place of time,
. . . always moving, always

into cosmology, and sometimes science falls a little short of Indigenous knowledge. So I like the interplay of both."

In conversation with Chandra, settler farmer Dianne Kretschmar also recognizes the need for an Indigenous perspective on our relationship with the land, and the limitation of "the European fixation on land ownership, because in actual fact, you can't own land, the land owns you, if you have any respect for the land."

Perhaps we need more poetic forms of language to express this world view rather than the academic discourses that often reflect Eurocentric ways of knowing. Joy Harjo, member of the Mvskoke Nation and the first Native American U.S. poet laureate, captures this ultimate integration of all our relations.

Food Tensions: Corporate Food Regime versus Food Sovereignty Movement

> Download the Facilitator Guide (ettl.ca/fg) for this section.

Our Legacies Exchange is basically a response to what we see as a crisis (environmental, political, cultural, and epistemological) represented in the capitalist model of industrial agriculture and a global food system shaped in the past sixty years by corporate concentration, environmental destruction, dispossession of peasant and Indigenous land, distancing between producers and consumers, neoliberal trade policies, and increasing health issues.

The focus should not only be what we are against, but what we are for.
—Fulvio Gioanetto

Rather than dwell on what we were up against, we chose to focus on the more sustainable and healthy food system we are trying to recover or create, epitomized by the term food sovereignty.

Living Food Sovereignty: Legacies Partners Speak from Where They Stand

The Legacies project started as an exchange among friends actively creating alternatives to the industrial food system. So, our conversations about food sovereignty were grounded in people's everyday lives.

Chandra reflected on the concept while breastfeeding her baby: "The first time that I heard the term 'food sovereignty'. . . it took me a while to wrap my head around that phrase. But the work that I do IS food sovereignty, it's just living that food sovereignty."

Like the Indigenous practice of passing a "talking stick" so that everyone has a chance to speak their own truth, we asked each of the collaborators to define food sovereignty in their own words, related to their cultural context and food work. For example, Dianne, who epitomizes the "Earth" end of our "Earth to Tables" metaphor, focuses on the work of growing food: "Food sovereignty to me means that we have the ability to produce locally most of what we need to eat; to provide the population with good, nutritious, culturally appropriate foods. It's a human right to have food and water."

Chandra, representing the "Table" in our conceptual framework emphasizes the eating end of the process: "Food sovereignty is being in control of what is on the end of your fork. That includes knowledge about and access to what it is that should be on the end of your fork. It includes support while in recovery from food-related trauma and trauma that is being played out through food."

Likewise, the responses of our Mexican partners depended on their identities and contexts. So Mayan food activists brought their particular Indigenous perspective to the conversation. In fact, Valiana noted, "The word sovereignty doesn't exist in our Mayan language, so we focus on Janaal, or eating, the broader act of recovering our traditional ancestral knowledge. It's about weaving ourselves into a community, inhabiting the land in its living forms as the woods, the winds, the ocean, the fire around which we come together to eat, as a celebration of life."

Ángel contrasted this holistic perspective with a narrow dominant view in the corporate food regime: "We view food sovereignty as a way of life; we call it 'reclaiming the art of eating' without involving transnational corporations. It means facing the challenges of growing our own food, caring for seeds, watching our plants grow, sharing our passion with others."

P'urepécha María and European-born Fulvio, raising their family in an autonomous village in Mexico, reflect on their own positions within the food cycle. Maria grounds her definition in the home and community: "Food sovereignty is to take care of the food we have and that we can produce without buying it. Here in our village women grow food in pots around their homes which they can harvest and use with their families."

As a social justice advocate shaped by a global perspective, Fulvio sees "food sovereignty as the right of each person to eat well and to produce their own food, with a distribution system that is direct and has a short chain. What is important is to produce food for the majority who don't have enough to eat."

Fernando, a non-Indigenous food activist promoting urban agriculture in a large Mexican city, offers the perspective of urban consumers and potential producers: "Food sovereignty is the right of people not only to eat a diverse diet but to have access to nutritious food and having access to land to grow our own food, and to produce the food in a way that respects nature. It's a commitment we make to take care of the Earth."

Back in Canada, on the Atlantic Coast of Quebec, settlers Anna and Adam reflect the perspective of a young family trying to be self-sufficient in food: "Food sovereignty for us means having choices and we feel very lucky to have so many. We work hard for it but growing, raising, processing, and preserving our own food lets us not only decide what we eat but how it is grown. Gardening and gathering from the forest is our work, our entertainment, our exercise, and our children's classroom for the summer and fall."

As an African-Canadian immigrant living in Canada's biggest city, Leticia brings a critical antiracist and gender perspective to the discussion: "The food movement is based on the backs of Black and Brown people. Globally Indigenous people are putting their lives on the land to protect the land, to grow good healthy food for all the beings. So dismantling racism is a big piece of food sovereignty, as well as patriarchy; racialized women are dominant in farming, but they don't own land."

Two other Haudenosaunee collaborators living in so-called Canada bring a historical perspective on the impact of colonialism and the current political process of recovering control of their food system. Rick recalls, "Years ago, I was surprised to find out the wide variety of foods of my ancestors. A seed of thought was planted that maybe our foods are important. I learned the elemental nature of crop cultivation and

animal harvesting within our culture. With John Mohawk and others, we got involved in communal farming, cultivating white corn as a defiant act against capitalism."

Similarly, for Ryan, "food sovereignty is strictly political to me. It's about control of land. As Indigenous people with distinct governments, we need to break free from the control of colonial governments, to feed ourselves and control our food system."

Perhaps not surprisingly, four members of our production and editorial team, immigrants and settlers living in Canada's largest city, Toronto, speak about the ideas that have influenced their local and global activism and allyship:

Colombian-Venezuelan-Canadian codirector Alex focuses not only on food, but on ways of being: "Ultimately, food sovereignty is based on good relationships: with your surroundings, with what you eat, and with the nonhuman, promoting new modes of thinking and inhabiting the planet."

For John, food sovereignty is "a worthy aspirational goal that seeks to provide food security, sufficient, even abundant, culturally relevant nutritional food for all, produced in ecologically sound and sustainable ways respecting

the rights of consumers, farmers and their workers to define their own food and agricultural systems consistent with social justice."

As a leader in local, national, and global networks, Legacies coeditor Lauren notes that her "ideas about food sovereignty were deeply shaped by the People's Food Policy Project. Inspired by La Via Campesina, it was a grassroots response to the crises in our food systems, which engaged 3,500 people over three years to come up with A People's Food Policy for Canada."

Editor/director Deborah offers the perspective of a settler activist from the Global North who has worked with and learned from Indigenous and peasant movements in the Global South: "Most of us urban dwellers have become disconnected from the land, from other living creatures, and thus from ourselves and each other. The reclaiming of this connection and of community control of food production has been initiated by millions of Indigenous peoples and peasants who remind us that food is not a commodity but is sacred medicine that can sustain and heal us physically, culturally and spiritually."

Where do you stand? How does your location, identity, and engagement with the food system affect your perspective on food sovereignty?

In honoring these multiple definitions grounded in diverse local places, we are not denying the usefulness of other attempts by both international coalitions of activists and committed academics to define this framing concept from a global standpoint. Let's put the Legacies voices in conversation with some of these.

Eric Holt-Gimenez offers a useful continuum for looking at these tensions. Under the banner of the Corporate Food Regime, he includes food enterprise, which represents the market-driven neoliberal industrial model, as well as food security, which he labels as reformist, referring to the mainstreaming of organic alternatives that remain driven by the market. In contrast, he advocates for food movements that reject the neoliberal market-driven system and promote food justice and food sovereignty. He considers the latter more radical, represented by international coalitions such as Via Campesina that aim to dismantle the corporate agri-foods monopoly and democratize food systems.

In 2007, five hundred representatives from eighty countries gathered in Nyéléni village, Sélingué, Mali for an historical Forum on Food Sovereignty.

"Food sovereignty is the right of peoples to healthy and culturally appropriate food produced through ecologically sound and sustainable methods, and their right to define their own food and agriculture systems.

"It puts the aspirations and needs of those who produce, distribute and consume food at the heart of food systems and policies rather than the demands of markets and corporations.

"It defends the interests and inclusion of the next generation.

"It offers a strategy to resist and dismantle the current corporate trade and food regime, and directions for food, farming, pastoral and fisheries systems determined by local producers and consumers.

"Food sovereignty prioritizes local and national economies and markets and empowers peasant and family farmer-driven agriculture, artisanal—fishing, pastoralist-led grazing, and food production, distribution and consumptions based on environmental, social and economic sustainability.

"Food sovereignty promotes transparent trade that guarantees just incomes to all peoples as well as the rights of consumers to control their food and nutrition.

"It ensures that the rights to use and manage lands, territories, waters, seed, livestock and biodiversity are in the hands of those of us who produce food.

"Food sovereignty implies new social relations free of oppression and inequality between men and women, peoples, racial groups, social and economic classes and generations."

Nyeleni declaration by Forum on Food Sovereignty, 2007, Sélingué, Mali

Organized by an alliance of international social movements, the conference crafted a definition of food sovereignty that has shaped the global movement.

Although many themes in the Nyéléni declaration echo the words of Legacies collaborators, elements named here not only challenge the politics of the current global food regime but propose its dismantling. And even as it resonates with some of our Indigenous participants' points about local control, culturally appropriate foods, and feeding the next generation, the language is still dominated by a Eurocentric productivist way of thinking; traditional practices of hunting and gathering are not included, and an understanding of the spiritual values of food as sacred medicine is not acknowledged.

Nonetheless, this collectively framed definition has impacted food movements in Turtle Island (North America) and is echoed in statements by Food Secure Canada: "Food Sovereignty is the right of peoples to healthy and culturally appropriate food produced through ecologically sound and sustainable methods, and their right to define their own food and agriculture systems."

In analyzing any of these groups and their definitions, we need to bring a critical eye and not fall into traps of homogenizing nations, organizations, and communities as monolithic. Power is always operating, and differences within abound. We need to create spaces for these differences to be acknowledged, shared, debated, and worked through. We are seeking honest conversations that embrace these differences.

Equity Tensions: Intersectional Identities and Power

Download the Facilitator Guide (ettl.ca/fg) for this section.

Food sovereignty movements (originating in the Global South) and food justice movements (originating in the Global North) are closely allied with other movements for equity. Integral to food system transformation are struggles for equity, intersectional identities, and power among all historically marginalized peoples who are defending and claiming multiple racial and ethnic identities, rural-urban differences, gender and sexual diversities, religious practices, age-groups, and other diverse identities.

The concept of "all our relations" is an important metaphor for understanding intersectionality within and beyond the food system. A historical perspective positions different forms of oppression as part of ongoing cycles of injustice based on white supremacy and extractive economics. Colonialism, neocolonialism, imperialism, development, and globalization draw on the logic of elimination and replacement, power, domination, settlement, expansion, and control.

The Legacies project acknowledges different manifestations of oppression, the pervasive nature of social inequality woven through institutional structures and individual consciousness. Legacies collaborator Leticia Deawuo describes in detail the structural and material ways food injustice is perpetuated in the neighborhood surrounding Black Creek Community Farm. "For me, the word apartheid makes it clear that these are systemically constructed communities, in the way that food is distributed across the city and the way that people experience food. The fact that you have the Jane-Finch community (in Toronto) with fast food restaurants at every corner, and a community that pays more than other communities for fresh produce, a community where police are surveilling the grocery stores, this is food apartheid." In Quebec, Anna outlines how food security is a structural privilege based on the services available and the way these services are made available.

The concept of "all our relations" helps us see that human and nonhuman communities are simultaneously marginalized by oppression.[12] The degradation and abuse of land and people through industrial agriculture, the subjugation and enslavement of Indigenous people and racialized communities, the imposition of what is "human" and what is "other" in European knowledge, the exotification of some food cultures, racial exclusion in some alternative food spaces, are all linked and interconnected issues. These are all themes that arise over and over again in our discussions with Legacies collaborators.

Equity issues, as they are expressed by Legacies collaborators, echo global movements working on food system transformation, decolonization, dismantling white supremacy, and equity. In their special report on climate and land, the Intergovernmental Panel on Climate Change (IPCC) outlines the gender and equity dimensions related to food security and climate change, highlighting the central role women play in agriculture and how climate change impacts are uneven depending on age, ethnicity, gender, wealth, and class, with poor and vulnerable communities facing greater impacts. The IPCC states that a rights-based approach that explicitly recognizes women is critical if we want to improve food security, as well as achieve global climate adaptation and mitigation targets.

Using even stronger language, the Intergovernmental Science-Policy Platform on Biodiversity and Ecosystem Services (IPBES) in its Global Assessment Report states that

the character and trajectories of transformation will vary across contexts, with challenges and needs differing, among others, in developing and developed countries. Risks related to the inevitable

uncertainties and complexities in transformations towards sustainability can be reduced through governance approaches that are integrative, inclusive, informed and adaptive. Such approaches typically take into account the synergies and trade-offs between societal goals and alternative pathways and recognize a plurality of values, diverse economic conditions, inequity, power imbalances and vested interests in society.[13]

Globally, momentum is growing for a "Just Transition." This term has its roots in labor and environmental justice movements and is being applied by climate and justice advocates. The Just Transition Alliance[14] outlines:

Just Transition is a vision-led, unifying and place-based set of principles, processes, and practices that build economic and political power to shift from an extractive economy to a regenerative economy. This means approaching production and consumption cycles holistically and waste-free. The transition itself must be just and equitable; redressing past harms and creating new relationships of power for the future through reparations. If the process of transition is not just, the outcome will never be. Just Transition describes both where we are going and how we get there.[15]

For food systems, the Just Transition concept is extended beyond organized labor to include agricultural, food processing, and food distribution workers who are often migrant, racialized, undocumented, and working in vulnerable or informal contexts growing, processing, cooking, and distributing food. In the past decade, organizing by racialized farmers,[16] small and medium-sized farmers,[17] migrant workers,[18] and food chain workers[19] has expanded significantly. Their vulnerabilities were exposed and laid bare during the COVID-19 crisis.

The experience of the environmental justice movement illustrates how communities of color and low-income communities have been disproportionately impacted by pollution and industrial practices, including industrial food system practices such as chemical intensive agriculture, confined animal feedlots, deregulated supply chains, and highly processed foods.[20] The environmental justice movement emphasizes centering

the voices, experience, and knowledge of those most impacted and engaging communities to "build thriving economies that provide dignified, productive and ecologically sustainable livelihoods; democratic governance and ecological resilience."[21]

The worldwide uprising against anti-Black racism and police violence that was sparked by the murder of George Floyd by police in Minneapolis, Minnesota, in the spring of 2020 revealed a convergence of movements against centuries of oppression against Indigenous, Black, and people of color. Many identified with the brutal action of the "knee on my neck." Thousands took to the streets in the middle of a pandemic that exposed a blatant disregard for racialized bodies, who were the majority of "essential" workers and a disproportionate number of deaths from the virus.[22] COVID-19 also revealed the frailties and injustices of the global food system. Youth activists, especially, showed a greater consciousness of the interconnectedness of all inequities—and of the necessity of alliances to work toward systemic change.

Political Tensions: Capitalism, Colonization, and Reconciliation

Download the Facilitator Guide (ettl.ca/fg) for this section.

The broader political tension within which we fight for healthy, sustainable, and culturally appropriate food is neoliberal capitalism and its history through European colonization and globalization, now being challenged by a resurgence and reconciliation process led by Indigenous peoples defending their land and culture, and joined by a growing number of non-Indigenous allies.

When we began this writing (December 2019), the political tensions resulting from more than five hundred years of European colonization, western imperialism, and neoliberal globalization were reaching a boiling point in a cauldron of conflicts over resources and protests of authoritarian austerity policies and human rights abuses.

Mass protests in the streets of Chile, Bolivia, Ecuador, Colombia, Venezuela, Nicaragua, echoed by social and environmental justice activists in the Global North, are connecting the dots between the struggles for political democracy and what Vandana Shiva has called "Earth Democracy." The uprisings in Chile precipitated the last minute moving of COP 15, the most recent international gathering to deal with the climate crisis, from Santiago to Madrid, Spain.

In Canada, in February 2020, the cauldron boiled over . . . with country-wide protests by Indigenous peoples and their non-Indigenous allies supporting the Wet'suwet'en hereditary leaders in their right to determine how their territory would be cared for and opposing the Coast GasLink pipeline project. Haudenosaunee activists in Kahnawake, Tyendinaga, and Six Nations held solidarity protests.

It's Columbus's mistake that unites us all.

—Vandana Shiva[23]

It's Always about Land

How did we get to this point? Many scholars, like Karl Polanyi, point to the "enclosure of the commons" in England in the 1600s as the roots of the history of land as property, and of earth as a resource to be extracted for human use.[24] He saw the subsequent processes of "civilization," "modernization," and "globalization" as contributing to the Great Transformation, disembedding humans from the Earth while promoting their mastery and control of nature.

European colonization of the Americas converged with the rise of industrial capitalism and promoted a world built on a distinction between traditional and modern, in which notions of "progress" and "development" were used to justify laws that dispossessed the lands and discredited the practices of Indigenous peoples.

For example, early colonizers in British Columbia saw the potential productivity of the soil for conversion into English-style farms and settlements, not recognizing "the subtle but significant Indigenous management practices of the area, involving the use of fire, weeding and clearing, pruning, selective harvesting, seeding while harvesting, soil aeration, replanting of bulbs and root

fragments, and transplanting from one area to another."[25]

Central to European colonization of the Americas were Christian and racist notions of the soul and the doctrine of discovery, which perceived Indigenous peoples similarly to nature, as wild and less than human, to be "civilized." The 1867 constitution of the colonial state of Canada reflected Eurocentric and white supremacist notion of superiority.

A recent gathering of Indigenous and non-Indigenous scholars concluded: "Unsustainable, non-reciprocal extraction, rather than sustainable, reciprocal regeneration, has become the dominant relationship to living earth and social systems."[26] This is more a "cradle-to-grave" system, rather than "cradle-to-cradle" systems in which trees in forests cycle from seed to nurse log, constantly regenerating themselves.

Key developments over recent decades are worth noting. In Canada, this struggle of Indigenous people to claim their inherent right to their territory has had numerous landmark moments. In the mid-1980s, a series of first ministers' conferences on self-government ended in an impasse. After the 1990 Oka crisis,[27] a Royal Commission on Aboriginal Peoples repudiated the doctrine of discovery and confirmed the inherent right of Indigenous peoples to govern themselves. The Supreme Court Delgamuukw decision in 1997 confirmed that the constitutional rights in Section 35 included real proprietary rights to their lands, giving weight to historical possession and to oral traditions.

The 2015 report from the Truth and Reconciliation Commission (TRC) on the history and impact of residential schools issued ninety-four recommendations based not on settler state frameworks, but on the UN Declaration on the Rights of Indigenous Peoples. Although the liberal government at the time pledged to implement the recommendations, it has become clear that it is too entrenched with corporate interests in land and resources such as oil. The TRC lead commissioner, Justice Murry Sinclair, synthesized the core criteria for moving forward: "Reconciliation is about forging and maintaining respectful relationships. There are no shortcuts."[28]

There is no political reconciliation without a reconciliation with the land. And that challenges all the tenets of advanced capitalism, neoliberal trade, and corporate globalization. Tully proposes a dual-pronged strategy linking two interconnected projects of reconciliation:

1. Reconciliation of Indigenous and non-Indigenous peoples (Natives and newcomers) *with* each other in all our diversity.
2. Reconciliation of Indigenous and non-Indigenous people (human beings) with the living earth; that is, reconciliation *with* more-than-human living beings (plants, animals, ecosystems, and the living earth as a whole).[29]

The nation-state is in question here. Because of the integration of corporate and political powers, the Canadian government continues to support fossil fuel industries and industrial agriculture. As Legacies partner and organic farmer Dianne concludes, "There's absolutely no political will for food sovereignty, zero. All the trade agreements, like CETA, NAFTA, the TPP, totally ignore the fact that we should be producing our own food and instead they mandate the globalization of commerce."

Our conversations across geopolitical borders revealed the differing impact of these agreements. We are all shaped by a globalized corporate food system, but the Mexican partners in our exchange deal with the legacies of policies that have turned countries self-sufficient in food into export-producing nations, the Global South feeding the Global North. Neoliberal trade agreements opened the way for the expropriation of communally held land; this allowed easy entry of transnational agribusiness to use the land as a resource to be exploited, a source of profit.

Our P'urépecha partners in autonomous Indigenous communities of Mexico also struggle to defend the legacies of both the rich biodiversity and cultural diversity of their territory. NAFTA gave the United States the comparative advantage in corn, supported by agricultural subsidies. This resulted in Mexico importing the cheaper corn and diminishing its self-sufficiency of maíz, which it had been producing for eight thousand years. The GMO corn of U.S.-based multinationals has contaminated the native corn and decreased maize diversity.

Timothy Wise summarizes the impact of NAFTA on Mexican campesinos: "while it opened land for investment, the manufacturing sector and agro-exports . . . it spelled death for campesinos; only 1 out of 4 got factory jobs."[30] It has also increased dependency on processed foods and shifted diets to U.S. style, exporting obesity. At the retail end of the food chain, supermarkets in

Mexico are controlled by multinationals such as Walmart.

The loss of land and livelihood has pushed even more Mexicans to move north to find ways to support their families, precisely by working in agribusiness in the United States and Canada, producing *our* local fruit and vegetables. They send back $20 billion in remittances, but even that is being threatened by recent efforts to stem the tide of the waves of migrants crossing the Mexican-U.S. border.

These legacies of migration and cross-border family relationships are being countered by our Legacies partners in their efforts to keep young people at home, defending food sovereignty in milpas and agroecological projects. Mayan Legacies partner Valiana leaves us with this question: "If *la comida* (food in the broadest sense) is what unites us in our lives, what we have in common, because all of us eat, how in this act do we ensure that we don't let the companies govern us but that we govern ourselves, in the large scale and at the level of family and friends?"

Through dialogue with our Indigenous partners, we settlers have been confronting the dark legacies of colonization, which separated communities from the land, children from their parents, people from their traditional practices of feeding themselves— through gathering, hunting, and fishing as well as cultivating. Similarly, our Haudenosaunee partners find hope in recovering the legacies of traditional foods and ceremonies, even as they create new forms and practices. Once again, food is at the center of these political struggles.

The year 2020 brought three major political crises that revealed even more clearly the systemic inequities upon which the global food system is built, opening up public discussion of the impact of colonialism and racism, and generating new alliances for systemic change. In early 2020, Canada was "closed down" for weeks, as Indigenous peoples and their non-Indigenous allies blocked the railways in protest of the Trans Mountain pipeline to carry bitumen from Edmonton, Alberta, to Burnaby, British Columbia, threatening the environment and Indigenous livelihoods. By March, COVID-19 had "locked down" not only Canada, but many parts of the world, revealing the unsustainability of the global food supply chain and exposing the disregard for the lives of migrant workers upon whom our food depends.

In late May, the videotaped brutal killing of black American George Floyd by Minneapolis police kneeling on his neck awakened the world once again to the anti-Black racism still rampant and sparked an uprising, led by Black Lives Matter. This new antiracism movement, while accentuating the disposability of Black lives, made the connection to the ongoing police violence against Indigenous peoples and generated a worldwide movement, joined by non-Indigenous activists as well.

The intersection of these three crises exposed both the horror of systemic racism integral to the corporate food system and the hope of new alliances to tackle anti-Black and anti-Indigenous racism in food justice and food sovereignty movements. The Legacies project has carried on our intercultural exchange, and we are preparing new videos to engage critical discussion of how these intersecting movements can push forward toward a truly just and sustainable food system.

CHAPTER 3

POLLINATING RELATIONSHIPS
Our Collaborative Methodology

Download the Facilitator Guide (ettl.ca/fg) for this section.

Listen! Listen for the buzz. No. Listen to the silence. Wild bees are dying off at alarming rates. One in three bites of food we eat depends on being pollinated by those bees, so our survival is intimately connected to theirs. Like them, we are threatened with extinction.

Seeing like a bee or like a plant or like soil challenges our human-centric view of the world, a view that, in fact, contributes to the global environmental crisis. Although the conversations in this book privilege human voices, we try to get inside the more-than-human forms of life in the images and stories in our videos and photo essays.

Pollination is a process that honors interspecies relations and describes the Legacies exchange well, a cross-pollination of people, knowledges, and practices. Since 2015, the Earth to Tables Legacies exchange has been pollinating relationships: across species, across generations, across borders, across ecologies, across cultures, across historical moments.[1]

Miguel Torres in the field at Plan B Organic Farm, Ontario

Lauren with Amelia (Anna and Adam's daughter) and Abena (Leticia's daughter)

Dianne with her son, Dan

Pollinating Generations

Our intergenerational process promotes dialogue between youth and elders. Canadian organic farmer Dianne has shared her knowledge with six young farmers in our exchange, including her son Dan. Mexico-based Fulvio has been mentoring his sons Bryan and Jorge in agroecological practices. Fulvio's daughter Serena and son-in-law, Miguel, have visited two Canadian farms, where their five-year-old daughter, Lindsay, learned to weed a garden. Our three gatherings of all collaborators have been family friendly: Anna and Adam brought their three kids to Six Nations, while Leticia came with her daughter Abena; they were cared for by Chandra and Rick's daughters.

While we produced multimedia tools to communicate to a broader public and particularly to youth, we experienced intergenerational tensions around the digital gap among collaborators. Everyone has their own preferred mode of communication. An elder partner prefers a landline telephone with no answering machine to speak with those who mainly communicate via Facebook or WhatsApp. Partners include those who prefer text messages over e-mail to rural Mexicans who have spotty internet service. Nonetheless, we have managed to bring some folks into conversations via FaceTime, Zoom, and Skype; one of the most interesting was between Chandra and Ryan speaking Mohawk over Skype!

The intergenerational learning around technology has definitely been a two-way process. For example, within the production team, Alex, my younger codirector, taught me many new technical skills: from framing video shots and recording good sound, to editing websites and creating hyperlinks. She also mentored other young people in the families we visited. And we both would sometimes pass the camera to an eager grandchild or aspiring young photographer.

Whether in the field or kitchen, intergenerational teaching and learning goes both ways. Ryan taught his mentor Dianne the Haudenosaunee skills of braiding corn and making corn soup.

Pollinating Borders

Indigenous peoples on Turtle Island (North America including Mexico) share a deep historical connection, with corn being central to the cultures represented in our exchange. Geopolitical borders are often seen as colonial impositions. The main north-south axis in our project runs from Ontario in "so-called Canada"[2] through New York to Ohio in the United States, and into central and southern Mexico (Jalisco, Michoacán, Yucatán, and Oaxaca states). Our project is built on personal histories of collaboration among some of us who live on Turtle Island:

Mexican agronomist Fernando spent the summer of 2002 learning organic agriculture from Dianne in Ontario. Dianne's family friend John met Fernando then and visited him regularly in Mexico.

Lauren invited Fulvio Gioanetto from Mexico to conferences in Canada in 2009; in subsequent years, he came to Ontario annually to work as a production consultant at Plan B organic farm.

In 2009, Deborah and Lauren hosted Gustavo Esteva from UniTierra in Oaxaca for a summer course on "Food Sovereignty, Indigenous Knowledges, and Autonomous Movements" at York University in Toronto. He introduced us to Mayan food activists Ángel and Valiana during a road trip to Mexico in 2014.

These Canadian-Mexican connections have been strengthened through the Legacies project and are evident in videos that are framed as exchanges of knowledges and practices.

- Fernando and Dianne have an ongoing dialogue about their deepening understanding of life of the soil.
- Fulvio and Dianne share information about not only agroecological techniques, but also about their common challenges of training younger people to take over farming.

When the Mexicans came to Canada for our gatherings, they also made new connections with each other, across regions and Indigenous nations. As a result, Mayans Ángel and Valiana invited Fulvio and María from their P'urépecha community in Michoacán to the Yucatán to offer workshops in medicinal plants and organic inputs.[3] All Latinxs[4] connected socially with our Colombian-Canadian production team

Mexican and Colombian collaborators connecting through language and food at an Ontario cottage

bilingual farmers market that integrates equally Francophone and Anglophone farmers and vendors.[6]

Raquel Bolaños, interpreter and artist/activist

Julieta María, interpreter and artist

(Alex, Juan, and Cristina); Spanish was a common language, human-plant relations a common passion, and a feast of homegrown food a way to both stomachs and hearts.

Pollinating Language

Language is critical to our understandings of culture and food.[5] Maternal languages of our partners include Mohawk, P'urépecha, Mayan, Spanish, French, and English. Although some of us are bilingual (Spanish-English), we required professional interpreters and wireless transmitters for our final gathering, an attempt to equalize participation. As important, Raquel and Julieta understood the issues and the cultural contexts of the participants.

In the Canadian context, French is an official language and a key political issue in the province of Quebec. Legacies partners Anna and Adam, who live in rural coastal Quebec, cofounded a

Pollinating Histories

A major goal of our exchange has been to challenge the colonial industrial agricultural system and learn from more holistic Indigenous food practices. In particular, we sought to develop relationships with Indigenous food activists in our own bioregion. In the current political context of truth and reconciliation in Canada, many settlers like ourselves are asking: given the brutal history of colonization and our ancestors' and our own complicity in it, how can we have a conversation that is respectful?

Food was our entry point, a vehicle for exploring myriad issues: land, non-agricultural food sources, cultural practices, and spiritual meanings of food, among others. As the project evolved over time, other activists in broader social movements such as the climate justice movement have also acknowledged the need for Indigenous leadership in shifting our minds to a deeper understanding of "all our relations."

Unearthing our complex and even contradictory histories is a lifelong activity for both settlers and Indigenous peoples, and the two-row wampum has been revived as a useful frame for constructing a relationship based on mutual respect. The two-row wampum first served as a treaty between the Haudenosaunee and the Dutch in 1613, an agreement for respectful coexistence, with each nation following its own path while not intervening in the path of the other. When Legacies collaborators gathered at Six Nations in Ontario in July 2019, our hosts, Chandra and Rick, introduced us to the wampum treaties and also to the longhouse, the communal living quarters of the Haudenosaunee, or "the people who extend the house." It was a profound way of welcoming us into their "homes," lives, histories, and shared future.

As guests[7] at Six Nations of the Grand River Territory, we were invited to participate in the traditional ceremonial protocol led by our Haudenosaunee collaborators, Ryan, Rick, and Chandra. As sacred ceremonies, they were not recorded, but our three hosts offer deeper introductions to the underlying Haudenosaunee cosmovision in videos and photos essays.[8]

Through the two days at Six Nations, we were able to ground our exchange in both historic and current food practices—whether gathering fresh vegetables at the local greenhouse or being served corn soup and strawberry

At our 2019 gathering at Six Nations, we visit a longhouse.

Legacies partners learn how to make cornbread at Six Nations.

When we met again in October 2016, we shared personal stories with objects everyone brought to honor ancestors who had influenced each of us in our current food practices.

Alex offers her monkey pot fruit reflecting her ancestry.

juice at the Everlasting Tree School. We learned about the storage of corn in the longhouse and the preparation of traditional cornbread in the Our Sustenance community kitchen. During our final feast of venison at Chandra and Rick's home, their daughters invited us to join an honor dance, reflecting the integration of food and art ceremony.

Pollinating Rituals

We opened our three gatherings of Legacies partners with a participatory ritual. These activities didn't always follow one spiritual tradition but were designed to help create a sacred space

Chandra and Rick's daughters lead us in a dance.

for deep dialogue, grounded in each person's history related to food.

In June 2016, we created a collective altar with objects people brought to introduce themselves through a story about their relationship to food.

During that second gathering, we also learned more about the ecologies and histories of the places we visited. We arranged with Jon Johnson of First Story Toronto[9] to give us a storied tour of the Humber River valley in western Toronto, the historic site of a Seneca cornfield and current site of salmon swimming upstream, highlighting the sacred meaning of both corn and salmon for Indigenous peoples.

At our final face-to-face gathering[10] at Six Nations in July 2019, we introduced ourselves in a circle locating our

Jon Johnson of First Story Toronto shares the Indigenous history of Humber River watershed.

migration stories on a map and sharing our icons (see page 73).

Throughout the five-year exchange, rituals have been part of our visits to each other's fields and kitchens as well. Dianne offered Chandra tobacco when she was invited to spend the day learning how to process corn; in Haudenosaunee protocol, tobacco is a sacred medicine offered to acknowledge and thank the person sharing her wisdom. Before any meal at Chandra's table, she lit a candle and welcomed us to join fingers in a circle, a ritual that is unique to her family but common in other forms in many households. The ritual of eating together has been central to our shared experience.[11]

These participatory openings were not only a way of getting to know each other more deeply, but they also prepared us to share our visions of the project and make decisions about its direction. We were always nourished with healthy meals at these gatherings of food activists. Chandra reflected on these gatherings: "We actually practice everything that we're talking about whenever we're together. We have a good meal. We have a great conversation. We come away having done something." She reminded us that "good food" is necessary for "good minds" (the gut-brain connection), which helped us reshape our goals over the years.

In our first gathering, we shared ideas about frameworks and methodologies for a collaborative production of a documentary film. At the second, we concluded that a multimedia package would be more dynamic and useful for education purposes than a feature-length documentary. At the third and final gathering, almost three years later, we reviewed draft videos and photo essays of the multimedia platform.

The themes of our videos and photo essays have emerged from these visits and gatherings. So, there are gaps in what we cover. The fact that this group was small and intimate made

Dan maps his migration story on a map of Turtle Island.

Dianne offers Chandra tobacco to thank her for sharing her knowledge.

communication easier in some ways but also limited us. We lacked fuller representation of urban agriculture and urban racialized communities,[12] LGBTQIA[13] perspectives, and U.S. cases. In terms of Indigenous participants, we mainly focused on one of our bioregional neighbors, the Haudenosaunee, and dug deeper into their history, but we lacked representation from other Indigenous communities in Canada or the United States surviving in different ecologies, with different treaty arrangements and food practices.

Although we didn't consider our project a conventional "research" process, we were funded by academic research monies, two Social Science and Humanities Research Council (SSHRC) Connections grants that support arts-based community-engaged research. The university affiliation required ethics procedures that didn't always fit our contexts or ways of working. For example, the ethics forms required by York University and by the Six Nations Research Ethics committee seem to assume that the process is led

by an individual academic, often an outsider anthropologist who will drop in, extract knowledge, and publish academic work for personal gain. This didn't fit the kind of process we were cocreating.

Pollinating Methodologies

We identify our process with alternative research methods[14] such as participatory research, community-engaged research, arts-based research, and decolonizing research,[15] all of which challenge conventional notions of research as individual, objective, neutral, and product-oriented. We have found many convergences between these more radical and collaborative approaches and the growing articulation of Indigenous research methods by Indigenous researchers.[16]

Although we were familiar with the four Rs of Indigenous education,[17] Jean-Paul Restoule recently expanded them, identifying six Rs of Indigenous research.[18]

Relationship is the overarching R, congruent with our framing of the Legacies exchange as one of "pollinating relationships." All other values fall within this primary principle.

Respect: This implies humility, respect for differences, and a commitment to building egalitarian relationships. Our research and production team had to learn about the different ecological and cultural contexts of our partners, and we visited their homes and communities many times over five years.[19] Partners had specific differences that we had to respect. For example, we learned not to visit Dianne's farm on a day that she was harvesting for the market, because she would be too busy to talk and would be distracted by filming on that day.

Sometimes we had to learn what respect meant in a particular context by making mistakes that were offensive. During our first gathering at an Ontario cottage, the classic flagpole bearing a Canadian flag was seen as an uncritical honoring of the colonial state, reflecting a lack of respect for the Indigenous territory on which we were meeting. But it sparked an important conversation about colonization and decolonization.

In Oaxaca, Mexico, we learned about cultural practices through unknowingly offending Indigenous beliefs: we had been invited to film Valiana and Ángel cooking typical Yucatán dishes, but when we set up the camera outside the kitchen at the dining table, Ángel informed us that for Mayans, eating is considered sacred and so should not be filmed. These uncomfortable moments were important in opening up honest conversation and helping to develop a relationship of trust over time.

Responsibility: We are responsible to the partners in our exchange as well as their families, to the knowledge they shared with us, and to ethical ways of working with this knowledge. We had many visits and conversations before bringing out the camera and filming interviews. And we regularly fed back material, sharing both footage and transcripts, as well as edited videos and photo essays. Our July 2019 gathering was an opportunity to review all material with partners, and they had an opportunity for feedback on the final website before it went live. So, though the production team bears ultimate responsibility for the final products, partners had many chances to feed in and sometimes complained of over-consultation!

Relevance: We began the Legacies project as an exchange among activists who identified with the common theme of "food sovereignty" and saw

Doña Yolanda sees herself in her milpa *in Oaxaca, Mexico.*

it as relevant to broader processes of decolonization and reconciliation. But the specific issues engaged in the videos and photo essays emerged from our conversations with and among partners. After the first year, we synthesized some of those themes and began to construct media pieces. The collective decision to produce a multimedia educational package rather than a feature-length documentary was based on its greater potential for critical use in communities, especially for potential young food activists. The real test of the relevance will come in the use of the tools by schools and communities.

Reciprocity: Reciprocity is a central principle not only of Indigenous cultures, but of many kinds of collaborative research. It took various forms throughout the years of our exchange. There was regular gift giving: from offering medicines to open conversations in a "good way" to sharing seeds (Fulvio's corn, Ryan's beans, Chandra's squash), Dianne's grass-fed beef and renowned lettuce, Valiana's and María's embroidered blouses, Deborah's photos and favorite books. We stayed in each other's homes and ate at each other's tables. The most powerful demonstration of reciprocity came in the form of an exchange of skills and work: Fulvio

and his family helped weed Dianne's garden; Chandra taught Dianne how to process corn; Valiana and Ángel introduced us to Yucatán cooking; we introduced them to farmers markets and multicultural foods in urban Canada.

Refusal: This principle, added by Mohawk Scholar Audra Simpson, is grounded in Indigenous self-determination in research. It refers to what communities may refuse to share and may represent a pushback against "ethical practices that protect institutions instead of individuals and communities."[20] We certainly struggled with this dynamic when requiring an Indigenous adviser to jump through multiple hoops of alienating research accounting forms required by the university in order to receive his payment. Silence was another response that may have implied refusal to participate, or may be related to other factors. At different moments throughout the five years, we connected with potential Indigenous co-applicants, advisers, and participants who had a strong influence on our thinking but chose not to continue with the project. We do not know all the reasons.

We hear loud and clear "Nothing about us without us!" as an important principle for all collaboration between

Indigenous and settler researchers, artists, and writers. We acknowledge the contradictions in our process with a production and editorial team that is intercultural but non-Indigenous, taking the lead in selecting participants, framing audio and video interviews, and processing stories in videos and photo essays. We created space and budget for videographers from all three Indigenous communities, and some material from those efforts is included. But there was a lack of training in some contexts as well as insufficient budget to hire established filmmakers.

Pollinating Mediums

At a deeper epistemological level, we share with Indigenous researchers an understanding of knowledges as "holistic and relational, interconnected and interdependent systems that encompass knowledge of the spirit, heart, mind, and body" (Abolson, 2011; Cajete, in Kovach, 2009).[21] This is the approach our collaborators take to their work with soil, plants, and food preparation: Dianne drawing on her embodied knowledge from years working the land to find new ways to regenerate the soil with mushrooms and wood chips, Chandra giving us the sensory experience of making cornbread at our 2019 gathering.

We locate our collaborative process within the field of arts-based research, an approach that honors other ways of knowing, artistic modes of inquiry, and alternative forms of cultural expression.[22] Central to all artistic expression is story—all of the pieces of the online platform are drawn from oral sources, people telling their food stories grounded in their own contexts. As collaborator Fulvio concluded, "This is the strength of the Legacies project—gathering life histories of real people in specific places." And when together, we always shared stories in a circle, another symbol of collective knowledge creation, counter to a western notion of knowledge as a product, even commodity, attributed to one person considered an "expert."

Photography and video were key tools in documenting the activities of our storytellers and feeding back to them their ideas and practices in edited form, as videos and photo essays. Some commented that it helped them understand their work in a new way, and they felt their knowledge and experience valued.

The camera could both enable and inhibit communication, depending on

Talking Treaties by Jumblies Theatre at Fort York

the circumstances. We never brought out the equipment during our first visits, and only after agreeing on the themes and sites for documentation. Still the setup and testing of multiple cameras and mikes required time and patience. Some, like Dianne, became so accustomed to the filming that she would stop us when a passing train threatened a good sound recording, or call us to

document her experiment of growing mycelium to regenerate the soil on her farm.

We hired a Haudenosaunee videographer to film the Thanksgiving Address and contracted Red Door Productions at Six Nations to edit all Haudenosaunee videos. The videos of Black Creek Community Farm involved Black filmmakers in documenting the multiracial project.

All videos and photo essays were vetted with the people appearing within them before going public.

In two cases, we gave cameras or microphones to young participants and asked them to film relevant activities in their communities. Often the young people made their own videos with cell phone technology; Chandra and Rick's daughter Olivia, for example, produced a short video of the corn-processing workshop Chandra offered in her kitchen and presented it to us at the end of the day. In Mexico, Fulvio and his sons got so used to the cameras and the visual methodology that now they are developing their own series of educational videos around medicinal plants in Spanish. This is one way that our process continues, especially as we may now create a new piece based on the coronavirus pandemic. These local productions are supported by monthly Zoom conversations of all partners, with Alex offering online technical support.

We made a conscious effort to promote intergenerational and intercultural dialogue by editing photo essays and videos to juxtapose collaborators from different places, ages, and cultures. We also asked them to comment on each other's stories, moving beyond a singular perspective and honoring multiple voices. Finally, we invited commentators with knowledge in a certain theme area to offer reflections at the end of those stories. Our hope is that this dialogical approach will encourage you, the reader/viewer, to enter into our conversations collectively, critically and self-critically. We encourage you to add your own experience and opinions to the discussion and, ultimately, to act upon new ideas and deeper understandings.

The multimedia package privileges the visual and digital—video and photographs allow us to tell stories in ways not limited to words. For younger people, the multiple digital forms speak in a language that they already know. But we are also challenged to "decolonize the digital" by offering frameworks and promoting processes that challenge dominant knowledge systems and honor Indigenous ways of knowing. In *A Digital Bundle: Protecting and Promoting Indigenous Knowledge Online*, Jennifer Wemigwans returns to Linda Tuhiwai Smith's classic *Decolonizing Methodologies* for a list of twenty-five projects or methodologies that can offer a framework for how online Indigenous knowledges can contribute to Indigenous resurgence. Although Legacies stories are not limited to Indigenous voices, the twenty-five projects speak to the kind of process that went into creating Earth to Tables Legacies digital pieces as well as how we hope they will be used: from reframing to connecting, from negotiating to envisioning.

There are many examples of digital technology feeding cultural renewal and education, multiplying voices of Indigenous peoples, marginalized communities, and food activists of all ages. But there is also a risk of becoming more disconnected from and destructive toward physical environments. Starblanket and Stark warn that "these technologies are transforming our approach to living in-relation, . . . and we forget the unique benefits of being situated physically in relationships."[23] This contradiction in the use of online tools has been accentuated by the coronavirus pandemic, with self-isolation and physical distancing pushing many to revert to creating and communicating through digital Web-based software.

Pollinating Organizations

Although our connections with each other were based on personal relationships and not on organizational links, most of us are part of coalitions or food movements, both local and global. In the Canadian context, for example, Dianne has connected with Ecological Farmers of Ontario, Canadian Organic Growers, and the National Farmers Union (NFU), while her son Dan was active with the NFU's Young Agrarians, which sent him as a delegate to meetings in the United States and Brazil of Via Campesina, the largest global food sovereignty coalition of eighty million peasants and Indigenous peoples in more than eighty countries. In Mexico, Fulvio founded an agroecological network, Red Coyote, and through workshops throughout the country, makes connections with innovative projects. He has also promoted an exchange with farmers in Ontario through his collaboration with Plan B Organic Farm.

Chandra and Rick are deeply involved with communities in Haudenosaunee territory, in both upstate New York and southern Ontario, from Six Nations to Tyendinaga to Kahnawake near Montreal. They are often featured speakers on issues of Haudenosaunee history and food in both Indigenous and non-Indigenous conferences and gatherings; in 2018, Chandra brought 130 people together in "The Law Is in the Seed: A Community CORNvergence."

During their work with UniTierra (University of the Land) in Oaxaca, Mexico, Ángel and Valiana became part

Alex filming Serena in cornfield

of food sovereignty organizations in the state and have been regular delegates to the National Indigenous Congress gatherings in Chiapas. Through ongoing student exchanges, they have developed strong links with Trent University in Peterborough, Ontario, and ChocoSol traders in Toronto.

Several of us are integrated into the urban agricultural community in Toronto. Leticia of Black Creek Community Farm was a member of the Toronto Food Policy Council and in late 2021 became executive director of a Canadian international NGO, SeedChange. Lauren has previously led the Toronto Food Policy Council, Sustain Ontario; was vice chair of Food Secure Canada, the major NGO of the food movement; and is chair of a new initiative, the Peoples Food Institute. Through her current work with the

Mexican Legacies collaborators visit First Nations House at Trent University.

Global Alliance for the Future of Food, she connects with food advocacy organizations around the world. Deborah has participated in Food Secure Canada and the Canadian Association of Food Studies, and with John has attended regular gatherings of the Agricultural, Food and Human Values Society.

Our hope is that this educational package will encourage users to seek organizations in their communities, regions, and nations that connect people working for just, healthy, and culturally appropriate foods. The videos can be used in cross-sectoral gatherings, as we did in 2019 when we screened "Why Farmers Markets?" in a local cinema as part of Toronto's Urban Agricultural Week. The Facilitator Guides include links to organizations that are relevant for each theme, promoting collective action growing out of greater awareness of food justice and food sovereignty issues.

The local, regional, and national organizations that Legacies collaborators are connected to are part of broader social movements. In many ways, the collaborators experience at a micro level the macro struggles for food sovereignty, truth and reconciliation, diverse ways of knowing and equity elaborated in chapter 2, "Navigating Dynamic Tensions on Common Waters."

Like the uncertain future of the bees that opened this chapter, our future pollinations—across borders, cultures, languages, generations, and mediums—are uncertain. If anything, the coronavirus crisis was a humbling reminder that we need to be constantly listening, in particular to the many ways that other beings—both human and non-human—are communicating to us.

What are we hearing?

What are we learning?

What are we doing?

Dianne digging in the forest of Grenville Farm

CHAPTER 4

DIGGING IN AND DIGGING DEEPER

Facilitating Dialogue and Action

Stop. Breathe. Think. Digest. Connect. Talk. Act.

We live in a culture where many of us browse and zap our electronic devices quickly from one story or image to another, leaving us isolated and our thoughts fragmented. This is not how we imagine the Earth to Tables Legacies educational package to be used. We have created Facilitator Guides for all of the videos and photo essays precisely to encourage critical, collective, and creative engagement with the stories and issues they raise. Look for this box at the start of every photo essay or video intro.

Download the Facilitator Guide (ettl.ca/fg) for this section.

Though the guides can be used individually to help a reader or viewer engage more consciously with the videos or photo essays, they are perhaps most helpful for a teacher or workshop facilitator. These guides are available online and can be downloaded from the website.

The guides all begin with a list of terms or themes that appear in the specific video or photo essay. We do not offer definitions for these terms. Rather you may choose to explore, discuss, or interpret them in a group.

The Facilitator Guides are divided into two sections, each identified by the icons below.

Digging In offers two kinds of questions for discussion: generic decoding questions and specific questions.

Generic Decoding Questions

These questions can be used to get groups to connect what they see and hear in the videos and photo essays with their own lives, both individually and collectively. They are based on a process developed by internationally known Brazilian educator Paulo Freire, who engaged literacy students in "decoding" images through a process that begins with description, makes both personal and collective connections, and hopefully moves into strategizing for action on relevant issues that arise from the discussion.

Specific Questions

In this section, we offer some questions that can both test the reader's or viewer's understanding and encourage a critical discussion of issues raised by the stories of Legacies partners. In some cases, we've extracted quotes from the videos and photo essays to encourage a deeper reading of the issues they raise.

Hands-On Activities

Not all of the themes of the Legacies material lend themselves to hands-on activities. But in those that do (such as "The Soil Is Alive" video), we encourage a multisensory engagement that deepens the learning. Creative facilitators may develop experiential learning activities that fit the particular context and give a group a chance to move from idea to practice.

Intergenerational and Intercultural Dialogue

The Earth to Tables Legacies exchange was consciously constructed to encourage conversations across generations and cultures. In many cases, the videos or photo essays themselves are examples of such a dialogue. For example, in "The Soil Is Alive" video, Canadian organic farmer Dianne Kretschmar reconnects with younger Mexican agronomist Fernando Garcia around their common analyses of the importance of the soil. In the photo essay "Mother's Milk: The Original Food," we have juxtaposed the stories of five different breastfeeding women in the project, revealing differences of age, culture, class, Indigeneity, and geographical location. Another way we encourage dialogue across differences is through

the commentaries that academics or activists outside the project have made in response to specific videos and photo essays.

In the guide, we have highlighted the border-crossing conversations of Legacies participants and raised some questions about the differences they reflect. Our hope is that viewers and readers will not only consider the differences reflected in the Legacies material, but will engage people of different ages and cultures in their discussion of the same material in their own contexts.

Individual and Collective Action

Action is the operative word here. Central to the popular education approach we are advocating through the Legacies project is the movement from discussion to action. In this section, we encourage viewers and readers to consider the relevance of the conversation to their daily lives and practices. These may include small steps in changing one's habits or becoming involved in group or organizational initiatives toward food justice and food sovereignty. If the guide is used with an organization that is directly invested in the issue, the Legacies material can be a catalyst for strategic planning for collective action.

Digging Deeper: Resources for Further Research and Action

Digging Deeper suggests resources for further research and action.

We recognize that our material is limited by our small group and their stories, which are not definitive statements but, rather, catalysts to get individuals and groups thinking. They can be jumping-off points for further research, so we have included some of the more comprehensive resources that we have uncovered. When testing the material with a university class, students added to this list, and we hope you will do the same.

Videos and Websites

Many others are making videos like ours, and organizations offer websites that are filled with useful articles, reports, images, and contacts. In some cases, we've also included relevant radio programs, podcasts, and music.

Books and Articles

We include specific articles and books that affirm, deepen, broaden, and even challenge the ideas within the Legacies material.

Organizations

Local, regional, national, and global organizations are working on the issues raised within the Legacies stories. This is not an exhaustive list and favors the Canadian context, so viewers and readers in the U.S. and global context will need to identify the groups that are most engaged in food sovereignty and food justice issues in their areas—not only name them, but contact them, check out their activities, and find ways to get involved.

Chandra leads collaborators in an activity during our 2019 gathering at Six Nations.

PART III
STORYTELLERS

Together, across generations, cultures, and borders, we cocreated the Earth to Tables Legacies. Part III of the book, chapter 5, provides an introduction to the storytellers and production team serving as an orientation to each collaborator's passions, perspectives, and place.

"Meet the Storytellers" shares a brief biography of collaborators involved in the project. You'll meet the storytellers in the photo stories and videos throughout the book and website, and these biographies share an insight into who you will meet in the chapters to come. In "Meet the Production Team," the coeditors and codirectors, Deborah Barndt, Lauren Baker, and Alexandra Gellis, share reflections on their deep roots and connections to food issues and to the people who form the foundation of Earth to Tables Legacies. These roots provided fertile ground for the cocreation of the project and shine a light on the relationships that grew and deepened through our conversations.

"Our Food Icons" is a playful way of getting to know each collaborator, each storyteller, through a food that they identify with. This highlights the interrelationship between people and food sources, how people shape food and food shapes people. In "Our Migration Stories" the collaborators share their histories of diaspora, movement, and migration, stories that connect us to the land as well as broader political, economic, and cultural processes and politics.

These introductions to the storytellers are also an invitation to join the conversation, to think about your own food biographies, your own creation stories, your own food icons and migration stories. We hope you'll bring these into our collective conversation as you read through the rest of the book and explore the Earth to Tables Legacies website.

Ángel Kú

Anna Murtaugh and Adam Royal

Chandra Maracle

Dan Kretschmar

Dianne Kretschmar

Fernando Garcia

Fulvio Gioanetto

Leticia Deawuo

Maria Blas

Rick Hill

Ryan DeCaire

Valiana Aguilar

CHAPTER 5

STORIES OF THE STORYTELLERS

Meet the Storytellers

Valiana Aguilar is a Mayan woman leader from the Yucatán who spent five years, with her partner, *Ángel Kú*, working with the University of the Land (UniTierra) in Oaxaca. Valiana and Ángel recently returned to their hometown of Sinanché where they are building a traditional Mayan homestead, a *Solar Maya*, and a *semillero de aprendizaje*, sowing seeds for learning.

"Food and its relationship to the land has a central role in our life as a community. We belong to a generation of young people from Indigenous communities who decided to leave the academic path behind and return to growing food on the land, to our ways of life and our ways of understanding the world."

Learn more about **Valiana Aguilar** (ettl.ca/c_va) and see her in the photo essay, "Mutual Nurturing," on page 106.

María Blas Cacari is a P'urépecha woman leader in Nurio, an autonomous community in the Mexican state of Michoacán. She has maintained traditional Indigenous practices and can explain the nutritional qualities of traditional foods of the P'urépecha culture.

"I was raised by my great grandmother, a *curandera* (healer), who taught me about plants and their medicinal uses. Currently, I'm working with my family to create organic inputs for fertilizer, herbicides, and pesticides."

Learn more about **María Blas Cacari** (ettl.ca/cmb) and see her in the photo essays "Mother's Milk" on page 118 and "Medicinal Plants" on page 96.

Ryan DeCaire is Kanien'kehá:ka (Mohawk) from Wáhta Mohawk Territory. He teaches immersion courses in Mohawk in Haudenosaunee communities, is a language professor at the University of Toronto, and a PhD student at the University of Hawaii.

"My work in language revitalization is guided by the thought that people revitalize a language, but more importantly, that a language revitalizes a people. I believe the same is true with our relationship with food."

Learn more about **Ryan DeCaire** (ettl.ca/crd) and see him in the video "The Thanksgiving Address" on page 17 and in photo essays "Language and Food" on page 91 and "Haudenosaunee Gifts" on page 84.

Leticia Deawuo was born in Ghana and moved to Canada at the age of twelve. She lived and worked in the Jane-Finch neighborhood of Toronto, where she was director of the Black Creek Community Farm. Leticia is now executive director of SeedChange, an international NGO headquartered in Ottawa.

"The food movement is based on the backs of Black and Brown people. So dismantling racism is a big piece of food sovereignty, as well as patriarchy; racialized women are dominant in farming, but they don't own land."

> Learn more about **Leticia Deawuo** (ettl.ca/cld) and see her in the photo essay "Food Justice" on page 160 as well as the video "Black Creek Community Farm" on page 170.

Fernando Garcia learned organic agriculture from Dianne Krestchmar in 2003. Returning to his home in Guadalajara, Mexico, he founded the urban agricultural project Cosecha en Casa, teaching residents to grow their own food. Since 2016, he has been an adviser for a Mexico-based multinational company producing healthy foods.

"I ensure that the raw materials are produced organically, promoting the values of sustainability and social responsibility. One of my projects is to train Mexican farmers to produce cauliflower and kale, hearty vegetables that are then processed into other nutritious products."

> Learn more about **Fernando García** (ettl.ca/cfg) and see him in the video "The Soil Is Alive" on page 127 and the photo essay "Promoting Organic Agriculture in Mexico" on page 144.

Fulvio Giaonetto is an Italian-Mexican agroecological producer and consultant living in the autonomous P'urépecha community of Nurio in Michoacan, Mexico. Fulvio has mentored many young P'urépecha youth in the creation of natural fertilizers, pesticides, and fungicides. With a PhD in ethnobotany, he often lectures in Mexican universities on issues related to food sovereignty.

"I grow vegetables in a bio-organic and agroecological way, and offer technical assistance to many small producers. I work with my family and with other healers."

> Learn more about **Fulvio Giovanetto** (ettl.ca/cfgi) and see him in two videos, "The Alchemy of Agroecology" on page 130 and "Who Will Feed Us?" on page 173, and the photo essay "Medicinal Plants" on page 96.

Rick (Hayadaha) W. Hill is Tuscarora of the Beaver clan and a leading community-based Knowledge Keeper at Six Nations of the Grand River. An artist and historian, he has worked with museums, taught at universities in both the United States and Canada, and has been awarded honorary doctorates from

both McMaster University and Guelph University.

"Working with community elders to produce an exhibition on Haudenosaunee history and culture helped me understand the elemental nature of crop cultivation and animal harvesting within our culture. The Legacies project is my last gasp to try to help others avoid what has been called the New World Syndrome—the intentional harming of Indigenous peoples by replacing their ancestral foodways with industrialized nonfoods."

> Learn more about **Rick Hill** (ettl.ca/crh) and see him in the three videos of the "Haudenosaunee Primer" on page 200 as well as the photo essay "Haudenosaunee Gifts" on page 84.

Dan Kretschmar grew up on Grenville Farm, learning organic agriculture from his mother, Dianne Kretschmar. He became involved in the political side of agriculture as a youth delegate for the National Farmers Union at gatherings of Via Campesina, the transnational coalition of Indigenous and small farmers.

"These international encounters shook the roots of my soul and reignited my dream to have an outdoor education center, agroecology school, and forest school on the farm."

Learn more about Dan Kretschmar (ettl.ca/cdk) and see him in the "Who Will Feed Us?" video on page 173.

Dianne Kretschmar was one of the first organic women farmers in Ontario and inspired the Riverdale Farmers Market, the first farmers market in a Toronto park. At Grenville Farm two hours north of Toronto, she has mentored many young farmers, five of whom are collaborators in the Legacies project.

"I had worked for fifteen years as a geologist in the bush on the Canadian Shield before farming. For the past thirty years, I've been trying to produce good organic food in the rocky Muskoka region of Ontario. I don't own this land; it owns me."

Learn more about Dianne Kretschmar (ettl.ca/cd) and see her in two videos, "The Soil Is Alive" (page 127) and "Who Will Feed Us?" (page 173), as well as the photo essay "The Animal Food Cycle" on page 133.

Ángel Kú was born in Ticul in the Yucatán peninsula of Mexico and learned about the Mayan culture from his grandmother. With his partner, Valiana, he collaborated with UniTierra in Oaxaca, learning more about the ways Indigenous communities relate to the land. Now back in the Yucatán, they are creating a project that honors the knowledge of the elders.

"We are committed to collectively recuperating our ancestral ways of learning, healing, eating, living, and speaking."

Learn more about Ángel Kú Dzul (ettl.ca/cak) and see him in the photo essay "Mutual Nurturing" on page 106.

Mohawk community food leader *Chandra Maracle* was born and raised in Buffalo, New York, and lives with her family on Six Nations of the Grand River Territory in Ontario. She is a PhD candidate in the Faculty of Environmental Studies at York University in Toronto.

"I have been a foodie and health food junkie for as long as I can remember. I am founder of Kakhwa'on:we/ Real People Eat Real Food and cofounder of Skaronhyase'ko:wa/The Everlasting Tree School."

Learn more about Chandra Maracle (ettl.ca/ccm) and see her in the "Thanksgiving Address" video on page 17 and the photo essays "Mother's Milk" on page 118, "The Mush Hole" on page 178, and "Cooking and Eating Together" on page 106.

Anna Murtaugh learned organic agriculture from Dianne Kretschmar and met her partner, Adam Royal, at Grenville Farm. Anna currently teaches and farms with Adam in New Carlisle, Quebec, on the Gaspé coast, where they live with their three children.

"We helped start the farmers market, and it has grown every year since. Our goal is to support local growers and connect them with local people, bringing together both the English- and French-speaking communities."

Adam Royal lives with Anna Murtaugh and their family in New Carlisle, Quebec, where they raise cattle, pigs, sheep, and goats, and have a large vegetable garden. Adam is a teacher and a seasonal butcher, especially for local settler and Indigenous hunters in the Gaspé region.

"Growing, raising, processing, and preserving our own food lets us not only decide what we eat, but how it is grown. Gardening and gathering from the forest is our work, our entertainment, our exercise, and our children's classroom for the summer and fall."

> Learn more about Anna and Adam at **Anna Murtaugh & Adam Royal (ettl.ca/caa)** and see her in the video "Why Farmers Markets?" on page 154 and the photo essays "Mother's Milk" on page 118 and "The Animal Food Cycle" on page 133.

Research and Production Team

Coeditor Lauren Baker has more than twenty years of experience working on food systems issues with Sustain Ontario, the Toronto Food Policy Council, the People's Food Institute, and the Global Alliance for the Future of Food. With a PhD on maize movements in Mexico (*Corn Meets Maize*), she has taught at the University of Toronto and Ryerson University.

"In my work on sustainable food systems, agroecology, biodiversity, health, and true cost accounting, I have the great privilege of connecting with people all around the world with diverse perspectives. As someone with a long-standing interest in urban agriculture, I take great delight in gardening, seeing plants grow, visiting the local markets, and cooking meals for my appreciative family."

> Learn more about **Lauren Baker (ettl.ca/lb)** and see her as narrator in the photo essays "Food Justice" on page 160 and "Promoting Organic Agriculture in Mexico" on page 144 and in codirecting the video "Black Creek Community Farm" on page 170.

Codirector and coeditor Deborah Barndt builds on twenty-five years of research on the NAFTA food system (*Tangled Routes: Women, Work and Globalization on the Tomato Trail*), teaching food sovereignty at the Coady International Institute, and creating art projects for the local food movement. She is a photographer, community artist, and popular educator, and professor emeritus at York University's Faculty of Environmental Studies in Toronto.

"Since the 1990s, I have gathered stories of people, mainly women workers in the global food chain. With the Legacies project, I focus instead on the stories, images, and voices of those who are resisting corporate food and reclaiming their own food production and cultural practices."

> Learn more about **Deborah Barndt (ettl.ca/d)** and see her work in most videos and photo essays.

Codirector Alexandra Gelis was born in Venezuela and grew up in Colombia, Puerto Rico, Mexico, and Panama before settling in Toronto in 2007. As part of a family of artists, she integrates video, sound, sculpture, and installation in multimedia exhibitions in Latin America, North America, Europe, and Asia. She is completing a PhD at York University in arts-based environmental studies.

"It was the call of the plants that brought me to food. My multimedia work has focused on the relationship between people and plants, both historically (through colonization) and currently (through globalization). I prefer to bring the media tools to communities through workshops on self-representation and collaborative creation."

> Learn more about **Alexandra Gelis (ettl.ca/ag)** and see her work in all the videos and many photo essays.

John Murtaugh came to Canada in the early 1970s as a draft dodger protesting the Vietnam War. Inspired by agricultural work with the Peace Corps in Tonga, he has remained an avid rooftop gardener and plant breeder. His friendship with Dianne Kretschmar seeded the Legacies project, and he has assisted all aspects of production for the past five years.

"I especially enjoy the self-seeded edible plants and leafy greens that come up everywhere each year as thick as weeds. I am an avid composter, using all my kitchen scraps, fall leaves, and plant residue produced on my small bit of land in downtown Toronto."

Learn more about John Murtaugh (ettl.ca/j) and see him in the video "Why Farmers Markets?" on page 154 and as a narrator in the photo essay "The Animal Food Cycle" on page 133.

Meet the Production Team

As the coeditors and codirectors of this book and accompanying multimedia platform, we each bring a different perspective of what the project is and how it came to be. Our creation stories are both personal and political.

Deborah Barndt, Coeditor and Codirector

I grew up in a small farming village in Ohio in the 1950s. My childhood memories are of playing in the haylofts of barns and sleeping with my friends and their cows in stalls at the county fair. We roamed the woods for berries and hickory nuts for snacks, and boiled sumac for tea. My mother tended a large vegetable garden and canned goods for the winter; my father chopped off the head of the turkey that became our Thanksgiving dinner. Potluck suppers in the local church basement were common. Food was local, fresh, inexpensive, and often shared.

On a visit to that community forty years later, I found a ghost town: the lone grocery store boarded up, the barns dilapidated, the fields empty. The current residents, perhaps the grandchildren of my farm friends and now commuters working in the closest city, drive a mile up the road to feed themselves from one of the fast-food franchise restaurants surrounding the exit of the interstate highway. Immense tractor trailers whiz by transporting fruit and vegetables from Mexico to my present home in Canada. Tracing the history of my hometown and the trajectory of those trucks is a lesson in the development of the global food system that transpired throughout my lifetime: the legacy of the corporate food regime.

In the 1990s, while teaching environmental studies and community art at York University in Toronto, I coordinated a collaborative research project, excavating the impact of the postwar industrial food complex I had witnessed along that Ohio highway. NAFTA, a free-trade agreement between Mexico, the United States, and Canada, had just been implemented. The Zapatista uprising in southern Mexico protested this latest entrenchment of the neoliberal model, defending Indigenous territory from multinational interests and claiming autonomy from the nation-state. Our team of women researchers followed the journey of a corporate tomato from a Mexican agribusiness to a McDonald's restaurant in Toronto. We gathered the stories and images of the women workers on the front line of the hemispheric system, the invisible and unsung producers, processors, sellers, and preparers in the tomato food chain. While unearthing the impacts of that globalizing system on the relationship between producers and consumers, we also stumbled upon many stories of resistance by peasant and Indigenous communities in the Global South. We also witnessed small farmers and critical consumers creating more sustainable and just alternatives to the corporate system in the Global North.

When I was approached in 2014 by a filmmaker hoping to produce a documentary based on our tomato book, *Tangled Routes: Women, Work and Globalization on the Tomato Trail* (Rowman & Littlefield, 2002, 2008), I decided that the cinematic world had enough exposure of what was wrong with the global food system. Rather, we should be highlighting these stories of resistance, resilience, and regeneration of more equitable and ecological food practices. I had met my partner, *John Murtaugh*, in 2012 at the first North American conference on urban agriculture, and during a four-month road trip in 2015 from Toronto to Panama, we reconnected with friends and coworkers in a growing global grassroots food movement. We found his family friend Fernando Garcia, for example, teaching organic gardening in suburban Guadalajara, Mexico, and my former colleague Gustavo Esteva nurturing younger food sovereignty activists like Mayans *Valiana Aguilar* and *Ángel Kú* at the Zapatista-inspired Uni-Tierra (University of the Land) he had founded in Oaxaca.

I had first met Gustavo in 2003 while in Oaxaca to visit *Lauren Baker*, who had been a key research assistant on the tomato project and was then completing her own doctoral research in Oaxaca on maize movements: *Corn Meets Maize* (Rowman & Littlefield, 2012). Together we designed the first food course in our Faculty of Environmental Studies at York and invited Gustavo to teach a summer seminar, "Food Sovereignty, Indigenous Knowledges, and Autonomous Movements." Lauren had gone on to become the first director of Sustain Ontario and then the coordinator of the Toronto Food Policy Council. Our collaboration in this new project represented an ongoing intergenerational exchange. Lauren brought her current transnational work, through the Global Alliance for the Future of Food, and connected us with Legacies collaborator *Fulvio Gioanetto*, ethnobotanist living with his partner, *María Blas*, in the P'urépecha community in Michoacán, Mexico, who had been sharing his unique agroecological experience and innovative techniques with Canadian farmers and food activists.

Back in Canada, John introduced me to *Dianne Kretschmar*, then a seventy-year-old organic farmer in the Muskoka region two hours north of Toronto, near the family cottage he shared with his late wife, Elizabeth Harris. It was Elizabeth's friendship with Dianne that led her to establish in 2001 the first organic farmers market in a city park, the Riverdale Market, to sell Dianne's produce. Their daughter *Anna* worked on Grenville farm for more than a decade, meeting her husband, *Adam*, there. Dianne had mentored many young farmers over thirty years, including her own son, *Dan*, Mohawk *Ryan DeCaire* from the nearby Haudenosaunee reserve of Wahta, and *Fernando Garcia*, who came all the way from Mexico to learn organic farming from Plan B Organic and from Dianne's Grenville Farm. This strong, curious, and committed woman represented a constellation of intergenerational and intercultural exchange of food knowledges and practices.

I began to see the threads—from my mother's garden to our small urban gardens, from my rural past to Dianne's struggle to continue farming, from her passion for the soil, the plants, and the animals to her protégés' food projects spread across the continent, in urban and rural, settler and Indigenous communities.

Stark questions emerged: *What food legacies are being passed on from one generation to another? Across cultures and borders? Who will produce our food in the twenty-first century and how?*

I invited Lauren as a younger food movement leader and *Alexandra Gelis* as a younger Colombian-Canadian multimedia artist and York PhD student researching human-plant relations to form an intergenerational research and production team. We began to build an exchange and to document the process, using photos and video as research tools. Longtime collaborator Min Sook Lee, documentary filmmaker and PhD student of film and migrant workers, served as an adviser, and Sylvie Van Brabant, seasoned human rights

documentary filmmaker, served as producer for our first phase.

My decades of research, education, and activism in the Americas had given me rich opportunities to work with and learn from Indigenous communities, and those voices were echoing in my ears: Guatemalan Mayans teaching me other notions of time;[1] Quechua women migrants in Peruvian literacy classes;[2] Miskitu and Garifuna popular educators on Nicaragua's Caribbean coast;[3] Indigenous migrants exploited in Mexican tomato fields;[4] Guna, Miskitu, and Mayan community artists in Panama, Nicaragua, and Mexico.[5] In Canada, I learned with Inuit adult educators in the Arctic, photographed solidarity with the Oka crisis,[6] organized workshops around the five hundred years of colonization,[7] and cocreated photo essays on Aboriginal self-government.[8]

During twenty-eight years of teaching in the Faculty of Environmental Studies at York, I've continued to learn from Indigenous faculty and students alike, beginning to understand how the Eurocentric Cartesian worldview has reinforced a disconnection of humans from the rest of nature and fragmented our understanding of the interconnections of all living things. Named by

some Indigenous nations as *all our relations*, these connections must be restored if we are to survive as one of multiple species on this planet. Indigenous voices have both challenged our thinking about knowledge and food, and offered alternative visions of how we learn and how we can feed ourselves.

I was convinced that any intercultural exchange had to include a settler-Indigenous dialogue. Since 2015, we have found ourselves in the midst of a very powerful resurgence of Indigenous communities in so-called Canada, where a Truth and Reconciliation Commission unearthed testimonies of survivors of government and church-run residential schools, part of a broader cultural genocide. To move beyond that horrific legacy, our government, and indeed all Canadians, were challenged to respond to ninety-four recommendations to decolonize and transform colonial institutions. Indigenous leaders had also sparked the Idle No More Movement, pushed for a National Inquiry into Missing and Murdered Indigenous Women and Girls, initiated multiple land claims, and led social and environmental struggles against hazardous mines and pipelines and for clean water and air.[9]

Although we initially sought connections with Indigenous food sovereignty leaders in British Columbia, we chose to "dig where we stand" and learn about and from the Indigenous nations whose stolen land we occupy. Closer to home, we found community food leaders such as *Chandra Maracle* and *Rick Hill* recovering traditional Haudenosaunee foods, creating alternative schools with Mohawk values, and helping us all to reconnect more deeply with all our relations through food.

And so, with both Mexican and Indigenous collaborators entering into this intercultural exchange, we asked deeper questions: *What can we learn from a dialogue between food activists in the Global South and in the Global North? How do we open up a respectful conversation between settler and Indigenous food leaders on Turtle Island?*

Food is an entry point, a catalyst for conversations across our very real differences. But our commitment to food justice and food sovereignty is also a common passion, one way of speaking back to this moment.

We want to pass on a different legacy. A more hopeful one.

Lauren Baker, Coeditor

When I was a child, I lived all over the world. Because of this privileged experience, flavors and traditions intermingle and connect to visceral memories. Dhal bat and chai in Nepalese tea houses. Grape crush and red licorice from the U.S. commissary. Exchanging lunches with my Japanese friend Atsuko. The bustle and vibrant colors of markets were deeply imprinted in me. When my family was traveling in the 1970s and early 1980s, American fast food and ultra-processed food were exotic around the world. Now, of course, you can find Walmart, supermarkets, fast-food restaurants, and really anything you desire in most countries. Through the course of my lifetime, the food system has transformed to profoundly impact our ecological systems, daily habits and diets, behavior, and cultural traditions.

This global experience led to strong passions for social justice and the environment. Engaging with the food system became a way to address all my interests—in global and local equity, in food security, in food waste, in agriculture and the environment, and in social movements and economic alternatives.

During my master's, I met *Deborah Barndt* and began working with her on the Tomasita project, tracing the trail of a tomato from Mexican field to Canadian table. This project was an incredible education in global supply chain complexity and the true cost of food. Firsthand we saw the ecological damage caused by monoculture production, how labor was shaped by gender, race, and class; we witnessed the health impacts of these systems as women breast-fed their babies while pesticides were being applied. Adjacent to the field, temporary communities made from cardboard and scrap materials housed migrant Indigenous workers.

This deepened my interest in alternatives to these industrialized systems, and I began to explore how food systems could be ecologically and socially embedded. I became engaged with Toronto's food movement. I cofounded Annex Organics and Urban Harvest, an urban agriculture business and organic and heritage seed company; and worked at FoodShare Toronto, a vibrant community food organization, often in partnership with organizations such as AfriCan Food Basket and Greenest City. Overtime I became fascinated by community gardens across Toronto and the incredible biodiversity and cultural diversity they reflected.[10]

I continued to explore the themes of biodiversity and cultural diversity in the context of post-NAFTA Mexico through my research on maíze in Mexico. Corn tariffs had just been lifted, and U.S. corn flooded Mexican markets. Mexico, as the center of origin for corn, was a dynamic place to better understand social movements promoting sustainable, diverse agriculture, policy, and practice. Through my connection to Mexico, I had the great fortune to meet and develop long-standing relationships with Legacies collaborators *Gustavo Esteva* and *Fulvio Giaonetto*.

My interest in corn led to meeting *Rick Hill* and *Chandra Maracle* during the Guelph Organic Conference, and I immediately resonated with their vision for Indigenous food sovereignty, Indigenous foodways, and the reclamation of Indigenous food systems with corn at their heart. I have been deeply inspired by how Haudenosaunee history and culture illuminate my understanding of food systems transformation. It has been a great pleasure to introduce collaborators from food movements in Mexico to collaborators from food movements in Canada through the Legacies project, deepening our collective understanding of the potential for ecological and regenerative food systems.

Over the past decade I have been involved in the leadership of a number of alliances and organizations working on food systems transformation. Sustain Ontario, the Alliance for Healthy Food and Farming, the Toronto Food Policy Council, Food Secure Canada, Everdale Environmental Learning Centre, the People's Food Institute, the Global Alliance for the Future of Food all strive to bring people together to build understanding, influence, and ultimately effect change across food systems. It was through this work that I met *Leticia Deawuo* and became involved in Black Creek Community Farm.

Through my current work with the Global Alliance for the Future of Food, I advocate for a food system that is resilient, renewable, diverse, healthy, equitable, inclusive, and interconnected. For the Global Alliance, these principles are a way to see the whole food system and to shape decisions about the future of our shared food systems so we avoid siloed approaches, unintended consequences, and limited, narrow, short-term solutions. Through this work with the Global Alliance, I am able to relate the conversations between Legacies collaborators to a broader "intercultural" dialogue with food systems actors around the world. The Legacies conversations help me more deeply understand parallel and entwined efforts to decolonize food systems globally.

Alexandra Gelis, Codirector

I was conceived in a darkroom where my parents developed photographs; hence, my fascination with cameras. My story is a mix of postcards, moving images, bright colors. and smells.

I was born in Caracas, Venezuela, and my childhood memories carry the smell of the Caribbean Sea between Puerto Rico and Cartagena, Colombia, where I spent my childhood. It was a women's house, with my great-grandma, my grandma, my aunt, and my mom. This gave me a female perspective on life based on solidarity, intimacy, and affection, far from the "normalization" of what a woman should be in an openly macho society in South America.

In my home there was always shelter and food for anyone who dropped in. As my grandmother would say, "Here there is always food for everyone, we just add some more water to the soup." I especially remember the smell of coconut rice, fish in coconut sauce, sweet "cocadas" or even a homemade coconut tanning oil on my skin at the beach. Life tastes better with coconut! Food was also fruits: in the patio of my house, I played in fruit trees of tamarind, guava, and mango. But the best smell was the one that emanated from

the fruit bowl of Mrs. María, who woke me up every morning with her songs: "Avocado! Banana!" I would run to the door to help her lower the heavy metal basin from her head. From San Basilio de Palenque, forty minutes from Cartagena, she brought caimito, guama, custard apple, delicious fruits that are scarce today because they're not part of the commercial market.

My great grandmother made me avocado juice with milk every morning, although that red juice with a strange name in English, "Kool-Aid," was already trendy among my friends, seemed to make them cool, and give them higher social status. I never understood their taste nor their fascination with Kool-Aid and soft drinks.

Cartagena has now become a city for tourists. Between the beach and the bay where I grew up, it has become impossible to eat fresh fish. They are more expensive and only come frozen; the best catches are for tourists. Fishermen are allowed to bring their nets to certain beaches far from tourists, where they only catch small fish, because the bigger ones have been taken by the large multinational fishing nets.

I have had a nomadic life, in constant migration from one city to another.

I became a woman traveler with a camera in my hands, sometimes into dangerous lands, capturing and reframing humans and nonhumans usually absent from the media. Other times I would bring the tools (DIY technologies) and cameras into communities for self-representation workshops or collaborative creation projects.

In my life of constant movement, I was "called" by the plants and became interested in the relationship of plants and people. Plants that "supposedly" don't move are the ones that taught me most about the politics behind migration. I started exploring how native, nonnative, invasive, and "migrated" plants are connected to the forced and unforced migration of people and colonization of territories. The bio-political presence of plants to control people and territories has been my main concern in the past ten years. My work deals with botanics as a form of resistance: plants that are used as territorial control technologies (TCT), both by those in a position of control and by subaltern resistances to those controls.

Since 2009, I have worked on two main projects: Corredor is an ongoing project exploring the elephant grass planted as a living barrier around the

Panama Canal by the U.S. Army during the Vietnam War. It was brought from Vietnam to control the Canal Zone and to keep Panamanians out of their military bases.

I initiated the second project, MAT: Medicinal Plants and Resistance, in San Basilio de Palenque, an Afro-Colombian town, known as the "First free town of the Americas." I investigate the history of seeds, medicinal and ritual plants that were brought by runaway enslaved persons, often hidden in their hair. Used to reshape the new free territories, these plants are today growing all over patios, land, and sidewalks.

Smells of the fruits of Mrs. María, all my childhood memories with my aunties (my mom's best friends—historians, educators, artists, women leaders—who shaped the ethno-education law in Colombia and the declaration of San Basilio de Palenque as a UNESCO Heritage site) brought me back to the town in 2011 with an invitation to give a media workshop. To access memories of the plants, I started an art-based collaborative research and creation project working with elders, who had the memories, and with youth, who were no longer interested in traditional knowledge.

We used media technologies as a connection device; cameras became the main tool for intergenerational communication, youth framing the plants with cameras while elders explained the visible and the intangible aspects of the stories of the plants. Over several years we captured hundreds of stories, recording for new generations the images and voices of many *abuelos* who are no longer with us. Rather than write a book that the youth would not be interested in reading, I created an online platform to gather the complex plants-human narratives, stories told in layers where the drum, colors, dance, the way of moving, the palenquero language, and their animistic beliefs became a unit. This project became the base for my doctoral research: "An Arts-Based Inquiry into Plant/Human Relations in Equinoctial America: A Case Study of San Basilio de Palenque, Colombia."

When I began my PhD in environmental studies at York University and met Deborah Barndt, my supervisor, the Legacies project was just being born. I have been able to bring both my research interests and my multimedia skills into this collaborative project as a codirector of the video documentation and part of the core production team. I am deeply convinced that at this moment we need to experiment with the arts and the senses, to radically disrupt dominant ways of knowing, and to learn other ways to see, feel, and know.

Our Food Icons

Each collaborator in the Earth to Tables Legacies project has a unique story, sense of place, and connection to food sovereignty. Each of us chose a food-related icon (plant, animal, insect, container) that we identify with. These choices reveal personal passions, histories, and personalities. And they highlight the interrelation between people and food sources: how people shape food and food shapes people.

Adam: On our farm in Quebec, we have goats, which are like part of our family. We milk them daily and cook with the milk. Anna makes yogurt and cheese.

Alex: The monkey pot fruit is a symbol of resilience, fragility, beauty, and healing. It grows on trees along the sidewalks in San Basilio de Palenque, Colombia. One of my first childhood memories was playing by the river, mixing wild herbs and flowers in the woody fruit pot. The seeds of the fruit are highly nutritious, medicinal, and antagonistic to cancer.

Ángel: The owl (*tunkilunchu* in Mayan) represents the transition to another life. My hahwal or spirit is Kimi—representing life and death, which is not the end of our existence. Like corn, we are planted in this world; when we die, we begin to rise again.

Chandra: Haudenosaunee white corn is my icon, but I most enjoy preparing it and feeding it to other people. Every single time I prepare it, I'm reminded of the creation story, and that corn that I love to prepare is older than time as we know it, and it never gets old for me.

Anna: I have a fond memory of planting thyme at Dianne's farm when I first worked there. Twenty years later, it has become a huge field of thyme.

Dan: When I was a kid, I wouldn't touch beets, and planting beets was the hardest job on the farm. As an adult, I love beets, and I've found a more efficient way to grow them through the paper pot planter.

Deborah: My name means bee in Hebrew. I like the connotation of being a pollinator, bringing people together and pollinating ideas.

Dianne: My icon is lettuce. Canadians eat lettuce all year around, and I love lettuce. Muskoka's a perfect place to grow lettuce; we have lots of lakes, so every morning there's heavy dew. And lettuce has this wonderful morphology, that their leaves catch the dew, and the dew goes to the heart of the plant and into the roots. Just engineered for success.

John: I chose lamb's quarters, because I love watching it grow up voluntarily in my rooftop garden. Even though some consider it a weed, it is very nutritious and edible. It came to America with the Europeans, colonizing the farmers' fields, as did the colonizers.

Lauren: My Ukrainian ancestors grew corn on the Canadian prairies; eventually, with the industrialization of agriculture, corn became part of monocultural production. Then I studied the movements to defend maíz in Mexico. Since then, I've been interested in the agency of corn, how it shapes and reshapes landscapes over time.

Leticia: My dad is from the aguna clan in Ghana; aguna is a tiger. So, my icon is a tiger.

Fulvio: My plant icon is lichen. One reason is that they represent a symbiosis between different beings. Another reason is the spiritual connection lichens have with other forms of life.

Fernando: My icon is kale, a hearty green vegetable. I taught urban residents to grow it in Guadalajara, and now I'm training farmers to produce kale for healthy dried snacks.

Rick: The Mother Earth offers her nutritious and medicinal bounty in a great dish from which we can all share. She asks us to only take what we need to feed and heal ourselves; leave something in the dish for others; and show our gratitude by keeping the dish clean and not wasting what she has provided. Thus, the Dish with One Spoon is how such gifts make their way from the earth to our tables.

María: My icon is the lavender plant. It is medicinal, helps us relax, and makes us feel good.

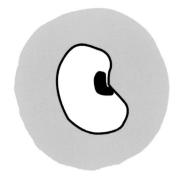

Ryan: I collect old heritage beans. I love breaking them open and seeing how beautiful they are. I love that they're a power food, and you can save them over time. I started with twenty-five Haudenosaunee varieties and now have about seventy-five different varieties.

Valiana: In Mayan, maíz or corn, literally means "women's breast." Corn is the being that first loves you and feeds you. The challenge to growing corn in the Yucatán is that it is planted in the middle of our rocky soil, which actually maintains humidity.

Our Migration Stories

When we gathered for the third time as a group at Six Nations in July 2019, we shared our diverse histories of migration along with the food icons described above. This activity, created by research assistant Tzazná Miranda Leal, connected us to the broader political, economic, and cultural process of global migration.

Although we all live in a narrow latitude of North America (or Turtle Island), we discovered that, in reality, all of us have migrated throughout our lives and have learned from diverse contexts, continents, cultures, and culinary practices.

Some of us have deep precontact ancestral roots in Turtle Island. Others have colonial histories in Europe and so have landed in North America (Turtle Island) as settlers on stolen land. Still others find a mixture of Indigenous and European ancestry in their family histories. Our complex trajectories perhaps reflect the reality of this era: most settlers have moved from their homelands and thus have different relationships to the land. Many Indigenous cultures, however, moved extensively across vast territories, yet still retained connection to the land.

Legacies collaborator Ryan DeCaire shares his migration story at Six Nations gathering in 2019.

Let's start with those who have the deepest roots in the so-called Americas (named after an Italian mapmaker).

Original Inhabitants Were on the Move

Our Indigenous partners represent three different peoples: the Haudenosaunee (known as the Iroquois Confederacy or Six Nations) straddling the border between the United States and Canada; the Mayan, located in the Yucatán region of Mexico (as well as in other Mexican and Guatemalan states); and the P'urépecha in an autonomous community in the central Mexican state of Michoacán.

Prior to European contact, the Haudenosaunee moved for food, across a wide swath from what is now New York State to Wisconsin. Today they are mainly located in upper New York State, southern Ontario, and Quebec. For them the border between the so-called United States and Canada was imposed; it is more an inconvenience, something they cross regularly to connect with family and friends. Both Rick Hill and Chandra Maracle were born in Buffalo, New York, where their fathers were Mohawk ironworkers. Rick's work trajectory crisscrossed the border over decades: he studied art in Chicago, taught at the University of Buffalo, then worked with the art program of Indian Affairs in Ottawa; back in the United States, he curated Indigenous art in Santa Fe, New Mexico, and at the National Museum of the American Indian in Washington, D.C. Since 2007, he has lived in Ohsweken, Ontario, on Six Nations of the Grand River territory, with his wife, Chandra Maracle.

Chandra's mother's family is Sicilian American; her father's family came from Tyendinaga, a Mohawk territory in Ontario. Her family frequently crossed the border from Detroit to Fort Erie, Ontario. Now living with Rick and her four children at Six Nations in Ontario, the family regularly attends gatherings in upstate New York. But when asked where she calls home, Chandra points to the sky and outside of the map: "After I studied our creation story and learned how connected the first woman was to food and corn, I felt deeply that's my home."

Ryan DeCaire is also Haudenosaunee, but his people came from the east and settled in the Muskoka region of Ontario. His home reserve, Wahta, means maple tree, which is considered the leader of the trees, or the first to provide us with sustenance. As a young man, he worked on Dianne's farm near his community. In his work on language revitalization, Ryan has taught at other Mohawk communities, Kanewake in

Quebec and Six Nations in Ontario. As he said, "Haudenosaunee people, if they're involved in community, travel constantly."

Our Indigenous collaborators in current-day Mexico have a different colonial history, as it was the Spanish rather than the British and French who invaded their territories. Ángel Kú's Yucatán hometown is Ticul, which means "settled, after the wars," perhaps referring to a major massacre in nearby Maní, where a Spanish friar had thousands killed and cultural codices destroyed in 1562. Ángel followed the path of many young Mayans, traveling to Chiapas to join Indigenous movements; then to Oaxaca, where he worked for five years with UniTierra, University of the Land.

Ángel's partner, Valiana Aguilar, shared that experience with him before they returned to her hometown of Sinanché, Yucatán, a Mayan community of two thousand near the Gulf of Mexico. Her grandparents worked in haciendas like slaves and had to fight for the land, finally secured in the Mexican revolution. Recently, her grandfather offered the family land to Valiana, confident that she would not sell it but would carry out her dream to build a working farm and educational center,

such as UniTierra, with youth in the community.

The third Indigenous nation in the Legacies exchange is the P'urépecha of Nurio, an autonomous community in the central Mexican state of Michoacán. María Blas Cacari grew up in a military family that moved regularly from state to state in Mexico. Then her family joined a majority of the residents of her hometown, migrating north to the United States for work—in California, Missouri, and Wisconsin. There is still a lot of movement back and forth among family members, and María has also traveled throughout Mexico, Central America, and Italy for agricultural workshops with her husband, Fulvio.

Colonizers, Immigrants, and Refugees

Fulvio Gionetto has spent his life on the move, migrating between continents and states. Born in Italy and educated in France, he worked with UNESCO and the Sami in Lapland before coming to Mexico as an ethnobotanist in 1997. Since marrying his P'urépecha translator, María, they and their four children have traveled around Mexico and Central America, offering workshops on medicinal plants and organic inputs. He also lectures at Mexican universities and advises producers on agroecology. His consultancy work has extended to the United States and Canada, where he has come regularly during the growing season.

Fernando Garcia was born in Guadalajara, Jalisco. His mother is from Saltillo, Coahulia, in northern Mexico, while his father is from Jalisco. As a youth, Fernando attended one year of high school in San Antonio, Texas. Then as a young agronomist, he spent a summer twenty years ago learning organic agriculture on two farms in Ontario, Canada. His current work of training farmers in organic production has involved travel all over Mexico and to Venezuela, Bolivia, the United States, and Ethiopia.

The only four Canadian-born Legacies partners reflect both deep and recent British colonial histories.

Dianne Kretschmar's ancestors came to the eastern coast of the United States with a sister ship of the *Mayflower* in the 1600s. They retreated to Canada as United Empire Loyalists after the Boston Tea Party (1773). Dianne's mother was born in Yorkshire, England, and came to Canada as a child. Both parents were raised on the West Coast, married in Vancouver, then migrated east, to Edmonton, to Toronto, and the suburbs.

Her move two hours north to the Muskoka region more than thirty years ago was to start a farm in a rocky area after working as a geologist in Alaska and other points north.

Her son, Dan, was born on the farm, and only as a young agrarian activist did he begin to travel. As a youth delegate for the National Farmers Union, he went to meetings of Via Campesina in Miami, Peru, and Brazil. These experiences sparked his vision for an agroecology school on the farm. For three years, he taught English in China, earning money to develop this dream in Ontario.

Adam Royal grew up close to Dianne's farm in Ontario and met his wife, Anna, while working there for several years in the early 2000s. He then moved his family back to the Gaspé region of Quebec, where his mother's great grandmother settled.

Anna Murtaugh's parents represent migration to Canada from two different wars. Her mom was born in England during World War II and came to Canada with her mother, a war bride, when she was three years old. Her dad (production team member John) came from Chicago (his grandparents were from Ireland and England) but arrived in Toronto in the early 1970s as a "draft dodger," protesting U.S. involvement in

the Vietnam War. Anna grew up in the center of Toronto, next to a city farm, and worked on Dianne's farm for ten summers. She then lived with Adam in Montreal until they moved to the Gaspé community of New Carlisle.

Since the 1980s, the massive influx of immigrants and refugees to Canada has been from the Global South, fleeing economic hardship, war, and various forms of discrimination.

Leticia Deawuo was born in rural Ghana, where she grew up with her grandmother, a corn and peanut farmer. Leticia's mom and sister immigrated to Canada in 1993, and she joined them in 1996. Leticia was director of the Black Creek Community Farm in Toronto, and now is the director of SeedChange in Ottawa.

A Border-Crossing Production Team

All members of the production team have complex migration histories.

Codirector Alexandra Gelis was born in Venezuela, grew up on the Caribbean coast of Colombia, and lived in Puerto Rico, Mexico, and Panama. In 2007, she moved to Toronto, but her multimedia artistic projects have taken her all over Canada and the United States, to Ethiopia, Peru, and back to Colombia. Other Colombian Canadians,

Jorge Lozano and Juan Pablo Pinto, have joined her on the video documentation and editing team.

Coeditor Lauren Baker's maternal grandparents migrated from Ukraine and settled in a farming community in Alberta. Her father's ancestors crossed the Atlantic from Scotland and England, arriving as new immigrants to farm on Turtle Island. Her parents grew up in Hamilton. Over many years, her father worked internationally, so Lauren was born in Malaysia and lived in Honduras, Rome, Sri Lanka, and Nepal. Although Toronto has always been her home base, her current work takes her around the world connecting with other organizations working toward food systems transformation.

John Murtaugh, production assistant, was born in the United States and grew up in the Chicago area. He spent two years working with the Peace Corps on agricultural projects in Tonga and traveled extensively through Central American and the South Pacific. In refusing to fight for the United States in the Vietnam War in 1970, he was welcomed to Canada as a "draft dodger": "I got advice to go to Toronto; the other option was to go to jail." He has raised his family in downtown Toronto over the past fifty years.

Similarly, codirector/coeditor Deborah Barndt has made her home in Canada since the early 1970s. Born in northern Maine in the United States, next to the Quebec and New Brunswick borders, she grew up in farming communities in Ohio, then studied in Ohio, Michigan, and France, and worked in Switzerland and New York City before moving to Canada. She migrated internally for work from Ottawa to Montreal to Toronto (where she has lived for forty-five years). Sporadically, she worked and lived in Latin America (Peru in the 1970s, Nicaragua in the 1980s, Mexico in the 1990s and 2000s); these intercultural connections have inspired and provided a base for the Legacies project.

These short migration vignettes reveal that, like many in our globalized world, we have complex identities and trajectories over space and time. A clear difference among us, however, is the relationship we each have to the colonial history of where we now live and work. Although the political contexts shaping this relationship are different in Canada, the United States, and Mexico, the fact remains that the history of the Americas is based on a brutal occupation of Indigenous land, the theft of natural resources, the suppression of languages

and cultural practices, and the loss of connection to land and healthy practices of securing and eating food.[11] Some of us with racial, class, and education privileges have benefited from this ongoing cultural genocide. One of the aims of the Legacies project is to use food as an entry to a conversation that leads us to a deeper understanding of Indigenous perspectives and moves settlers toward more active allyship.

Ruth Koleszar-Green offers us new ways to think about this relationship. She distinguishes between the term "settler" and the term "guest." A settler engages in a superficial way, participating in ways that do not unsettle the privilege, or equating settler's reality to Indigenous realities. In contrast, "a guest is an individual that is in relationship to the Land in a way that supports stewardship and not ownership." Guests develop relationships with Indigenous communities and "respect reciprocal engagement."[12] This is a worthy goal for our project, one that we must constantly work toward. We hope that it will inspire others to reconsider their relationship to colonization and reconciliation through the lens of food sovereignty.

PART IV
Conversations

We are gathered around a table with Mayan collaborators Ángel and Valiana in a palapa, thatched-roof cottage by the Gulf coast of the Yucatán, their ancestral home. A sea snail on the table offers an entry point to the kind of conversations we hope this multimedia package will generate.

We have organized the Earth to Tables Legacies videos and photo essays around four interrelated themes: ways of knowing, earth, justice, and tables. These four themes coincide with the dynamic tensions that frame the project: knowledge, food, equity, and politics. There is a linear logic from earth to tables, conventionally following the processes of production, distribution, and consumption. The sea snail spiral offers a more organic way of thinking about food and the issues and relationships explored through this project.

1. The underlying *ways of knowing* emerge from the tensions between Eurocentric knowledges and Indigenous ways of knowing, being, and acting.
2. These ways of knowing are grounded in the *earth*, a living organism as understood by food sovereignty movements challenging the corporate food regime.
3. Food sovereignty promotes social and environmental *justice* or equity for intersectional identities rather than hierarchical relations of power.
4. The *table* represents the political struggle between neo-liberal capitalism, colonization and globalization, and a decolonization and reconciliation process.

We introduce the themes here as one way to organize and work with the videos and photo essays in a class or a community-based workshop. A facilitator can choose to enter the material through any one of these four themes. Although the order has a linear logic to it, one can begin anywhere, mixing and matching the visual stories.

The four themes correspond to the dynamic tensions elaborated in "Setting the Table" and ground them in the Legacies exchange with selected quotes from our collaborators. Listen for these excerpts in the videos and photo essays to understand them in their specific contexts.

CHAPTER 6
WAYS OF KNOWING
Honoring All Relations That Sustain Life

Mayan people measure their time not in years, but in cycles: we open and close cycles.

—Ángel and Valiana,
Mayan activists, Yucatán, Mexico

Language isn't just a means of communication, there are thousands and thousands of years stored within the Mohawk language, and insight into how to live within the cycles of the earth.

—Ryan, Mohawk,
Wahta, Ontario, Canada

At the core of food sovereignty are ways of knowing, being, and acting in the world that value organic and cyclical processes, represent a holistic view of nature, and acknowledge the interrelationship of all the elements that sustain life. These ideas have come into our conversations over five years, through many different places and from many different voices, some of which you will hear in the five photo essays and videos in this chapter.

This perspective is challenged by Eurocentric knowledges that fragment our understanding, objectify living things, and focus on products over processes. Western sciences often work to explain the material world, whereas Indigenous perspectives see all life processes as spiritual. The Legacies exchange is part of the broader dialogue between western scientific knowledges and Indigenous knowledges, which are converging in new ways.

There's been a total new reconceptualization about soil biology and food webs. If we could hear the signaling and communication in soils, it would be a cacophony of loud sounds. It's so amazing, scientists have to admit they were totally wrong. Now they realize that the soil microbiata is in communication, including the plants.

—Dianne, settler farmer
in Ontario, Canada

I am a botanist and I think that the plants are spirits; they are a form of intense energy, and not just matter. When we eat plants, the energy or spirit of the plant enters our bodies.

—Fulvio, Italian/Mexican,
Michoacán, Mexico

The videos and photo essays in this section can catalyze conversations about these different worldviews, or what our Indigenous Spanish-speaking participants call "ways of living." Each video and photo essay is introduced with a short text, includes a link to a Facilitator Guide, and is followed by commentaries.

HAUDENOSAUNEE GIFTS: CONTRIBUTIONS TO OUR PAST AND COMMON FUTURE

Chandra Maracle and *Rick Hill* of Six Nations of the Grand River Territory
Ryan DeCaire of Wahta Territory

Download the Facilitator Guide (ettl.ca/fg) for this section. See hyperlinks (ettl.ca/6a) for this essay. Each photo essay offers a page with all the hyperlinks for that essay.

Deborah: The Legacies Exchange unveiled the shameful ignorance that we settlers in the United States and Canada have of the Indigenous history of the land we live on. This is land that our colonial ancestors stole and renamed as nation-states. I have only recently realized, for example, that most of the places where I grew up in the United States (Ohio, Michigan, and New York) are in the original territory of the Haudenosaunee. Nor did I learn in school or from my family about how the Haudenosaunee influenced the ideas of democracy in the United States constitution. The Haudenosaunee contributed to a vision of more equitable relations between women and men, to various agricultural practices from interplanting to storage of grains, and to an environmental ethic that is needed as

Chandra, Rick, and Ryan at Six Nations with Rick's paintings

we confront a global climate crisis. The Legacies Exchange has offered us settlers an intense educational experience that is an ongoing process.

Listen to Legacies collaborators Chandra Maracle, Rick Hill, and Ryan DeCaire highlight in this essay some of the gifts of the Haudenosaunee to our past and our common future.

Chandra Maracle, Mohawk activist and core Legacies collaborator, regularly offered us history lessons about our own countries that revealed the invisibility of Indigenous peoples in our education and the richness of their legacy.

Chandra: Haudenosaunees' Role in the Construction of the United States and Canada

Haudenosaunee refers to a group of people, known as Iroquois in French, and as Six Nations in English. The Six Nations Confederacy includes Mohawks, Oneida, Onondagas, Cayugas, Senecas, and the Tuscaroras.

So this is the original United Nations. These six nations came together under instructions of a particular prophet within history to create one confederacy of one mind, often known as *Ska'nikòn:ra*, or the good mind, or *Ka'nikonhri:yo*.

The boundaries included the area around what is now called New York State. After the American Revolutionary War, there were some folks who had remained loyal with the British descendants who became known as Canadians. There were other Haudenosaunee folk who chose to fight with the Americans in that war.

This is significant because Haudenosaunee history *is* Canadian history (ettl.ca/6a). To talk about U.S. or Canadian history without talking about the Haudenosaunee is leaving an incredibly large chunk out and doing a disservice to the European descendants

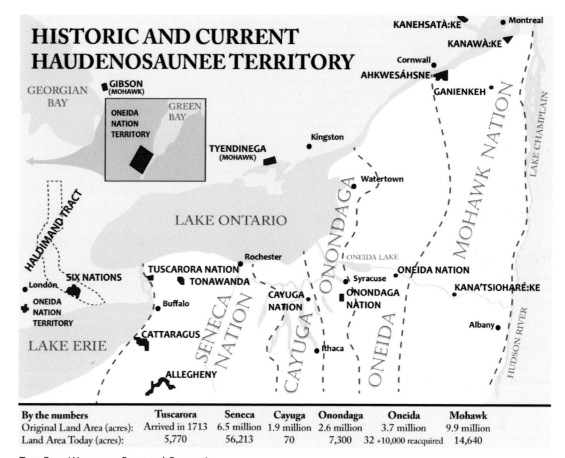

Two Row Wampum Renewal Campaign,
http://honorthetworow.org/learn-more/haudenosaunee-territory/

By the numbers	Tuscarora	Seneca	Cayuga	Onondaga	Oneida	Mohawk
Original Land Area (acres):	Arrived in 1713	6.5 million	1.9 million	2.6 million	3.7 million	9.9 million
Land Area Today (acres):	5,770	56,213	70	7,300	32 +10,000 reacquired	14,640

who became Canadians and those who became Americans, as well as to the Haudenosaunee people.

The Haudenosaunee were absolutely critical in the forming of the countries that have become known on this continent and therefore the influence that

North America has had on the world. That influence first came in the form of how the Haudenosaunee shaped those who became known as Canadians and Americans.

The Haudenosaunee have a unique history. They had about two centuries

Chandra at Food Secure Canada Assembly in Toronto in 2016; painting by Rick Hill

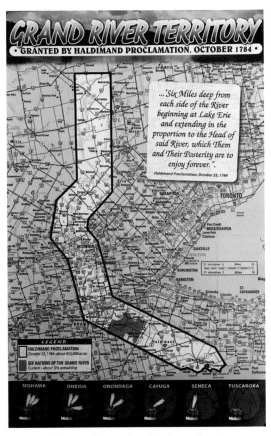

"The Haldimand Tract, land in Canada given to the Haudenosaunee by the British for their loyalty during the Revolutionary War, the red represents what it has been reduced to." —Kyle Martin, O. H. Multimedia, Six Nations Elected Council

of diplomatic relations with the first European arrivals, before folks went west of the Mississippi. At the beginning, there was much more reciprocity between the original inhabitants and the colonizers. For example, often folks think that apples were indigenous to this area, but actually they were introduced by the English. Haudenosaunee were renowned agriculturalists at that time. I think they would have readily welcomed new seed, and probably said, "Oh, apples, we'll do that, we can grow anything." That's what agricultural people do; they don't discriminate against good food.

There's a lot of documentation that also reveals bio-agricultural warfare. Europeans knew how closely the Haudenosaunee were tied to the land agriculturally, so there were campaigns during which troops were ordered to burn thousands of acres of cornfields and other crops. This started with the first U.S. president, George Washington, who became known as *Ranatakárias* or the town destroyer, so now the word for the U.S. president still means "town destroyer."

There's a lot that went on in colonial history, that became U.S. history and later became Canadian history, that

has to do with the relationship with the Haudenosaunee.

I don't really consider myself to live *in* Canada; rather I live *within* Canada. I feel the difference when I'm in Ohsweken (at Six Nations of the Grand River Territory) and when I'm in Caledonia or Brantford or Hamilton or Toronto or anywhere else. It could also be because I have the perspective of having grown up "within" the United States (Buffalo).

Deborah: Rick Hill, Tuscarora historian and Legacies adviser, grew up in an area north of Buffalo, and identifies as Haudenosaunee, not as a citizen of either colonial nation-state, the United States or Canada, within which his current home, Six Nations, is located. Rick has helped to bring to current public consciousness the treaties that govern the relationship between First Nations in the traditional Haudenosaunee territory and the United States and Canada. In the area now known as Toronto (in the so-called province of Ontario and the so-called nation of Canada, all Indigenous names), the treaty that governs us is known as the Dish with One Spoon. Rooted in the Haudenosaunee creation story, this treaty is elaborated by Rick below.

The Dish with One Spoon Treaty

Rick: In our Creation Story, humans are made out of clay, which comes from the Earth. That is why we refer to the Earth as our mother, because we are

Chandra introduces Legacies collaborators to the wampum belt representing the Confederacy of the five Haudenosaunee Nations.

made from that. The Creator finished our bodies out of clay, he breathed into them, he put some of his flesh and some of his mind and told us to come alive. This is why they say the earth is alive. It produces life, it keeps generating.

One of the instructions he gave to the first people was to be thankful for everything he had provided. He made a beautiful world for us. Everything we need is in this world. He gave us five hundred medicine plants, fifty different food plants, as well as animals, birds, trees, bushes, all kinds of things. You don't need a grocery store, you don't need a pharmacy, you don't need Walmart. Everything you need to be happy and healthy is here.

Think of it this way: He put everything into this big dish—all those things we give thanks for. Then he said: "Here, take from this dish what you need, use what's in this dish to be healthy, to feed yourself. But there are some rules."

Nature is like this dish, this great dish with one spoon (ettl.ca/6a). Out of it comes all the bounty that we are meant to share. There's an ecological premise to the dish.

First of all, everybody has an equal share to what's inside the dish, but you only take what you need. So, you don't hoard food, collect things, and store them, and think I'm just going to keep this for myself. Second, you always leave something in the dish for other people. When you go to pick a medicine plant, you don't take the first one, or the second one, you don't clean out the whole field. You always leave something there because plants have intelligence, they're looking at what we do. Third, you've got to keep the dish clean. Now with the environmental holocaust that we're facing, it's very challenging. It's this notion of sharing and connecting that we have to get back to.

This agreement was codified in the Wampum belt of a Dish with One Spoon. What the Peacemaker said is that the chiefs should eat from this common dish. We should never use a sharp instrument, because we share the land. And everyone has an equal right to go hunting and gathering on all parts of the land. It's one land meant to be shared.

In this dish is a long-term health plan (ettl.ca/6a).

Deborah: Ryan DeCaire, professor of Mohawk, offers insight into the agricultural practices of the Haudenosaunee and the deep philosophical underpinnings of their complete food system.

Haudenosaunee Agriculture

Ryan: I've traveled to different Haudenosaunee communities and taken as much knowledge as I can from elders and other growers about heritage seeds and old ways of growing crops.

You could talk about the way our ancestors grew mounds. But what inspired the thinking? It wasn't that they just one day woke up and had a good idea. When we talk about organic or sustainable food systems, we don't often talk about the spiritual side. As Haudenosaunee, all our knowledge comes from a spiritual origin (ettl.ca/6a). For thousands of years, anything we've been inspired by we've always learned from nature.

They say that at the time of the creation of the world, there were three primary original instructions:

One was to love one another.

The second was to constantly give thanks to everything in creation, to remind ourselves that everything in the environment has a responsibility, so that the cycles and balances of life will continue. We also have a responsibility to see that life continues, and to remind ourselves of those responsibilities that we agreed to at the beginning of time. Today we need to ask: have we forgotten those responsibilities? Human beings forget, so there comes a time that we have to remember.

The third instruction is to live within the cycles and balances of the natural environment. Let nature be our teacher, always listen to the environment; not only to dissect the environment but to actually become the environment, to be spiritually connected to it. So that we never lose that ultimate or spiritual connection.

It's a connection to our ancestors, because there are people who planted corn, for example, for thousands and thousands of years, and that's come to us today. In one Seneca village, at the time of European colonization, they found one million bushels of stored corn. They realized that Indigenous people weren't just growing for that one year. They weren't just growing for next year or three years from now. They had enough stored for up to ten years! That

Rick explains the Dish with One Spoon Treaty to Legacies partners in 2019 at Six Nations.

Ryan with Wahta's original corn propagated at Grenville Farm

different ways they stored corn: they braided corn together, they hung it in a longhouse (now in a barn), or stored it in corncribs. They would also slightly char it and store in the ground, so it wouldn't sprout or go rotten. Power foods such as squash and beans can easily be stored. So as a culture, we focused on food security, with a deep connection with food.

When the colonizers attacked Haudenosaunee villages, they concentrated on finding the corn storage and understanding of food security, of having food in case something goes wrong next year or the following year, was a lot more advanced than in our modern food system.

That's a mechanism for controlling the food system, and it's been going on for hundreds of years now. There were fields, and laying waste to that. It was understood at the time of colonization, that if you control somebody's food system and how they survive, then you're ultimately controlling them.

When you look to Indigenous people and food systems, Haudenosaunee are often talked about as agriculturalists. That's very simplistic; it's not that way at all. The ceremonial cycle revolves around the food system, which takes place in every ecosystem on the earth, whether it be hunting in the fall,

Iroquois white corn that Chandra harvested and braided

harvesting in the fall from gardens, making maple syrup in the spring, gathering wild strawberries, fishing. When we talk about food, we can't separate farming from other land-based activities that provide sustenance for us.

When we think of agriculture we should also think of the forest and the role it plays. Especially with this new interest in sustainable agriculture, in organic agriculture, food sovereignty, or food security, we forget about the role that forests play, that oceans play, and mountains and rivers. They all play a role in food sovereignty, food security. The Haudenosaunee had what could be called a complete food system (ettl.ca/6a).

LANGUAGE AND FOOD: A WORLDVIEW IN VERBS

Ryan DeCaire, professor of Mohawk language, University of Toronto

Download the Facilitator Guide (ettl.ca/fg) for this section. See hyperlinks (ettl.ca/6b) for this essay.

People revitalize a language but really a language revitalizes a people. And food revitalizes a people.
    —Ryan at Legacies gathering, 2019

Language is such an amazing thing. It's similar to corn. It's so different from English. When you learn your language, Kanien'kéha or Mohawk, it connects you to generations of your people who have passed. Like corn, it reconnects you to your community and gives you insight into how your ancestors thought and how your people continue to think today.

Ryan talking with Dianne Kretschmar in the forest of Grenville Farm

When you have a language that's built like that, what kind of thinking does that perpetuate? You have this kind of symbiotic relationship between the language and the way people think.

Rethinking Food through Language

Corn, beans, and squash in the Three Sisters mounds of Chandra and Rick Hill

One word that comes to mind is *Tyonnhekhwen*. It's what we call our life sustainers, all the vegetables and fruits, in particular the corn, beans, and squash, which we also call the three sisters. *Tyonnhekhwen* means they that sustain us and provide us with life. So, when you have a people who refer to their food in everyday speech as "They provide us with life," how does that guide your behavior? How does that remind you of your relationship to that food?

When we go to a grocery store, we too often see food as a commodity, with a label and a price tag. And we start to

Language isn't just a means of communication. There are thousands and thousands of years stored within the language, as well as deep understanding about how to live within the cycles of the Earth.

You can look at the Mohawk language in linguistic ways, and say it's a verb-based language, because 90 percent of the Mohawk language is based on verbs. This perpetuates an understanding that everything constantly has a role and a place, is doing something, and has a responsibility. Mohawk is a polysynthetic language, so things that we'd say in English in a paragraph we'd say in a sentence in Mohawk. It means you can't separate who's doing an action from what the action is and when the action is happening.

understand it like any other thing, like a watch or pair of shoes or clothes. When it becomes a product, we have no connection with that food. But if you have a word like *Tyonnhekhwen*, or they sustain us, it's very clear what that word means. It's a constant reminder, built within the language, and therefore, it perpetuates how people use the language as a way of thinking.

Everything's expressed in verbs, like cups and tables and shirts; they are all verbs. When we talk about objects, we talk about what they do *in relation* to us. Therefore, there is knowledge built within a word. For example, east means "where the sun rises."

We need to bring the words back to a cultural story. When you learn your language, it connects you as a people. If you look at our Indigenous communities, you see social breakdown and disease, and loss of social cohesion. Language is something Indigenous people truly connect with, which they can't

Dianne Kretschmar helped to propagate Wahta's traditional corn at Grenville Farm

do with English. It's something they all share, that they have an ultimate connection with, so it helps to restore social cohesion. They feel, "Hey, this is mine. I'm proud of this language, and I want to continue to perpetuate that in our communities."

That's similar to something like corn. It's extremely nutritious and a lot better than the Doritos corn chips you're going to get in a bag. It's a connection to our ancestors because there are people who planted that corn for thousands and thousands of years. They had a connection with the Earth, and that's still with us today. It's similar to how we all have a belly button: we're constantly connected to our mother, and to their mother and their mother . . . which goes back to the Earth. Corn's like that; it connects us to who we are, to our identity; we have helped to propagate

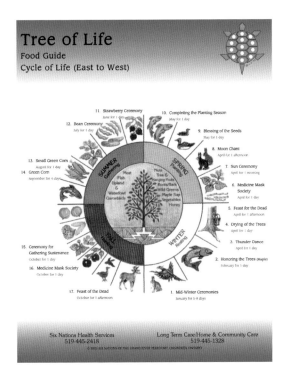

Tree of Life
Food Guide
Cycle of Life (East to West)

11. Strawberry Ceremony
June for 1 day

10. Completing the Planting Season
May for 1 day

12. Bean Ceremony
July for 1 day

9. Blessing of the Seeds
May for 1 day

13. Small Green Corn
August for 1 day

8. Moon Chant
April for 1 afternoon

14. Green Corn
September for 4 days

7. Sun Ceremony
April for 1 morning

6. Medicine Mask Society
April for 1 day

5. Feast for the Dead
April for 1 afternoon

4. Drying of the Trees
April for 1 day

15. Ceremony for Gathering Sustenance
October for 1 day

3. Thunder Dance
April for 1 day

16. Medicine Mask Society
October for 1 day

2. Honoring the Trees (Maple)
February for 1 day

17. Feast of the Dead
October for 1 afternoon

1. Mid-Winter Ceremonies
January for 5-6 days

Six Nations Health Services
519-445-2418

Long Term Care/Home & Community Care
519-445-1328

© SIX SIX NATIONS OF THE GRAND RIVER TERRITORY, OHSWEKEN ONTARIO

it. It reflects that relationship between human beings and the Earth. Because corn doesn't grow if you let it grow on its own. It grows really well when connected with human hands.

Recovering Language and Culture

Throughout the cycle of a year, we have ceremonies, such as strawberry ceremonies and maple ceremonies; our ceremonial cycle revolves around the food system. It is still thriving in certain spots; a small percentage of our population is still very engaged with the traditional culture.

People are working hard to bring that back to life, but it requires a lot of sacrifice to not take jobs that pay well, so you can always be in your community, always working hard to restore your language, to restore that way of thinking. There's so much to learn: songs and dance and stories and speeches, to do birthing and funeral ceremonies, to raise your kids as first-language speakers. You have to shelter your family, because if you're not careful, you lose it all. It's a challenge.

But the culture has changed. Now it's not outlawed to speak the language. Before, people of my grandparents' age weren't allowed to speak their language; they were beaten, they weren't allowed to gather in groups. So, they went underground. But now it's becoming more mainstream. There is a renaissance, but there's still a lot of work to be done. When it comes to restoring Indigenous knowledge systems, we need to concentrate on the community, where it's continuing to be perpetuated. Those are the people who dedicate their lives to this.

Although I enjoy teaching the language at the university, my priority is not in Indigenizing institutions. We need to support Indigenous people and their work at the community level, rather than trying to bring it into the university. Language acquisition, cultural acquisition, revitalization isn't just about the people learning the language. There's so much other work to be done, whether it be activism, governance, food production.

I have students from China and Korea as well as from Indigenous communities such as Six Nations. All students have a need and want to understand what it means to be Canadian after being lied to for their whole lives. They feel a responsibility to right the wrongs that have been done in the past. For those who are not Indigenous, that's the kind of work they can do as partners, as allies. They can be part of a broader Truth and Reconciliation process.

Continuing the Conversation
"Language and Food" Photo Essay

Dr. Lorna Wanosts'a7 Williams
"Language, Voice of the Land"

Ryan DeCaire is sharing insights into his Kanien'kéha (Mohawk) language and relationship with the Earth in this essay. Indigenous peoples around the Earth are working to restore, reclaim, revitalize, vitalize, and maintain their languages while also working to replenish, cleanse, restore, and care for the Earth that nurtures and sustains all that depend on it to live. Indigenous peoples know that languages grow from the land. It is natural that learning the language takes an active place in learning on the land and in ceremony.

A strategy by colonizers to control the land and the people was to silence their language. Religions, institutions such as schools and governments actively undermined the use of Indigenous languages wherever they settled. Homelands were diminished, and Indigenous people confined to reserve lands, snippets of their home territories, making it a challenge to care for the land and to maintain a full relationship. At the same time, every social institution contributed to silencing the presence of Indigenous peoples and sought ways to dislocate people from their homelands and separated children from their families and communities and ancestors.

This multimedia educational resource and Ryan DeCaire's essay demonstrate that Indigenous people have kept the voice of the land and the voice of the ancestors in their minds, hearts, and spirits so that they are living today. The unique understandings are once more shared, uncovered, and lived. This resource will serve as a model for other Indigenous peoples around Planet Earth as they rebuild and reconnect with their languages and knowledge systems.

Dr. Lorna Wanosts'a7 Williams is professor emerita of Indigenous Education, Curriculum, and Instruction at the University of Victoria and Canada Research Chair in Education and Linguistics. Member of the Lil'wat Nation, she was awarded the Order of Canada in 2019 for her contributions to Indigenous education and her advocacy of Indigenous language revitalization programs.

Medicinal Plants in the P'urépecha Cosmovision

An Intercultural Partnership between
María Blas Cacari and *Fulvio Gioanetto*

> Download the Facilitator Guide (ettl.ca/fg) for this section. See hyperlinks (ettl.ca/6c) for this essay.

Lauren: This is a love story—a love of territory, of ancestral knowledge, of plants, of culture, of family and of people, in the P'urépecha Indigenous communities of Michoacán, Mexico.

The collaboration between María Blas Cacari, P'urépecha medicinal plant expert, and Fulvio Gioanetto, Italian-Mexican ethnobotanist, is unique, as they combine their different cultural histories and worldviews in the work they do with medicinal plants.

Fulvio: I came to the Indigenous community of Nurio in 1995, invited by the European Union and a Mextec organization to evaluate traditional medicine and to work with 100–150 youth learning about their culture through plants. It brought together more than one hundred healers to share information and improve their medicinal products.

I didn't speak P'urépecha, and María was my translator as she understood the language and came from a family of healers. Over time I fell in love with her, and stayed in Nurio, where we live and have raised our four children.

Fulvio and Maria with her parents at their wedding in 1997

María: I learned the use of traditional medicine with my grandmother in Nurio. She was a healer and knew a lot about medicine. When I was a child, I spent a lot of time with her, because as the oldest of her great grandchildren, I was able to help her out. Over time, I realized that what she knew was very interesting and could be useful to people.

My grandmother was asked by many people to share her knowledge about medicinal plants, and because

she didn't speak Spanish very well, I had to translate for her. I traveled in the territory and did more research because I knew the plants in our P'urépecha language.

Fulvio and I worked together to recover and research plants that could be used in traditional medicine. Based on the knowledge of about one hundred healers in four regions, we produced a book in 1997 about plants in the P'urépecha plateau, identifying their scientific names and functions in both Spanish and P'urépecha.

Fulvio: I have a doctorate in botany and in pharmacology. I chose not to work in big companies because they are often taking ancestral knowledge and exploiting it for profit. I'd rather work with the people and look for viable options for them to live more decently, more humanely, and more sustainably.

I am a botanist, and I think that the plants are spirits (ettl.ca/6c); they are a form of intense energy, and not just matter. When we eat plants, the energy or spirit of the plant enters our bodies.

I'm interested in animism and totemism. Not just in the anthropological sense, but more profoundly, in understanding how a territory functions and how we interact with life.

María: In the territories of the P'urépecha Indigenous nation, our subsistence is based on a holistic vision of the territory and of the beings and spirits that live and interact. It is also based more on ecological exchanges (with nature) than on economic exchanges (with markets). We interact with the landscape and the territory maintaining and favoring the mosaic of habitats, biological and genetic heterogeneity, and functional biodiversity (ettl.ca/6c).

In the spatial dimension, the territory becomes an agroecological complex in which cultivated fields, cornfields, fallow areas, forests, and bodies of water are all functional units of the complete food system. This increases biodiversity (e.g., the milpa agroecosystem) in spaces where the strategies of multi-species, polycultures, agroforestry (edible forest gardens) rather than monocultures are favored.

We also attribute positive spiritual values to components of biodiversity;

everything in nature has a "spiritual owner," and we have to ask permission to use it.

Fulvio: Through living and working in Mexico for more than twenty years, I have learned that gastronomy, food, and medicine are part of a cultural reality, a way of connecting to a spirit called "plant." For example, María has taught me that in the P'urépecha culture, there are many levels of reality.

Cosmic Planes of the P'urépecha Tradition

María: The P'urépecha cosmogony is similar to that of other Mesoamerican traditions like that of the Mayans, where the universe is conceived in three planes:

A. Aunadarhu (firmament), where the celestial gods dwell;
B. Echerendi (the earth), intermediate plane inhabited by humans and the provident spirits, of the mother of the earth Xaratanga;
C. K'umajchukuarhu (where you are with the gophers), the place of the underworld.

There are four types of calendars—solar (Juriata Miiukua), agricultural lunar, astronomical, and the oldest ritual or festive (Kuiuchukuaro)—all related to fire and its characteristics. The element of fire, reflected in the energy of the sun, is at the center of our cosmovision and all our rituals. Every year on February 5, we offer a ceremony to the new sacred fire.

Invocations are still offered to Tata Jurhiata, or Father Sun, and Nana Kujtsi, Mother Moon and goddess of the night. During the Day of the Dead, we honor the idols of the ancestors, protective deities, and guardians of the family and of the houses of the Tharhésicha, or elders. The People of the Plateau think that some supernatural beings like the spirits of the forests, the hills, and the ravines (the Hapaingua, Japingua, and Phitsikorhekata), the black spirit (Sumbatsi), and the Lord of Death (Achvarhikua) sometimes cause illnesses and nothing less than death.

The Meaning of Specific Plants

Fulvio: Within this cosmovision, the cultivation of chia was important because it was strongly linked to the solar cult and the four cardinal points; a deer-shaped bread is made. A similar ritual worked for corn, corresponding to the cultivated varieties of white, pinto, colorado, blue, and yellow corn. The animals are also related to spiritual elements, setbacks, and/or beneficial

events and are thought to possess extrasensory insight and clairvoyance.

Around 2,500 species of plants, including 18 species and subspecies of ferns, 86 species of lichens, 195 species of mosses and liverworts, and 235 fungi, have been botanically inventoried in the four P'urépecha bioregions. Of these, around 43 percent have ethnobotanical uses (as medicines, food, fodder for animals, dyeing).

There are about fifty different variants of tziri, or criolle corn, grouped into more than a dozen varieties. These landraces of corn are sown at different times throughout the annual cycle and in diverse geographical spaces, allowing our people to cultivate this plant throughout the year, to take advantage of environmental diversification and to develop a vast culinary culture.

Women's Work

María: In our current work with natural plants, whether for medicine, food, or organic inputs, it is the women in our community (ettl.ca/6c) who gather them in the forests, fields, and meadows.

Cornfields outside Nurio, Michoacán

Healing Practices

María: Tradition teaches us that life is an equilibrium between worlds and interconnected beings, and that illness is caused when this equilibrium is broken.

Healers and traditional therapists, in addition to the visible observation of the body, use different divinatory techniques to identify the origin and cause of the disease, either by removing the spell or by cleaning whatever is "dirty" in the house. Another technique consists of a diagnosis by means of a fresh chicken egg, with an interpretive reading of the yolk and white forms.

Maria gathering lavender

Women in María and Fulvio's family

In healing practices there are aspects of intercultural syncretism derived from the process of acculturation in colonial times. The healers used to cover traditional practices with a veil of Christianity to avoid persecution by the Inquisition. Simultaneously, the Spanish conquistadors began to incorporate native drugs into colonial academic medicine.

As in most of the other Indigenous populations of Mexico, traditional P'urépecha therapists use plants and perhaps animal raw materials, which are sometimes combined with mineral substances, in herbal preparations and in usual forms of administration, such as infusions (*Kanelita*), cooking (*Jamakata*), maceration in water (*t'okeman*), vinegar (*shalipera*), maceration in alcohol (*alcohol-ejatziman*), serenades (left to macerate in lunar light, *angatap xaliperan nanakutsiri tzantzqua jinguñi*), tinctures, poultices (*sanucuntan*), soaps (*xapú*), *horchatas*, syrups, ointments and poultices with oil, petroleum jelly, or animal fat.

How does the spiritual practice of a healer affect the healer herself? When one is curing someone spiritually, she uses

In 2018, Fulvio produced a new book, which includes many more medicinal plants he has identified with their characteristics and uses. We asked him to name three different examples of plants that are commonly used in Mexico; he suggested the broadleaf plantain, Spanish sage, and *Argemone Platyceras*.

Examples of Common Medicinal Plants

Broadleaf Plantain
Plantago major
There are more than three hundred uses of this plant. The leaves are boiled and applied as a plaster for skin infections. It's considered a diuretic, expectorant, emollient, and healer. In liquid or syrup form, it can be used to fight colds, bronchitis, and asthma. It can also be used externally on burns or ulcers. It can be gargled to relieve angina and used as eye drops for conjunctivitis and inflammation of the eyelids. Recent research has shown its cytotoxic effect on cancerous cells.

Spanish Sage
(Salvia hispánica or chia)
The leaves can be heated on embers and used as a muscle relaxant, and the seeds can be macerated in water and taken by children with dysentery. It can also be used as a laxative, demulcent, and pectoral, to cure diarrhea, dysentery, and hepatitis.

Argemone Platyceras
(xate or chicolote)
Many parts of this plant can be used for medicinal purposes: the roots can be boiled and used as an immune booster; the seeds can be macerated in water and used to cleanse the eyes; the liquid from the stems can be also be used in the eyes; the crushed leaves applied to the temples are good for headaches; and an infusion of the petals can be taken for coughs.

plants. She must be very focused and draw upon energies to help the person feel better. The work of trying to capture the bad or negative energy and transform it into good or positive energy can be very exhausting. Still, some people keep doing this work, at times because their economic survival depends on it.

But in my case, it was too demanding emotionally, so I eventually left the work. There are special cases, perhaps when my grandchildren feel sick, when I can return to this practice and offer spiritual healing. But healing work can also affect you physically; for example, it can give you headaches. So you have to focus on healing yourself as well.

Passing on the Knowledge

Fulvio: Now our children and grandchildren are learning about how to use plants for their own healing.

Our daughter Serena with her husband, Miguel, gather resin from pine trees for medicinal use (ettl.ca/6c), and our granddaughter Lindsay helps to gather pine cones, which can also be used to treat skin infections and coughs. Our sons Bryan and Jorge assist me in the medicinal plant workshops I offer around Mexico.

This is our legacy—carried on through the next generations.

Continuing the Conversation
"Medicinal Plants in the P'urépecha Cosmovision" Photo Essay

Amber Meadow Adams

Starting with the invasive "medicinal plant" broad plantain described by Fulvio in this essay, Haudenosaunee scholar Adams excavates the impact of colonial plants on women's "illnesses" also produced by colonization. She asks us to dig deeper into the destruction of the social fabric that supported women in childbirth.

"An Imported Medicine for an Imported Ill"

Plantago major. In 1938, Albert Jones, Onöndowa:'ga' from Ohí:yo (Allegany), told newly minted ethnographer William Fenton about some of the uses of plantain. Fenton recorded that it was "good for what whites call 'nervous breakdown,' or when [a] female overworks. When she has many children to look after . . . She feels badly, dizzy in the head."* Jones describes what Fenton identifies as both *Plantago rugelii*, a species indigenous to North America; and *Plantago major*, a Eurasian import. Whether Jones referred to one species or two, *Plantago major*—so aggressive in its spread that it earned the name "Englishman's foot" among some Indigenous nations— had by the twentieth century eclipsed *rugelii* in many parts of the Haudenosaunee homelands.

It was the imported medicine for an imported ill. Until the 1790s, the Haudenosaunee continued to live in houses designed for extended families, organized around one's clan. Children had not only *ista*, a *Kanyen'kehaka* term

encompassing both *mother* and *aunt* in English, but also uncles, cousins, grandparents, siblings, and friends to share the responsibilities of feeding, teaching, and caring for them. Women typically spaced their pregnancies three or four years apart, avoiding the physical overtax of carrying and breast-feeding children, sometimes simultaneously, that their European contemporaries often faced. Haudenosaunee women in the seventeenth and eighteenth centuries had regular access to something many North American women in the twenty-first do not: reliable, economical, and effective care, not only for their children, but for themselves.

Breaking the longhouse into single-family homes—"single" counted as that proletarianized unit of production, the nuclear family—has taken centuries. Removed from the insulation of extended family, losing access to birth control as traditional herbalism was driven underground and habitat was urbanized, Haudenosaunee women were forced to meet greater responsibilities with fewer resources. European invasion transformed a rich biome into a state of poverty: land theft, disease, war, and internment in residential schools meant higher average rates of morbidity and mortality in Indigenous populations. As the primary caregivers in more isolated households sheltering poorer, sicker people, a Haudenosaunee woman in Albert Jones's time could expect at least some periods of extreme overwork. The "dizz[iness]" he describes is a clinical

(continues)

presentation of dehydration, malnutrition, anemia, hypo- or hypertension, migraine, and panic disorder—all conditions associated with physio-neurological stressors. Even the menstrual retirement traditional to longhouse life was no longer possible, nor the period of care of the woman, self-given or offered by others, that privileged her health and well-being rather than her dependents. Also, as capitalism overwhelmed the more matrifocal Haudenosaunee economy, women began to lose voice in Council, both within communities and between their nations and the Crown and its daughter states. This displacement, though never complete, further eroded the social space women's *kasha'tstenhsera*—capacity and autonomy—had occupied for centuries, marginalizing them within their own eco-legal system and further increasing burdens of stress.

Jones's reporting of *Plantago species* as treatment for an individual's disease stands as a sign of pragmatism and defiance—uprooting and metabolizing an invasive species as an act of resistance to being uprooted and metabolized. In that respect, a Haudenosaunee woman was not taking plantain to reverse the disease process but to fortify herself by absorbing a form of life, no matter its origin, like her and her peers: tenacious, adaptable, and capable of surviving and growing under hard conditions. Yet I wonder if, in 1938 or a century later, the question, "What are your medicine plants?" drives healers toward answers that Western medical philosophy can only misinterpret. The Haudenosaunee woman having a "nervous breakdown" can swallow her *Plantago* privately and privately return to all the things that made her sick. No public change, no structural disruption, no biomic recovery is needed.

The Haudenosaunee healers for whom I have greatest respect treat illness as systems reaching beyond the borders of any one body. *Ka'nikòn:ra*, the spirit, will, desire, and consciousness manifesting as physiological phenomena, exists only in relation to all other *yoti'nikonhrashon'a*. All parts touch, and all parts move. How would the work of rescue ethnobotany change if curiosity about medical systems, food systems, and even ecosystems became curiosity about the matrixes of macro- and microlife? What if the acknowledged treatment for one woman's nervous breakdown were the regrowth of a forest, or a renaissance of the kind of equity-in-care that capitalist medicine cannot accommodate? A sick woman and the sick Earth, our Creation story tells us, are one body. Where do we look for the medicine and the respite care for our shared mother?

Amber Meadow Adams is a writer living and working at Six Nations Grand River Territory. She received a BA in literature and writing from Columbia University and her PhD in Indigenous studies from the University at Buffalo.

*James Herrick, *Iroquois Medical Botany* (Syracuse, NY: Syracuse University Press, 1997), 61.

Valiana Aguilar and *Ángel Kú*[1]

> Download the Facilitator Guide (ettl.ca/fg) for this section. See hyperlinks (ettl.ca/6d) for this essay.

Of yellow corn and of white corn its flesh was made; of corn dough its arms and legs were made . . . only corn dough made up its flish.

—Popul Vuh
(fragment of creation story)

To Sense Ourselves in a Weave

Our grandmothers used to tell us stories about a hidden trunk in the Mayan community of Maní, south of Yucatán. The trunk contained the rope of life that united communities. When the Spanish came, they cut the rope. Since then, it has been our duty to reweave ourselves, meaning, reuniting the threads of *Kuxan Suum* (the living rope).

The world we know is unraveling in our hands; knots of threads are detaching and falling. It has become urgent to find ways, paths, roads that can weave us back together, even though we are aware that the resulting weave will not be the same as the original one. We feel

Doña Rosa shows Valiana how to weave a hammock.

that one of the main prerogatives now is to regenerate that weave.

To achieve this, we think we have to collectively heal ourselves first. That healing must be rooted in our elders, our grandmothers and grandfathers, learning from their paths. They have left us with the task of walking our paths while healing.

The weave makes reference to hammocks, which is where our bodies can rest. However, to make a hammock we have to make knots as well. That is why we say we are knots in networks of relationships, that is what forms community, what makes us into a "real us."

To Walk in the Footprints of Our Elders in Different Geographies

For the Añú people, as we learn from José Ángel Quintero Weir, elders are our footprint. They are our past, our present, and our future. Our life would not have meaning without those footprints, meaning their steps give direction to our steps, with the possibility of opening new paths that will offer footprints for others.

Among the Mayan peoples, grandmothers raise us, share creation stories, show us the rituals, the language, the dances, the food, the ways of the community. They show us the way to relate to the world, with all the animals and beings of the natural environment. Our grandfathers teach us to walk in the natural environment, to explore it and see ourselves in it. Through this, they teach us to see our land and defend it, because the natural environment is our sustenance. All of these elements keep our peoples alive, despite the strategies of death that the system has wanted to impose on us for more than five hundred years.

One of the legacies left to us by our elders is a small gap that allows us to see and understand what our people are—this is where we say our elders have left footprints, and those footprints are the past and the present at the same time.

Our Rituals, Legacy of Our Elders

Gourd filled with saka *for ceremonial offering*

One of the rituals that we are taught when we are little is to ask permission of the mountain or the natural environment before carrying out any work. The grandparents prepare the *sakab*,[2] made by cooking corn by itself to make the dough that is to be brought to the mountain. We use a large bucket to dissolve the dough in water and add honey, which is then offered in gourds to the four directions.

To the heart of the sky and the earth, to the winds, to the animals we ask permission to work the land with no problems and so the harvest can grow.

For the Mayan peoples, it is not frowned upon when a young person leaves the community. They are leaving so they can walk their own path and experience other places. In all of our ceremonies we speak of the four directions, which represent the world for Mayan people.

Both of us had the curiosity to leave and to come to Oaxaca to learn about the experience of other communities. When we made that decision, we asked our direct grandmothers and grandfathers in the Yucatán to accompany us in our hearts, in our way of resisting and existing. We invoke their memory in our day-to-day life, and thanks to them, we are able to keep on existing despite barriers we face along the way.

In the ritual of *Jeets Meek* that Mayan people perform for babies a few months after they are born, the child is gifted a needle and thread. Children are told that it is so they can learn how to knit, be it clothing or relationships, that needle and thread accompany us throughout our journey.

Previously when we traveled within our territory or visited other states with other Indigenous peoples, when we speak to other sisters and brothers, we find that it is not just what Valiana and Ángel think about the world. Rather, what our elders have seen and have left to us from their own path is manifested through our words. We have found that the way of thinking of our people coincides with other Indigenous peoples: the way of seeing life, of experiencing the world, of listening to and sensing it coincides with ours. And we could not know or experience this if we were not these knots or nodes in the networks of relationships that we are. This is the result of the shared lived experience of our elders.

What has pushed us to walk our path is the quest for knowledge, but also to recognize and reconnect ourselves with other lands and geographies regenerates who we are. That is how what we do and what we live is meant to help us return to our home and share with our elders what we have learned, and in doing so we root ourselves even deeper.

Mayan people measure their time not in years, but in cycles: we open and close cycles.

Another element that is given to us in the ceremony of the *Jeets Meek* are keys, precisely keys to open and close cycles. In a sense this is what brought us to Oaxaca: opening a cycle of knowledge that is getting to know and learn from the communities and also to know more about UniTierra in Oaxaca (ettl.ca/6d). We did this so we could propose in our own community to build a space of learning where young people can walk with us in order to be able to regenerate the community weave that is disintegrating more and more every day.

Arriving in Oaxaca implied learning collectively and getting involved in "mutual nurturing" (or *crianza mutua*). This is an expression we adopted from our Andean siblings. They teach us the notion that everything is nurtured: human beings and Mother Earth have an interrelationship that allows us to exist and survive. Without this relationship life itself would not be possible. Now we use the expression "mutual nurturing" to describe the ability to learn from others' lived experiences and to allow ourselves to be mutually raised. This means learning from others in order to then continue on our path and in the struggles of our communities.

In Oaxaca we have remained involved in community life to continue being true to ourselves. It has allowed us to become rooted here and to heal. Our growth would not have been possible, and in fact is never possible without the teachings of our elders. Those true elders who have built a life, who have shared with us and from whom we can learn to build a different life for ourselves as well. We listen to the joy and the sorrow in their life. Their pain in seeing and recognizing that a world they once knew is no longer, the pain of this world unraveling. It seems like we do not know where we are headed, but deep inside they know and hold within their hearts that way of life that can reweave us together again. This however requires not just to listen to them, but to carry out the work and to heal.

Doña Yolanda and Don Toño were the first elders who opened the doors of their house to us when we arrived in Oaxaca. They are from San Agustín Etla, the first community we visited when we arrived. Doña Yolanda and Don Toño have a farm with some cows, and they grow a milpa and vegetable gardens. They have resisted their whole lives and have refused to depend on an employer. They are autonomous. What they call "work" is actually a way of life they are passionate about and that they have managed to build throughout their lives. For us they are an example of how to build community: their way of relating to one another, to the community, to the farm, to the animals, to their vegetable gardens, while they work on their *milpa*.

Don Antonio with his compost pile

Doña Yolanda and Don Toño have a painful history. Like in many communities in Mexico, women are not taken into consideration by their father to inherit

Doña Yolanda in the milpa

land. This is the case of Doña Yolanda, who since a young age observed that taking care of the land and working the land for sustenance was a way of living with dignity. With a lot of effort and dedication, after a few years, she was able to buy a piece of land together with Don Toño. It is also a joyful story because they have cared for the land and grow food with no agrochemicals. They produce cheese from their cows' milk in Oaxaca's traditional way, and they grow their milpa every year. They are proud of their work and their way of life. They watch the world today with

concern, they look around them and notice that young people are no longer interested in working the land. They ask themselves what will happen when they can no longer work the land. We see this also as our duty and responsibility. Not to simply sit with them through this, but to build our lives trying to re-create that which has been lost.

We ask ourselves: Despite all the difficulties, how do we form our path and build that "us" that we are talking about? Without depending on the state, on institutions. For many, that "us" doesn't exist anymore. Instead, people

only care about themselves as individuals, and through this individualism, they abandon that love for the land and that love for growing our own food, for sharing food with others. For many Indigenous peoples sharing food with family is the most sacred; it's what makes us siblings.

Knitting together the life experiences of Doña Yolanda and Don Toño with the experiences of our Mayan elders, we found each other as family. That leaves us with the responsibility of figuring out how to heal the family tree of pain that they have lived through and how we will walk alongside others while we build "us."

This includes what we have learned with Gustavo and Nicole, grandparents of UniTierra, from Oaxaca and Marseilles, France, who have embraced us over the past five years. They arrived at San Pablo Etla to a piece of land on a hill thirty years ago. They had lived in Mexico City for fifty years. When they arrived, the land was completely depleted; a peasant sold them land that has been a pasture of his goats. For us they are role models, since they represent the regeneration of life.

Nicole had tried growing her own food in Mexico City in small spaces, the ones found in city homes. When she arrived in San Pablo Etla, she started

Visit to Gustavo and Nicole's house with Deborah and John

creating her own compost and adding it to the soil. She then tried different types of vegetable gardens and milpa. Gustavo is a deskilled intellectual who has dedicated the last few years to writing and reflecting on the state of Indigenous peoples alongside them. He has also closely followed the trajectory of the Zapatistas and developed a radical critical analysis of the school system.

They left their life in the city to go live in a rural community and to create UniTierra with other Indigenous organizations as part of their lives. They have regenerated the land and cultivate vegetables, raise chickens, and grow their milpa. Their little house is made from adobe (soil and clay), with no-flow toilets, gray-water filters, and rainwater-catchment tanks. Opposite to the

A Mayan palapa, a meeting place in the Solar Maya created by Ángel and Valiana in Sinanche, Yucatán

mainstream development model, they believe that the art of inhabiting a place does not necessarily mean using expensive or commonly called "good quality" materials. Their path has inspired many people who have come through UniTierra throughout the past eighteen years. It has been the same for us; we live by their example and follow their advice.

The Footprints That Open the Roads of Autonomy

Sometimes we talk about switching nouns with verbs. We see that in everyday life the elders are doing it. Our grandmothers never talked about going to the doctor when they had an illness. Rather, their patio/garden is a type of pharmacy that heals. When somebody has a stomachache, a fever, or a bruise, they head to the patio/garden and bring "medicines" such as a twig of rosemary, sagebrush, spearmint, peppermint, and so forth. Each plant can heal us; that is the true art of *healing*. Within the art of *eating*, grandmothers possess a large repertoire of recipes with the same ingredients: corn, beans, squash, chili, tomatoes. If one talks to a grandmother about these ingredients, she can name within minutes a hundred recipes that they know how to make. Similarly, we can say that in the art of inhabiting Mayan houses, they use around fifteen different types of wood that are found in different parts of the bush or forest.

When we walk with them, our grandfathers show you while they walk and explain "this wood is good for a roof or as a beam, etc." And they always mention "we have to ask for permission before cutting any wood, otherwise the alux[3] can take you."

It isn't something new; this individualism has been imposed upon us for a long time. It's like a blindfold that forces us to keep depending on a system that sickens us, that invalidates us, that makes us dependents, that makes us deaf, that prevents us from mutual upbringing. These legacies we are receiving are allowing us to build a

Don Antonio Mukul in Maní blessing the seeds for the milpas

different "us," to recuperate the idea of an "us." It is urgent to rebuild that "us" so we can keep living in that world we want.

Our elders are not telling us what we have to do, they are not telling us each day where we have to go. And there is no need since we can see for ourselves what world we are living in. What they do is inspire us; they move us by their example and not through their discourse, like often happens in universities. Their actions are a way of living

and feeling the land, the milpa, the wind and the rain. It is in that practice of the milpa that we see ourselves and we feel a part of that "us."

The Milpa

The milpa is our way of life. It's comprised mainly of three elements or three sisters: corn, beans, and squash. At different times within one same cycle one can also grow *yuca*, *macal*, jicama, tomatoes, chilies, flowers, other beans, and so forth. It begins in January or February by walking through the land and finding a place to offer the sakab. At that time, one asks animals to stay away, such as snakes. If the land has alux, that is when they need to be nurtured so they are able to work the land. Next is weeding or cutting down trees in the land. If the land is big, it can take a longer time, and it can be done collectively.

In March/April the seeds that will be planted are collected. At this time the winds have died down a little and one can burn the land. This practice is important because it allows any plagues that are in the soil to die and it also helps fertilize the soil. This is also a good time for a ceremony asking for rain and for a generous harvest.

At the end of May, the first rainfalls are expected. It's important to check

that the land is well-watered before planting the seeds. The planting can be a collective activity for men, women, grandmothers, grandfathers, girls, boys, everybody. The corn takes different amounts of time to grow, between a month and a half to three or four months. The first corn is offered to the four directions, the heart of the sky and the heart of the earth, as an appreciation. Similarly, from all the meals that are prepared, a small portion is offered to the land to return part of what we are eating.

The corn can be harvested early to make atole, *iswua*, new dough bread, and so forth. Then the corn is bent so it can dry and later be harvested. When harvesttime arrives, many communities still practice a ceremony called *wajicool*. At this ceremony, a large meal is prepared and offered to the land as a sign of gratitude. This is around October/November, when we are preparing for the fiesta of the dead.

This is also the season for *ibes* (white beans), *spelón* (the beans that are eaten young), of jicama, of marigolds, of tangerines, and so forth. These are all harvested from the milpa, and meals and offerings are prepared. The land then rests for December, and in January, the cycle of the milpa begins once again.

We always remember Don Toño working in the milpa and telling us: we have to add nutrients to the soil to heal it! And if the soil needs healing, why shouldn't we heal ourselves too? If the milpa is an "us," why do we think we are individuals?

We are in this circle with our elders who have shared their life experiences, their way of living and surviving in this world. It has been vastly enriching, all this learning, all this mutual upbringing, all this listening. We are at a point in the cycle where there is no choice but to fight to keep and maintain this life that they have shared with us.

When we talk about eating, we see the threats to corn like GMO corn, such as corporate patenting of seeds, herbicides, agrochemicals that damage the land. We see the future of Indigenous

Peoples and their way of life affected by these threats. They have fought all their lives to maintain the diversity of life: all that can be planted, all that can be built, every living thing with whom we can relate. Speaking of "good eating" is not just to defend food but also to keep growing it.

When we talk about the world unraveling it's because we are trying to liberate ourselves from a war against that "us," a war against our ways of living and feeling. This is where our elders' teachings come into play. Learning from their mistakes implies healing and taking responsibility for the things we do as well as the things we do not. What are we doing and not doing and how do we take responsibility? How do we do that, learning from them again?

Hopes, Dreams: Creating Our Own Space of Learning in Sinanché, Yucatán

While in Oaxaca, we nurtured the dream of creating our own space in the Yucatán. Two years ago, we spoke to our family about the possibility of returning to our community. In that moment the grandfathers agreed that they would give the community-ejido[4] rights of

more than ten hectares to Valiana. This was because every day tensions grow over what will happen to the community when the next generations abandon the land completely. Many former ejidos have been privatized or rented to companies to construct wind farms and other uses.

The land also has a history. In the 1980s there was a henequen hacienda, with large plantings of henequen monocropping, an agave plant that is used to make textile fibers. This devastated the natural environment, and since then there has been an intention to regenerate the land and the community weave through the formation of an ejido.

Cultivating hennequen in Sinanché, Yucatán

We returned to the Yucatán in October 2019, to begin constructing

Mayan sculpture in Ticul, Yucatán

our dream. We decided to settle here in Valiana's hometown of Sinaché, where there is a strong weave among the community. There are many problems: young people are leaving the community; the older people are no longer working the land. This project has to be born with the *abuelos/as*, the young people, with the community. We never thought of doing this alone. It even includes people who are not here, but people who know about the project.

This was an opportunity to heal not just the land, but also the pain that was caused in the community by the hacienda. Our project needs to be a space to denounce all the death that is being sown. This includes struggles against the Mayan train,[5] corporate wind-power projects, solar panels, and the threat of our seeds being patented by companies.

Ángel and Valiana forging a path on family land outside Sinanché

So our project is not isolated from the other battles of our people.

We hope it can generate strategies that will help the Mayan people remain alive. This is our final battle. If we don't resist the wave of megaprojects, we could lose our autonomy, our ways of living, our language . . . and this includes la comida, water, the ways we relate to the land and each other. We're thinking about how to construct autonomy with others. To speak our language, to respect the land, to prepare our ancestral food that our *abuelos* taught us is part of this autonomy.

We are trying to create a space where we can grow our food and provide an alternative way of life and inspire young people to return to the land. For us that

means returning to our ways of eating, healing, and inhabiting. We want young people to learn freely about different societal tools that will allow them to return to the community and apply what they have learned in a way of life full of joy.

Continuing the Conversation
"Mutual Nurturing: Reweaving Community with Our Elders" Photo Essay

Monique Mojica
"Of Bodies Born from Stardust and Cornmeal"

I am responding to the photo essay on "Mutual Nurturing (*La Crianza Mutua*)" from the point of view of a performer and playwright engaged in activating and animating land-based, embodied dramatic structures for the purpose of telling Indigenous stories theatrically. Many things in this essay resonate with my artistic practice, a practice that spans six decades and four generations. It is itself a process of retrieval of culture and language, reclamation of identity and reconnection with kinship, land, and place. The "reweaving" of the self and the community is conceptually similar to the story weaving technique of building organic theater that I inherited from my immediate elder generation, Spiderwoman Theater. Presencing and embodying the warp and the weft of the weave, the knots and the umbilical cords that tie us to our origins, the layers of encoded meanings within textiles, effigy mounds, and earthworks complexes or the abstraction of iconic forms in petroglyphs, pictographs, or patterns on ceramics all provide guides and pathways toward reinventing the "real us." In this way, stories reenacted within earth cycles and a space-time continuum reflect a mutual nourishment rooted in the interrelatedness of the human body to land, waters, and the nonhuman world, because as much as we "perform" the Earth—the Earth performs us.

Corn. The Three Sisters. Many Indigenous nations are linked by these primary sources of sustenance. Through Corn Mother, we are relations. Our bodies are formed from her substance mixed with the ashes of extinguished stars. Our kinship ties can be traced to Corn Mother's long-ago migration north and to the many stories, songs, dances, and ceremonies enacted and reenacted across these lands now violently dissected along geopolitical borders. I am reminded of when my son was a sullen, crabby fifteen-year-old, and I brought him with me to visit Chiapas in the years just preceding the Zapatista uprising. Oh, he scowled at everything—except maybe *caldo de pollo*. But, then, there was a transformation. We were high in Los Altos in the community of Chenalhó when my scowling boy looked up and saw cornstalks growing at odd angles out of the rocky mountainside. He said to me, "I know this, Mom. They grow corn—these are my people." He located himself on that land through corn.

We carry Corn Mother in our DNA. What happens, then, when corn is so altered by pesticides and GMO practices that we can no longer turn to her as a source of nourishment? It seems to follow that the genetic modification of Corn Mother's DNA must alter us humans in profound ways. About twenty years ago, I was told that I am allergic to corn. That was a very emotional moment for me. I cried. I grieved the loss of Corn Mother. I can occasionally eat corn from unaltered, original seed grown in Indigenous territories, but only ever her "real self."

Toronto-based actor/playwright Monique Mojica is Guna and Rappahannock, which means that her Indigenous roots are in both North and Central America. Her artistic practice includes land-based, embodied research toward creating Indigenous dramaturgies that place Indigenous Knowledge in the center of her process.

CHAPTER 7
EARTH

When we go to a grocery store, we too often see food as a commodity, with a label and a price tag. When it becomes a product, we have no connection with that food.
—Ryan, Mohawk professor, Ontario, Canada

When you eat fry bread, you are literally eating the trauma of the generations.
—Chandra, Mohawk leader, Six Nations, Ontario, Canada

Many Mexican workers who migrate to Canada or the United States, when they come back, they are sick from the use of pesticides. So, this is the price they pay.
—Fulvio, Italian/Mexican, Michoacán, Mexico

The dominant corporate food regime is market driven and has disconnected us from nature, as many consumers no longer know where their food comes from. Indigenous peoples have borne the brunt of this disconnection, grounded in colonialism that brought new industrialized and often unhealthy foods, such as fry bread, to the Americas. The current impacts of the North American industrial food system are aggravated by the systemic inequities between Mexico, the United States, and Canada, which forces migration north with consequences for poorer workers from the south.

Legacies collaborators are challenging the globalized corporate system, starting with claiming our bodies as part of nature and even sources of food. All the efforts represented in these stories counter the disconnection from food generated by the global food system and industrial agribusiness.

If we're talking about local food, you can't get more local than mother's milk.
—Anna, mother/teacher/farmer, Quebec, Canada

Nature is like this dish, this great dish with one spoon. And out of it comes all the bounty that we are meant to share. There's an ecological premise to the dish.
—Rick, Tuscarora artist, Six Nations, Ontario, Canada

Through a settler-Indigenous exchange, we have learned to think deeply about how we feed ourselves, which also reflects how we care for the environment. Non-Indigenous collaborators working closely with the earth have developed similar holistic and integrated perspectives on food and growing food. The young agroecologists in our exchange have developed a more personal relationship with a closed-loop process of growing food that involves animals.

For plants, soil is like their stomach,— the way the plant eats is by the roots, the mouth of the plant is the roots, and they need a good quality of soil with a lot of life, just like we need life in our stomach to be able to synthesize the food that we eat.
—Fernando, urban agriculturist, Jalisco, Mexico

The treatment of the animal is the number one thing people want to know about when they buy meat. Was it grass fed? What is the history of the farm? What are the farmers like? What do they care about?

—Adam, teacher/farmer/butcher, Quebec, Canada

Ultimately, food sovereignty challenges the capitalist notion of property, the basis of the corporate food regime, and suggests another relationship with the earth.

We don't own the land. The land owns us.

—Dianne, farmer, Ontario, Canada

MOTHER'S MILK: THE ORIGINAL FOOD

A Cross-Cultural Conversation of Legacies Women

(Chandra Maracle, Anna Murtaugh, María Blas, Hilda Villaseñor, and *Serena Gioanetto)*[1]

Download the Facilitator Guide (ettl.ca/fg) for this section. See hyperlinks (ettl.ca/7a) for this essay.

With baby Theo in her arms (ettl.ca/7a), Anna revisited the field of thyme she had planted when she worked on Dianne Kretschmar's farm in the Muskoka region in the early 2000s.

The Legacies project brought Chandra and Anna together at the farm in July 2016; Chandra came from Six Nations in Ontario, and Anna was visiting from her home in Quebec.

Sitting down to share food and stories (ettl.ca/7a), they nibbled on the nutritious cornbread that Chandra had made from Iroquois (Haudenosaunee) white corn. As both mothers were still nursing their babies, they discovered a common passion for breast-feeding.

Chandra and Vyolette: "Cosmic or Spiritual Food"

Mother's milk is the original food (ettl.ca/7a), what we call Kakwa'on'we or the go-between food. There's the food a baby gets in the womb, fed from Mom on the inside. But as soon as the baby is born, she doesn't eat earth food just yet. She gets cosmic food, which is spiritual food.

That connection remains between the Skyworld and babies before they can actually physically eat human food or earth food. I like talking about breast milk as an important link in the food chain. It says a lot about my food sovereignty and Vyolette's food security.

Breast-feeding hadn't really happened in my family for a couple of generations. My parents were very supportive, but it was a process that I had to learn myself. And a couple of my kids had serious health issues, so couldn't breast-feed. In the hospital, having your pumped breast milk be dumped down

the drain accidentally is one of the worst things I've experienced.

Breast-feeding is a lifestyle choice. Some women make other choices and have a much easier lifestyle. It's the harder road in this culture and in this climate. Once a waitress in a restaurant said that my breast-feeding was making another customer uncomfortable. That's not something you want to say to me. I firmly but politely said, "Well, she's almost done," and kept going about my business.

People are generally more accepting now; breast-feeding is again the norm. Once an older woman came up and thanked me for breast-feeding my child. That we need acknowledgment shows that it's still not back to where it used to be.

The first time that I heard the term "food sovereignty" (ettl.ca/7a), it seemed over-politicized. It took me a while to wrap my head around that phrase and see it as important. The work that I do *is* food sovereignty; it's living that food sovereignty. It's not about pumping a fist and holding a picket sign. It's about sitting down with a stool and just feeding my kid . . . anywhere.

That's my pitch on food sovereignty and food security—the humble beginnings of breast-feeding.

Anna and Theo: "The Most Local Food"

Breast-feeding, or nursing my babies, was the obvious choice for me. It was what I experienced as a baby and toddler, and watched as my mother nursed my younger brother.

I was breast-fed until the age of about three or four. Not so much for nutrition at that point but for comfort. Many people find that to be very weird, if not totally wrong. I don't remember being nursed per se, but I do remember

the closeness and playing with the gold chain around my mother's neck.

Not only that, but my mother was a vocal champion of breast-feeding. She liked to boast about having helped other babies and mothers get the hang of it by feeding them herself and teaching them a proper latch. Imagine that—nursing someone else's child!

I had a strong role model, good personal experiences, and a family and community that were supportive of breast-feeding. So, when my first child, Katherine, was born, it was an obvious and natural choice. I know that is not everyone's experience. Although I had my mother as a role model, she was not around when my children were born. She had died two years before.

I was also very lucky to have my children born in a place where a mother's choices are respected. The nurses and community health clinics in Quebec are so supportive of families. We were given information, even pamphlets for fathers and grandparents on how to support breast-feeding. The nurses at the hospital taught me how to nurse a newborn and proper latching.

We had a visit from the nurse twenty-four hours after coming home, and she put us in touch with an organization in the area called "Suportons-lait." They provide

information for prospective parents about breast-feeding and can connect a new mother with a breast-feeding "godmother," or "marraine," who offers support when needed by phone, Facebook, or in person.

I enjoyed the social support of group gatherings and outings at local family centers, cafés, even a museum visit during world breast-feeding week to see a lactation-themed art exhibit. I didn't know any other mothers at that time, so meeting people was very important to me. I like to joke that Katherine is the poster child for breast-feeding as she is featured in the pamphlet for Suporton-lait, the photos taken at one of the monthly "causeries," or chat groups.

Katherine quit nursing on her second birthday, saying it tasted "yucky." I think the flavor had changed as I was pregnant at the time. And with my second child, Theo, it was my choice to stop nursing him when he was just over two years old. I was pregnant with my third child and felt I needed a break. I took a vacation for a few days without him and told him the milk was all done when I came home. He told me to go to the store to get more milk.

Nursing our third child, Amelia, was good but a little more challenging. Theo was a little jealous, and climbed all over

struggle to breast-feed without the kind of support that Anna enjoyed.

Breast-feeding creates a beautiful connection. But in Mexico right now, it is highly criticized. There's criticism for moral reasons, for example, for exposing your breast in a very conservative culture. Ads showing women exposing their breasts are not considered bad, but breast-feeding is seen as bad. It's hypocritical.

We're a very elitist and classist society. When upper-class women saw me breast-feeding, they said in a derogatory tone, "You're like an Indian!"

me as I tried to nurse. With three kids it was hard to sit down and relax into it.

I had a bout of mastitis that was so painful, and really knocked the energy out of me, but again with supportive health care I was able to get over it quickly (thanks to a nurse phoning in a prescription during a snowstorm). One of the main perks of breast-feeding for me was not having to get up at night to prepare a bottle. Just roll over, feed, and go back to sleep.

On the farm (ettl.ca/7a), we also see breast-feeding with our animals. Our kids get to see the goats and the rabbits being breast-fed from their mothers.

If we're talking about local food, you can't get more local than mother's milk.

Hilda and Diego: "A Beautiful Connection"

Hilda Villaseñor was a third breast-feeding mother at the Legacies gathering in 2016 accompanying her partner, Fernando Garcia, to Canada from Mexico. She recounts her

Fernando and Hilda with Diego

They also criticized me for carrying Diego in a rebozo to keep him close to my body. They thought he should be in a stroller or carriage. But when we came to Canada (ettl.ca/7a) for the Legacies project, people did not think it was strange for me to carry him in a snuggly, close to me.

My mother couldn't breast-feed me; she had problems, and it worked for only one month. So, I was bottle fed with formula.

I wanted to give my son the best food when he was a baby, but I also did it for the strong connection it would give us. Through breast-feeding, I was giving him more self-confidence and a strong relationship between mother and son. And I can see the results in him: he's very loved and very secure.

I was criticized for breast-feeding for more than two years. Many mothers only breast-feed for three months, and that's it. Instead of seeing it as natural and normal, they see it as abnormal. They think you are spoiling the child.

I visited many pediatricians who said that it would damage my son psychologically. I went through eight doctors before I found one who would support me!

Many of the things I did were criticized: carrying my baby close to my body, breastfeeding, having him sleep with me. Even cesarean birth is now more normal than natural childbirth.

I fought to keep breast-feeding. I even lost friends over this. Once in a restaurant with a friend, I breast-fed Diego under a cape. My friend criticized me for breast-feeding (even covered) in front of the waiter.

I believe very firmly in breast-feeding not only as a method of healthy nutrition, but as a way to nurture and connect with my son. So, if I had to lose friends and family, so be it.

María and Serena: "Backward or Modern?"

Legacies collaborator María and her twenty-one-year-old daughter, Serena, live in the autonomous P'urépecha community of Nurio in Michoacán, Mexico.

Maria with grandson Felipe in 2020

María: When my sister Ana was a baby, almost forty years ago, we couldn't buy bottled milk in Nurio. Everybody breast-fed.

In the past, women would have children every year, and it was considered not acceptable to breast-feed while pregnant, though there were some women who would breast-feed both the older and the new baby at the same time.

I had an aunt who breast-fed her eight-year-old child. She would do it before she went to school and when she came home. It was less about feeding and more about giving the child comfort.

Many years later they started to sell formula. It was offered to support the women who had a small child and a new baby. And it was more practical for women who were working.

We had to boil water and keep it warm in a thermos. You had to buy formula, but the federal Health Ministry offers it free as a social service for people who can't afford it. Companies would donate their products and distribute them to people who needed it.

Now many people buy the formula, because if they breast-feed, they are seen as backward, stuck in the past. They are considered modern if they use formula.

Twenty years ago, people still had their children at home. There were midwives, but some women gave birth alone. Later they were encouraged to go to clinics to have their babies.

They now do more cesarean births as a form of birth control, because you shouldn't have more than three cesarean births. It's more expensive to have children in the hospital. Natural births are cheaper. Normally women don't want cesarean births, because they say that God sends you the children that He wants you to have.

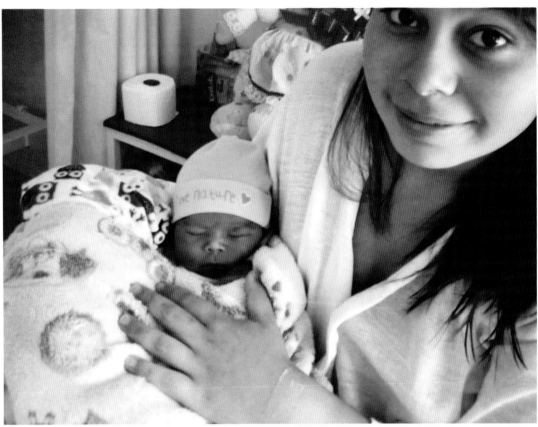

Serena with baby Lindsey

But we still keep the tradition of using medicinal plants that we know are good for our health. And I continue to find new seeds and gather plants (ettl.ca/7a) that I might use for my family.

Serena: I decided to breast-feed my daughter Lindsey because I knew that it was beneficial for her and for me. It's very nutritious and prevents certain diseases. I breast-fed her for six months, and she didn't get sick. It is a beautiful experience as a mother, to have the baby so close while breast-feeding.

Before, all women breast-fed their children. Older women, like our mothers and mothers-in-law, think it is better.

But women who have migrated to the United States come back saying that formula is best. Women in the United States don't breast-feed their children, because they are only with the baby for a short time after they are born before they have to go to work.

When you have a baby, you have to be there constantly, breast-feeding every few hours.

Now I think if a woman has money, then she will buy the formula.

But once our children start to eat solid food, they always have the nutritious corn tortillas that we make (ettl.ca/7a) on the comal by the fire.

Marta and Sirena making blue corn tortillas

Continuing the Conversation
"Mother's Milk: The Original Food" Photo Essay

Penny Van Esterik

How wonderful to see nurturing practices such as breast-feeding acknowledged as an important part of women's legacies. These stories are a reminder that breast-feeding is food security for infants and an important aspect of food sovereignty for families. They also illustrate that the nurturing and breast-feeding experiences of every mother and baby are unique. Less often do we hear that nurturing practices such as breast-feeding are also helping the environment. Breast-feeding is the most environmentally friendly way to feed an infant. It safeguards the health of mothers, children, and Mother Earth, now and for future generations, because it produces no garbage, no greenhouse gases (GHG), and requires no water, unlike the production and distribution of ultra-processed, expensive, industrial foods such as infant formula.

The stories remind us that the knowledge of nurturing practices passes from generation to generation and can be easily lost. We learn of the broken links between generations from Chandra and the threats posed by infant formula marketing and poor maternity entitlements from Hilda and María. In my case, my mother was impressed with the formula samples given by the hospital when my daughter was born decades ago. I was not breast-fed but given the newest fad, lactic acid milk mixed with corn syrup. My mother felt sorry for me and assumed that I was breast-feeding because I was a poor graduate student. Peer support helped me succeed. Anna was lucky to have her mother as a role model. Serena explains that migrants from Mexico to the United States can be taken in by this image of infant formula as the best and most modern, western way to feed an infant. This marketing, combined with poor working conditions and no maternity entitlements, makes it difficult for parents all over the world. Yet most parents can reconstitute the knowledge and skills needed to nurture our children.

My area of interest is Southeast Asia. I have learned about nurturing practices from mothers in Indonesia, Thailand, Malaysia, and Lao PDR. The parallels in these stories resonate with my experiences in those countries—the importance of mother's milk as a spiritual food connecting the generations; the view of clinic births, cesarean sections, bottles, and carriages as more modern and western than midwives and carrying shawls, nursing another woman's baby; free samples of formula provided by social services, and concerns about breast-feeding in public. Humor serves us well in these days of politically correct expectations and vicious mommy wars that pit breast-feeding moms against formula users. Here is one of my favorite responses to people who criticize a woman for breast-feeding in public: "If seeing a mother breast-feed her child in public bothers you, put a blanket over your head."

Penny Van Esterik is a nutritional anthropologist, retired from York University, Toronto, and a founding member of WABA (World Alliance for Breastfeeding Action). She works on food issues in Southeast Asia, as well as advocacy around maternal and child health.

Continuing the Conversation
"Mother's Milk: The Original Food" Photo Essay

Laura Solis

Chandra's naming of mother's milk as "cosmic and spiritual food" really resonated with me. And someone should make a T-shirt with Anna's phrase, "You can't get more local than mother's milk!"

Breast-feeding is a skill that requires time and practice and doesn't go without some challenges. Formula feeding is then sometimes seen as a quick-fix solution that ends up being a very expensive and not very nutritious alternative. All this extends to the way we eat now. Instead of planting the seeds and caring for the food to grow to harvest, today's society goes for the quick, easy, premade yet less nutritious option.

When a baby is born, the mother's milk takes at least three days to come in. The waiting can be anxiety-inducing for the people who don't know how their bodies work and are used to quick food availability. The first days of life, babies get colostrum from their mothers, which is commonly referred to as "liquid gold" because of its high nutrient content. But it only took a few generations for formula companies to market their product to make mothers believe that the natural process is unnecessary when you can have a readily available "food."

Bridgette Lynch, one of the first registered midwives in Toronto, has done a lot of research on the forty days after birth. During a workshop, she described how formula companies switched an entire generation of breast-feeding mothers to formula feeding and changed breast-feeding history for generations to come. This on its own brings changes that affect how soon a person can get pregnant again, as breast-feeding has a certain level of contraceptive protection. With formula feeding substituting for breast-feeding, people were getting pregnant sooner. Less breast-feeding equals more babies. And according to Bridgette, that is when the baby boomer generation emerged. Listening to her reflections was such an eye-opening statement on how food sovereignty was taken from women, with a ripple effect impacting many other circles for decades.

Laura Solis is a Mexican-Canadian registered midwife and proud mother of two children who were breast-fed before she knew how revolutionary breast-feeding could be.

"THE SOIL IS ALIVE" VIDEO

Download the Facilitator Guide (ettl.ca/fg) for this section. See the video here (ettl.ca/7b).

When you think about "soil," do you imagine it as "dirt," or as a universe of millions of microorganisms interacting with each other? In other words, do you see it as "dead" or "alive"?

This video invites us into a conversation between Dianne Kretschmar, seventy-seven, an organic farmer two hours north of Toronto; and Fernando Garcia, forty-six, a Mexican organic agricultural consultant based in Guadalajara. In 2001, Fernando had completed an agronomy degree and worked for the Mexican Ministry of Agriculture but had learned nothing about organic agriculture, so came to Ontario for a summer to work with Dianne. For Dianne, the relationship with Fernando was magical: "There was quite a difference in our ages, like huge, I could be his mother, but we were soul mates."

As part of the Earth to Tables Legacies exchange, we brought Fernando back to Grenville Farm in 2016. They

reconnected easily as they shared some of the same questions about the problem of overcultivation and their lack of understanding of the soil. As Dianne concluded, "What I realized is that both conventional and organic farmers, through excess cultivation, have destroyed the fungal component of the soil." In this video, she describes their common awakening as "morphic resonance," or a convergence of ideas where

Dianne and Fernando at Grenville Farm

everyone's saying, "Oh, oh, we have to change what we're doing."

Western and Indigenous sciences are coming together around this deeper understanding of the soil, of the fungal networks transmitting information as the internet of the soil, communicating between plants and trees deep beneath the surface. Dianne suggests shifting from a growing system based on cultivation to preparing seedbeds of cover crops and planting into the cover; this will keep living roots in the soil and maintain its water-holding capacity. She recognizes that Indigenous practices probably are built on this understanding of the soil as alive.

To generate an intercultural conversation, we asked project adviser and Tuscarora knowledge keeper Rick Hill to offer a Haudenosaunee perspective of the soil. This is Rick speaking in an excerpt from that video: "When you think about the earth, the soil, it's nothing more than everything that lived before—all the plants, the birds, the animals, the trees, the bushes, and people, my ancestors put into the ground. They become the soil; they give life to the soil. This is why our people say there's a spirit in everything— there's a spirit in the ground, in the stone, in the tree, a spirit in the animals. Because it's that spirit that makes the Earth come alive."

The accompanying Facilitator Guide can be used to catalyze deeper conversations about the issues of over-cultivation, soil structure, fungal networks, and morphic resonance.

Continuing the Conversation
"The Soil Is Alive" Video

Gilberto Aboites

The vision of the soil is of something alive, not a dead element, or just a layer of dirt. Seeds, too, are seen as alive, representing a spirit, as with maíz, or the culture of corn. This form of agriculture sustains life—at the personal, family, and group level—if you work with nature and integrate yourself into nature. It's the opposite of modern agriculture, which is mainly about producing quantity.

Just like the farmers in the video, the Nahuat in Teotítlan, prior to European colonization in Mexico, transplanted seedlings with roots into floating gardens called *chinampas*.

This system of growing created very rich soil; if you put your hand in a chinampa, it was so hot that you could feel it decomposing.

Gilberto Aboites is director and research professor of the Socio-economic Research Center at the Autonomous University of Coahuila in Saltillo, Mexico. His research and publications focus on poverty and marginalization, peasant rights, food security, and intellectual property rights.

![camera icon] "The Alchemy of Agroecology" Video

Download the Facilitator Guide (ettl.ca/fg) for this section. See the video here (ettl.ca/7c).

When you hear the word "weed," what do you think of? As Fulvio Gioanetto suggests in this video, we have learned to think about weeds as "bad," reflecting a Eurocentric way of thinking, predominant in industrial monocultural agricultural production. In fact, weeds can refer to all kinds of wild plants growing naturally within an ecosystem. And they can have many positive uses, from healing illnesses as medicinal plants to being transformed into natural fertilizers, herbicides, and fungicides.

Fulvio is an Italian-born ethnobotanist trained in Europe but living within the autonomous P'urépecha community of Nurio in the state of Michoacán, Mexico, where he has been creating natural inputs from "weeds." His P'urépecha wife, María Blas, a medicinal plant expert and healer, organizes women in their village to gather the plants and manages the selling of the natural fertilizers and herbicides to local campesinos, or farmers.

P'urépecha women gather plants and firewood.

Fulvio has spent his life developing his practice and sharing his knowledge through intercultural and intergenerational relations. In this video, you will see him passing on knowledge to his son-in-law, Miguel, in the forests of Central Mexico, while also teaching his sons how to create natural fertilizers on a farm in southern Ontario in Canada. For Fulvio, this is an important part of "food sovereignty" in that it frees campesinos from being indebted by buying expensive and often toxic inputs year after year. When local materials are used, a local economy is being built.

Fulvio "cooking" organic herbicides

Fulvio teaches his son Bryan about medicinal uses of wild carrot at an organic farm in Ontario, Canada

He sees this approach to farming as an important part of agroecology, farming that "centers on food production that makes the best use of nature's goods and services while not damaging these resources." It applies ecological principles to the design of farming systems; uses a whole-systems approach to farming and food systems; and links ecology, culture, economics, and society to create healthy environments, food production, and communities.

This video can serve as a catalyst to explore the meaning of food sovereignty and agroecology, and the related themes of functional biodiversity, migrant labor, biopiracy, fertilizer debt, and local alternatives, and Indigenous knowledge and identity.

Continuing the Conversation
"The Alchemy of Agroecology" Video

Harriet Friedmann

Fulvio Gioanetto is one of the new practitioners linking formal science with Indigenous and practical knowledge. He also connects places that seem very different in Canada and Mexico. Two points stand out for me in this video. One is how Fulvio links different kinds of knowledge. The second is what "local" means, and how that relates to "markets."

Fulvio shows us "how easy it is" to use plants that have been discarded and disdained by industrial agriculture—so-called "weeds"—to make fertilizers and pesticides. He says, "If you need science, use a book." Fulvio is a trained agronomist as well as an agroecologist, so he is familiar with both industrial and ecological farming. In this video he demonstrates how to combine formal science with practical knowledge. This shows that experts can work collaboratively with farmers, whether experienced or new farmers just starting out. And now everyone can learn more easily on the internet. It opens the possibility of "citizen science," in which farmers can define problems and contribute data to investigate them. Imagine farmers in a region with an insect problem sharing data, even photos, on smartphones. This kind of citizen science is being done for wildlife; why not for farming?

It is helpful to think about Indigenous knowledge as place-based but interconnected across places. Colonial empires and industrial agriculture suppressed local knowledge and practices everywhere, in Europe as well as in colonies. For instance, stinging nettles, which are native to parts of Europe, Asia, and North Africa, were used for centuries as medicine, as attractor for pollinating insects, as animal feed, and as fibers for textiles. People in different places discovered these uses despite stings from touching the plant. In each place they gave nettles a distinct name, which can reasonably be called "Indigenous,"

such as "hot and sharp biting plants." As colonial empires moved plants from one part of the world to another, a standard system of Latin names developed (for nettles, *Urtica dioica*). With industrial agriculture, nettles came to be considered a weed in both Europe and the colonies, even though some gardeners and farmers continued to use nettles as well as tea. Agroecologists in many parts of the world can now recover its uses. Now Fulvio takes knowledge from one place to another. This is a very different kind of "global" connection than those from the top down that make every place the same and turn that knowledge into private property.

What do these other ways of being "global" imply for "markets"? It might be easy to conclude that food sovereignty means no markets at all. However, Fulvio and his partner, María, make natural farming inputs and medicines to sell locally. This is efficient and helps everyone, the sellers and the buyers. The challenge is to keep these exchanges at the proper scale. It is the chemical manufacturers who create "global" markets that disrupt the circular, place-based relations that Fulvio demonstrates in both Mexico and Canada. Part of agroecology is reshaping markets so that farmers, people making natural inputs, and people preparing and buying food all connect at the proper scale. People with specialized skills can exchange them, and growers, cooks, and eaters in distant places can learn from each other.

Harriet Friedmann is a retired professor of interdisciplinary food studies. She writes and lectures internationally on political ecology of food and works with the Toronto Food Policy Council, food movements, and international organizations to change the food system.

The Animal Food Cycle: We Feed Them, and They Feed Us

Anna and Adam's Approach to Farming in Quebec

Download the Facilitator Guide (ettl.ca/fg) for this section. See hyperlinks (ettl.ca/7d) for this essay.

A Father's Perspective

Legacies collaborator John Murtaugh is the perfect person to introduce us to the farming practices of his daughter Anna Murtaugh and her husband, Adam Royal, who are almost self-sufficient in food in the Gaspé peninsula of Quebec, on Canada's eastern shore. He visits them regularly and helped gather these stories over the past four years.

John: In the early 2000s, Anna met Adam working in the summers with Dianne Kretschmar on Grenville Farm in the Muskoka region of Ontario. They were married in 2012 at our family cottage near the farm. Dianne offered a lamb she had raised to be cooked on an open fire for the wedding feast.

The Legacies project brought them back from their current home in Quebec to visit their mentor, Dianne, in 2016, when they showed the farm to their two children, my grandchildren, Katherine and Theo.

Adam: I'd say Dianne taught us everything that we know.

Anna: She taught us that in order to grow good vegetables you have to have animals; you have to have manure; they complement the garden. We now have a couple of sheep, one cow, and a few goats. We're starting to build up a manure pile.

Adam: Dianne has a spectacular manure pile (ettl.ca/7d). I know most people wouldn't say that, but we love manure!

John: Adam and Anna have followed Dianne's example in practicing closed-loop agriculture, in which the animals are fed by plants grown in a garden fertilized by their manure. They were eager to eat meat that was not factory farmed. This was also Dianne's motivation when she started farming with cattle

our weeds and excess plants to the cows across the fence, so they're very close to us.

We were consciously making them grass-fed beef, which we couldn't buy in the area.

They eat from the six acres of pasture recently pastured with clover and grass, and we supplemented that with some organic barley. So, they got grain, pasture, and stuff from the garden. In fact, a couple of times, they broke out and got into the garden . . . and that was a rodeo! They had a little feast on everything. They ate raspberry canes, potatoes. They eat a lot of the same stuff we do. Lots of space, wide open, good water, no hormones or antibiotics.

thirty-five years ago: **to eat healthy beef (ettl.ca/7d)**.

Adam: Like Dianne, we started with the idea of including beef in our diet regularly. In an isolated community in Quebec, if you buy meat from the store, it could be bad in two days. We decided to raise cattle for beef, designed for that from day one.

The process of connecting with the animal is a bit tricky. We say it won't be here next year; we don't dwell on it. On the other hand, we got the bull as a calf and raised it for two years, so you get to know it a little bit. Our garden is part of the pasture, so we could be in our garden, and the cattle are literally five feet away from us, watching us, drooling over whatever we're picking. We give

The Menagerie:
Animals in the Family

John: Since 2012, Anna and Adam have been raising a family along with many animals on the land of his mother's ancestors in New Carlisle, Quebec, on the Gaspé peninsula. When we visited them there in the summer of 2018, they introduced us to the animal members of their family, whom they feed and who feed them. Let's start with breakfast.

The Chickens Offer Their Eggs

We got the idea for the chicken tractor from Dianne (ettl.ca/7d); it's a movable fence that allows us to rotate the poultry from one grassy space to another. We pretty much raise them for ourselves. This year, we have fifty-five; we'll keep thirty-five for ourselves, and some are for friends and neighbors. We have a few laying hens that wander free range, and *if* we can find their eggs, we have eggs.

The Goats Offer Their Milk

Anna: I love goats and always have. When I was about twenty-two, I worked as an intern on a dairy farm in France that had goats and made cheese. My host Nadia said, "I can see you having your own fromagerie, Anna." And I said, "Yes, someday I will."

I always thought I would have my own goat someday. When we moved here and had a barn, it seemed possible. We said let's go on a road trip and get some goats. It was our Christmas present. We found them on Kijiji. We drove three hours to New Brunswick, bought them from a farm, and came home.

In the summer, we milk them twice a day, in the morning and the evening. In the winter, we just milk them once in the morning.

I'm slowly learning how to make different kinds of cheeses (ettl.ca/7d). I ordered a book online: *Artisanal Cheese Made at Home.*

Turkeys for Thanksgiving Dinner

Adam: We started the turkeys indoors under a heat lamp for the first couple of weeks, because it can be cold in May. Then we move them to the pasture until August. They're in a portable cage (ettl.ca/7d) that we move from patch to patch on the grass every day. They're very happy outdoors. Turkeys are so much fun, like little pets. We usually keep one turkey for Thanksgiving, one for Christmas, one for Easter. The black turkey is kind of a pet; her name is Molly.

When they are grown, the males can be 32–35 pounds. We debone them and turn them into sausage. And we keep five for roasting. One year we had a communal Thanksgiving dinner with the others involved in our local farmers market.

Food from the Sea

John: New Carlisle is perfectly located geographically to offer food from three major sources: the forests, the fields, and the sea. Although Adam is only a recreational fisherman, he speaks about the nearby coast as a source of many rich seafoods.

Adam: We have a good ice fishing season and smelt run in February/ March, and then by April, the crab and shrimp and lobster start up again.

Taking a Life to Feed a Life

John: Many people who question the eating of meat see the killing of animals as a violent act. But when you are raising them to feed your family, you must reconcile that their death gives you life. Adam describes his first experience of having their bull killed and efforts to make this a more humane process, as painless as possible for the animal.

Adam: We knew the day would come when this bull becomes our dinner. We were very nervous about the end date, when we had to put it in the freezer. He weighed in at seven hundred pounds in quarters of meat, not including skin, head, or guts. It was a beast.

My dad was very stressed. The bull was getting very big and not as friendly. We wanted to do it at home, but we knew that we needed someone to show us how to do it before we try it on our own. The guys that we got were cattle farmers, and they had done it many times. They were also big moose hunters and deer hunters, so it's just second nature. It's fun working with people who know what they're doing. We didn't have a clue.

It's harder than you think; it's not just bing bang, and it's over. It has to be perfect. It was 6:30 in the morning, the sun was just rising, it was freezing cold. My dad and I were there when they showed up. They said, just make life simple—he'll follow a bucket of grain. Pour it on the ground, he'll put his head down. They'll do the rest.

So, I dumped a bucket of feed on the ground, and the bull just very leisurely came to it, with no stress whatsoever. I turned around and walked the other way. I could not watch. Then I just heard

"bang!" He dropped right where he fell. He never knew what hit him; he never flinched; he never suffered. He was shot in the base of the neck of the spine, so it's over quickly. It was perfect, a flawless process. I'm still learning from them but could not do it without more assistance. I don't think I would ever do the shooting.

In factory farming, stress affects the meat. We had heard horror stories. Stress can make the meat tough. This beef was fall-apart in your mouth, super tender, not too strong.

Nothing Is Wasted

After the bull was killed, we hung it for 7–8 days. You just have to get the blood out, then skin it, gut it, and quarter it. We were apprehensive about the whole process. So, we said if we're going to do this, we're eating the whole thing: the heart, the liver, the tongue, the prairie oysters, everything. We really wanted to use every part.

We got so much from that one beast. If it was just ours, it would last easily two years. But with my mom and dad and my grandmother, I wouldn't be surprised if it fed half the town. A lot of things were shared and given away.

The liver was the size of our kitchen table, and we gave chunks to our neighbors and gave meat to people as a thank-you. That's the way the community works—sharing the meat and the garden.

We kept it simple—steaks, hamburger, and a few roasts. Out of all that, the tongue was the hit. A tongue's not really an organ; it's a muscle. We made *tortilla a la lengua.*

Even the off cuts—the guts, skin, head, and bones—went into a trapper bucket for bait.

Trapping is not as dead as you would think. The trapper we dealt with has an elaborate trapping line. A big forest fire about 10–12 years ago has pushed animals out to the coastline—animals that were elusive before: cougars, bear, lynx, and with them come deer, moose, coyotes, wolves.

We could have dried the bull's hide. I sawed down a few leg bones into marrow bones. We have them in the freezer, and sometime we'll make a marrow soup.

John: I asked Adam what it felt like to be raising, killing, and eating this bull.

Adam: We get quite a sense of joy and pride. It was a big event. Two years of waiting, and wondering—could we do this? Do we want to keep this as a pet? It was getting too big. A lot went into it. It's not something I want to do every year. I'd rather save up and have one nice big bull that would last two years. There are a lot of dairy farms around here, and the bull calves are of no use to the dairy. People will buy them in the spring and slaughter them in the fall.

Hunting is what most people do to feed themselves with meat. Farming is a thing of the past. If you see photos from fifty years ago, everything in forests was cut for big family farming. But that has totally shifted. There were socioeconomic factors: from the collapse of the cod fisheries to the big exodus, brain drain, and joblessness. Just fleeing the country for the cities and suburbs.

All that land has since grown up (basically brush). Abandoned land and wild animals have moved back in. So, hunting has been revived.

John: When the local butcher retired, Adam saw a need for a part-time butcher, especially during the hunting and slaughter season in the fall.

Becoming a Butcher

Adam: We raised a couple of pigs one year and when they were full grown, we didn't really know what to do with them. We got to this point, and now what? So, we started watching YouTube videos. We also asked around to get pointers from different people. We had someone who did the slaughtering for us and kept them in a cold storage for us. He said come pick it up and deal with it yourselves. So, we got Ziploc bags from the store and, without any great knowledge, we did the best we could with the knives and cleaver. It went well, taking maybe two hours per pig. They were huge, and we had meat for a long time. That was my first encounter with butchering.

Around the same time, I met an old butcher here in town who was selling an old grocery store with cold rooms, a meat saw, and a grinder. We thought about it, and said, OK, let's try it. We fixed it up, so it's all up to code now. And it's a good business.

The season varies from August to early December. There's not much the rest of the year. Chicken, turkey, and pigs come out in August. Then the hunting season in October is only seven days. So, it's a marathon; a rush when it comes on, then it's over. This year was a really strong year for pigs and moose. Deer were down; a lot of coyotes have moved in, so the population was down by half. We're subject to forces bigger than us. If there are coyotes that eat all the deer, that's what it is. We become conscious of the whole process.

The hunters go way out in the middle of the forest and stay for days on end and don't see a thing. A neighbor was out there, reading a book, and he fell asleep, then woke up to a big buck. The season for native hunters is indefinite.

They can go from the last full moon in September until the snow is too deep.

It's nice to have repeat customers, people who raise pigs or turkeys or hunt every year. For the most part, people want to sit in and help, just be part of the process.

The old butcher gave me the rundown many times. Learning to cut one moose is easy enough, but how do you manage twenty moose at a time? Then there's the cleaning, the saws—it's a big undertaking.

I get people with lots of experience working with me, like an old guy seventy-four with a lifetime experience cutting meat. Then I have younger guys, who are salmon guides on the river. They are pretty well immersed in it. They knew more than I did.

It's scary for an adult when you're up against a huge beast that's bigger than you, but for them it was ten times their size. But they were surprisingly comfortable with him, even though he was so big. I'd like them to just simply know where it came from. It's not a factory; it's not a truck; not a processing plant. There's the field, there's the fence, there's the cow, there's the freezer, there's the dinner table. Field to fork approach.

John: Like many young children of their age, Katherine at five and Theo at three are obsessed with the excrement of the animals. Listen to them talk (ettl.ca/7d) about the turkey poo and the pig poo.

Katherine and Theo have grown up with many animals who have become a part of their everyday relations while alive as well as on their dinner plates after death.

John: By growing up with animals (ettl.ca/7d), my grandchildren are learning more about all the natural processes of living and dying and how interrelated they are. They understand through their experience that other beings have died so that they may live. And they feel a connection with them that most of us have lost.

John: Adam the butcher is also sometimes Adam the teacher, as he shares his knowledge with the people when they bring him animals, and he cuts their meat for them.

Adam: You can influence what people eat throughout the year, by offering different cuts (ettl.ca/7d). I always ask how they cook it, and they will tell you about the different recipes they use. Everyone's different. The treatment of the animal is the number one thing people want to know about when they buy meat. Was it grass fed? What is the history of the farm? What are the farmers like? What do they care about? Hunting's different, because the animal is wild.

Growing Children and Animals

Anna: Katherine and Theo also got to know the bull (ettl.ca/7d).

Continuing the Conversation
"The Animal Food Cycle:
We Feed Them, and They Feed Us" Photo Essay

Fred Metallic

I see most farming based on an ordering or hierarchy of humans over animals and the right to enclose the animal. It's about humans having dominion over animals.

We Mi'kmaq people see it differently; we take these relationships seriously in our hunting practices.

For example, we don't see the moose as an animal. It's not a pound of beef, like a cow, that you can just pay $8.99 for. The moose is a part of our life; it's another being. We're trying to reeducate people on how we got to this place that we're so disconnected, as humans from animals, as people from territory. We've largely depended on science versus Indigenous knowledge. Now we're trying to bring a more balanced approach.

There are a lot of protocols in terms of what you need to do before you kill an animal. There are practices in terms of how much of the animal you should use, how you share that animal, how you share those teachings with others, so that it really does sustain life. It doesn't just sustain *my* life, because the animal isn't here just for me, but we're here for each other, now and afterwards. When I get moose meat from my brother, I'm connected and obligated to the moose and to my brother. When we're connected, there are obligations.

We're trying to get back on the land, to establish those relationships and understand the cycles. As human beings, we are born and we die in this territory. And we want to be buried in the same territory where the animals are buried.

Fred Metallic is a director of natural resources for the Listuguj Mi'gmaq government in so-called Quebec, Canada.

CHAPTER 8
JUSTICE

Many young people in my community need to survive, so there are two options: migration (the majority illegal) or work like a slave in big agribusiness, avocado, blueberry, or mango.

—Fulvio, Italian/Mexican, Michoacán, Mexico

I prefer the term food apartheid over food desert because it makes it clear that these are systemically constructed communities, in the way that food is distributed across the city and the way that people experience food.

—Leticia, food justice leader, Toronto, Canada

Within our exchange between generations and cultures, we recognize the complex relationships among all historically marginalized groups who challenge systemic inequities. Food activists are also engaged in intersectional struggles against racism, classism, sexism, homophobia, and transphobia, and discrimination based on religious beliefs (even though our materials don't touch on all of them). Food sovereignty movements are part of larger movements for environmental and social justice, in both the Global North and the Global South. Although the personal stories we share are grounded in very specific local contexts, we locate these experiences within a systemic analysis of unequal power relations that shape our daily lives. We have to acknowledge the many contradictions within each story shared here, because these multiple inequities are present and need to be challenged.

Definitely the debate is how accessible is organic food. In the city it can be extremely expensive, and before you know it, your pockets are empty, and you don't have that much to show for it. It seems like organic food is only accessible to people who either have a lot of money or put a lot of importance on what they're eating.

—Anna, teacher/farmer, Quebec, Canada

Lauren Baker interviewing
Fernando Garcia
Guadalajara, Mexico

Download the Facilitator Guide (ettl.ca/fg) for this section. See hyperlinks (ettl.ca/8a) for this essay.

Lauren: Fernando is at his house, in front of a living wall on his patio. He jokes that he set up the living wall, complete with drip irrigation, to satisfy his wife who told him as he is an agronomist they needed something green at home.

In the late 1990s, Fernando completed an agronomy degree and began work with the Mexican Ministry of Agriculture. Interested in learning more about organic agriculture, he got a leave to go to Canada in the early 2000s. First, he worked at Plan B Organic Farm near Hamilton, Ontario, and then moved to Grenville Farm in the Muskoka region of Ontario. He learned organic practices from Dianne Kretschmar, developing a special relationship with her based on their interests in agroecology, soil, and farming.

Once established back in his hometown of Guadalajara, the second largest city in Mexico, Fernando experimented with various agricultural enterprises, from retail and delivery of organic foods to large-scale organic lettuce production. He then founded Cosecha en Casa, an urban agriculture company that he ran from 2013 to 2018.

Since 2017 he has worked for Semillas Globales,[1] a multinational company that harvests and processes high-quality oils from seeds, nuts, and fruit such as sesame, chia, peanuts, and avocados. In describing his work with

Fernando teaching Cosecha en Casa students in Guadalajara

Cosecha en Casa and the company he now works for, Fernando raises critical agroecology issues: urban and rural specificity, issues of scale, community capacity and connection, and economic viability.

The Blooming: Cosecha en Casa

Cosecha en Casa was an urban agriculture business in Guadalajara. The project focused on establishing gardens of various sizes and scales, from balcony and patio gardens to community gardens, as well as running workshops and training events. Cosecha en Casa was an opportunity to do what Fernando loved most—growing food, sharing knowledge with other people, and supporting people to grow vegetables.

Cosecha en Casa was a well-known business in the community, and Fernando was well respected for his deep knowledge and understanding of urban agriculture. He inspired many young people and women to start their own gardens and brought them together for community dinners to share their experiences and build a suburban support group.

Over the five-year period that Cosecha en Casa existed, urban agriculture became very popular in Guadalajara and across Mexico. Fernando explains: "Urban agriculture is blooming. Lots of

people wanted to do it, but didn't know they need science and knowledge. Doctors, dentists, people without experience became interested in urban agriculture."

Over time, lots of people began offering urban agriculture workshops, and it was harder to get customers, because there was more competition. What concerned Fernando wasn't the competition, but that some competitors were teaching the wrong ideas, which meant that people weren't successful and were discouraged.

Community Connections through Urban Agriculture

According to Fernando, there isn't a sense of community in Guadalajara. The prevailing feeling is that it is a dangerous city. People hear about kidnapping and robberies, which creates fear. This impacts any sense of community. Urban agriculture was one positive response to the violence, to help neighbors get to know each other and to build community.

Urban agriculture offers a big opportunity to start developing community, but this requires government support. Because urban agriculture was a trend and in fashion, the government wanted to get involved in some projects. Fernando tried to work with the government many times, but the willingness to invest just wasn't there. For example, one government-started community garden looks abandoned.

"It isn't maintained," described Fernando; "you don't want to be part of it. When you look at it, you don't see a garden producing diverse good quality food. You see an abandoned piece of land that says 'community garden.' But you don't see community at all.

"I've seen community gardens in New York and Toronto. They are very different, and it is a different experience. It requires investment to start this kind of project. I am certain that the community will participate, but we need the spaces and ongoing help to establish and maintain the garden."

Cosecha en Casa helped me to find ways to share my knowledge with others, it helped me connect food production to consumers. We're accustomed to consuming food even though we don't know where it comes from, even from other countries. To have the capacity to grow your own food in your family context and then to consume it, completely changes the relationship you have with the food that you eat.

Transitioning from Cosecha en Casa to a Multinational Company

In 2017, Fernando was offered a full-time job at a multinational company that produces organic products and exports them to thirty-five countries. It buys raw materials from all over the world, many of which aren't available in Mexico. The company is concerned with sustainability, social responsibility and the way these raw materials are produced. Fernando was hired to ensure that the raw materials are produced organically and to promote the values of sustainability and social responsibility to the producers. Fernando brings his expertise on the technical aspects of organic agriculture to his work with the company, as well as the social skills to teach and encourage

Malocca garden at York University, Toronto

people to move toward more sustainable organic practices.

Fernando struggled with the transition, and for some time tried to maintain Cosecha en Casa while working in his new job.

Urban agriculture was a business that depended on me. People wanted me to do the workshops, to build their gardens, and I didn't have time to do that with my new job. And my son was three, so I wanted to spend time with him,

Fernando teaching deep digging to Noé, his garden assistant

food sovereignty. With Cosecha, it was more about self sufficiency and building community. At the company it is more about supporting the economic viability of smallholder farmers.

Giving Up the Huerto (Garden)

I had a vegetable garden in front of my house. This was stressing me out because I didn't have time to maintain it, especially when I was traveling. It became stressful and distracting. The owner of the land wanted to sell it, so it was time to give it up. The huerto fed me and my family for a long time. It is sad not to have this healthy organic food for my family.

Fernando tending his tomato plants in 2016

too. I felt like I was losing control of the business and people were expecting more than I could give. Cosecha en Casa is something I can start again when I want, because I built a community and developed some techniques. I decided to stop Cosecha en Casa for now and focus on this new adventure with the company. It is

a totally different scale, but uses many of the same agroecological techniques. The company offers a big opportunity to do things differently, to work on a different level with different people.

With both Cosecha en Casa and the company, the work was about supporting people to survive by increasing their

Especially now that I have a three-year-old kid and want to feed him responsibly. In one way it is frustrating. I look in my fridge

Fernando with his partner, Hilda, and son Diego in 2020 harvesting cabbage at the experimental farm near Chapala, Mexico

responsible way. It was a very intimate moment for me in the *huerto*, walking around, feeding and caring for the plants.

It was very hard for me to see the garden of Cosecha en Casa locked up and sold.

Working with a Multinational

At Semillas Globales, Fernando works as a rural agricultural development manager. He is working across a wide range of scales of agriculture with hundreds of farmers, some of whom have 1–2 hectares and others who might have thousands of hectares.

Fernando's work involves supporting farmers to improve their agro-ecological practices. For Fernando it is critical work, as the farmers are economically reliant on agriculture to maintain their families and communities. Each region, farmer, and scale of farm requires different strategies, planning,

and doubt what I am eating again. It wasn't only about food, but also community. It was a point of connection to people who think the same way and want to learn about food and agriculture.

It was a nice community that I miss. Building friendships, life, community. It was a hobby for me as well. A place where I connect with myself, this way of living, thinking, connecting with the mystery of agriculture in a and concentration in order not to make mistakes that would cost either the farmer or the company money. It is a big challenge.

"The farmers need to make a living from this land," explained Fernando.

All of them have the same problems—they don't get enough yield and spend a lot of money on inputs. Farmers think the industry is guilty and doesn't pay enough. I have a different point of view. What could you produce, what is the potential? If you were able to produce one tonne instead of 100 kilos, you would be earning lots more money with the money industry is paying. The strategy is to find a way to produce more and spend less.

We work in different stages. First, we sensitize farmers about this idea—so they understand a new approach, what they are doing wrong, and what they could do to improve. Second, after they become interested, they often realize soil is alive. Then it is easy to teach them techniques to make organic fertilizers and inputs and manage their resources in a sustainable way.

"This requires technical support and agricultural science." Fernando continues.

Farmers have lots of experience, and know how things must be done, but they don't always understand the importance of soil in agriculture. They don't know the soil is alive, that microorganisms are the stomach of the plant, and that if you don't have good soil you won't be able to produce good quality food and high yields.

In the Mexican context, there are risks involved in the direct approach of working with farmers the company takes. The approach is used because the company believes in business development in the field and not through intermediaries. This approach brings better profits for the producer, and better business for the company. But the agriculture sector in Mexico is exposed to drug trafficking activities.

These areas have been invaded by narco-trafficking. It's a risk for us who work in these areas, but it's almost throughout the country. We have to be very neutral, because we're constantly being watched, so we have to be careful. They [the narco-traffickers] see government

and industry as the enemy, so we are not welcome in these areas. We have to convince them that we really are trying to help the campesinos. They see us as foreigners. To manage this, the company has policies for people who work in the field: That they always travel in the daylight, for example, or that they have vehicles that don't get stuck in the rainy season. There's a whole security policy: we are trained on what to do in case of an ambush, what documents to take. This is a preventative policy, to avoid problems.

Because the company works globally, Fernando has learned a lot from his visits to other countries.

In Bolivia, Venezuela and two African countries, farmers' problems are almost exactly the same. There is a lack of strong farmer organizations, the state of the environment is poor, there is poor access to markets, and a lack of quality technical assistance.

There are fake technicians trying to sell expensive inputs and other things. There aren't real technicians or agronomists who are capable of diagnosing problems, accessing good information,

Fernando talking with farmers in rural Ethiopia, 2018

planning, and providing information to inform decision making. Local Indigenous knowledge is being lost by the use of remedies that work fast, but aren't focused on the root of the problems. This implies more mechanized soils, more exposed soils, the excessive use of chemical inputs, without understanding that when we use a pesticide, we can control a pest in the moment, but we are also killing insects that in a way maintain an environmental equilibrium. We need many microorganisms to work in the soil to maintain a natural equilibrium.

In our company, we are aware of the ideal conditions that must exist in the ecosystem without affecting living beings, microorganisms, or bees. All these relationships must continue to exist and work naturally so that we are able to produce quality food and good yields in time.

In 2019, the company secured an experimental farm outside Guadalajara, where Fernando has been able to mass-produce organic cauliflower that is then cut, cleaned, and dehydrated as healthy snacks. He is also working with local farmers to test other organic vegetables that could be cultivated and processed.

Fernando is very interested in the agroecological techniques that Michoacán-based Legacies collaborator Fulvio Gioanetto uses and the results he gets. It is very difficult for agriculture to be profitable with higher and higher production costs, low yields, and little attention to caring for natural resources like soil. Fernando talks about

Fulvio gathering "weeds" to produce natural inputs in Michoacán, Mexico

the importance of Fulvio's work and approach.

There is so much knowledge that Fulvio has, and I would like to test out some of these techniques, and learn more. What Fulvio does is very important right now. For me, a good farmer is a farmer who produces soil before producing vegetables. If you don't have good soil, you won't be able to have good yields, or good quality with low cost. The system will demand a lot of inputs. What Fulvio does is produce inputs that are affordable; farmers have what they need to produce them on their farms and in their communities. There is an opportunity to collaborate in the production of organic crops at my company.

For me, agroecology is the ability to produce food respecting all production factors—such as soil, water, the environment in general, without negatively affecting them and guaranteeing their health over time. It is not to apply a product to control a problem, but rather to try to understand why the problem arose and to understand the problem at its root, to recover the microbiological balance of the soil, to respect the entire relationship of the crop with insects, with animals, with water sources. Agroecology is to respect and maintain health across all these resources. We do not have to leave the natural world to turn agriculture into a practice.

Through the Legacies project, Fernando has had the opportunity to exchange his food knowledge with settler and Indigenous people in both Mexico and Canada. The project brought him back to Ontario for a reunion with his mentor, organic farmer Dianne Kretschmar. He was inspired by Mohawk community food leader Chandra Maracle at Six Nations to consider the table end of the food system, and to organize community dinners with his former students. Since 2017, he has been involved in scaling up, by trying to influence a multinational company to support small farmers to produce organic products in a more sustainable way.

Continuing the Conversation
"Promoting Organic Agriculture in Mexico: From Urban Gardens to Multinational Companies" Photo Essay

Samantha Trumbull

This story really cuts to the heart of some of the major barriers both for urban agriculture and small agricultural producers. There is a constant struggle for balance between capitalist multinational companies that have a fiduciary duty to their shareholders, and small justice-minded farmers or organizations that see a different world that doesn't center so much around profits. One thing I found particularly interesting and poignant about this story was that Fernando not only left his urban agriculture business to work at a large multinational corporation, he did so because his small business couldn't compete in the environment that those corporations created.

This observation led me to many questions, the primary one being whether corporations that aren't Certified B Corporations* can ever really be socially responsible. There is now a whole industry of corporate social responsibility, and, indeed, my farm receives both funding and volunteer support through these channels. However, at the root of many of the inequities and injustices in the food system is the fact that those same corporations have already chosen to feed the rich rather than the poor. Often when considering the food justice work that we do, I am forced to ask myself whether the changes necessary for an equitable food system are even possible within our current economic structures. Mostly I think the answer is no.

Despite that conclusion, the work that Fernando is doing is really important. Undoing much of the damage caused by the Green Revolution and the growth of pesticide and herbicide usage, GMO seeds, and monocropping is the work of generations. I do hope that governments take notice, so perhaps the question we should be asking is how can I get my local/state/ national government to take agricultural sustainability seriously? As was mentioned, the Indigenous agricultural practices are being lost, or have been lost. Luckily, we know so much more about plant and soil science. Once farmers have the knowledge and tools to collectively stand up to corporations, because they can grow their own seeds and make their own compost, then we can start to dismantle the whole structure upon which our food system is built.

Samantha Trumbull is the former executive director of an urban farm in the United States that aims to create a vibrant, informed, and well-nourished community through urban agriculture. Her belief in the power of food systems and the right of each person to have access to fresh, healthy, and sustainably produced food is her driving force. Before joining the nonprofit world, Sam served in the U.S. Peace Corps in Honduras and worked on a food security program for the U.S. government.

*Certified B Corporations are businesses that meet the highest standards of verified social and environmental performance, public transparency, and legal accountability to balance profit and purpose. https://bcorporation.net/about-b-corps.

"WHY FARMERS MARKETS?" VIDEO

Download the Facilitator Guide (ettl.ca/fg) for this video (ettl.ca/8b).

This is truly a story of legacies, passing food knowledge from generation to generation, and from country to city to country again. We follow Anna Murtaugh's twenty-year journey from downtown Toronto, where she learned to prepare food and create markets with her mother, Elizabeth Harris, to Ontario's rocky Muskoka region, where she learned to grow food with Dianne Kretschmar.

Anna met her husband, Adam, on Dianne's farm, and in 2012, they headed east to New Carlisle, Quebec, and to the homestead of his grandmother. As teachers and part-time farmers, they are raising three children as well as various farm animals and tending a bountiful garden that makes them almost self-sufficient in food.

Drawing on the legacies of Dianne's farm and of Elizabeth's markets, they were cofounders of a farmers market that brings anglophone and francophone farmers and vendors into a local park in the summer.

Dianne and Anna at the Riverdale Farmers Market in Toronto in 2002

Farmers markets have been proliferating in urban centers such as Toronto, reconnecting consumers to producers, in response to the distancing and alienation of a population that has little sense of where their food comes from. They become gathering places both for farmers to connect with other producers and for local residents to re-create a sense of community.

But there are many obstacles to farmers markets becoming truly accessible to all communities. As Anna mentioned, "It seems like organic food is only accessible to people who either have a lot of money or put a lot of importance on what they're eating."

This also means that large markets such as Toronto's Brickworks appear awfully white, not reflecting the multiracial population of the city. An antiracist critique of urban agriculture has led to initiatives such as another Legacies partner, Leticia Deawuo, who helped build Black Creek Community Farm to serve the racialized Jane-Finch neighborhood. An on-site Harvest Share market is open to local residents on an honor system. New immigrants to the neighborhood bring their agricultural knowledge from their countries of origin, creating a unique fusion of food practices on the farm.

"Ontario still imports around twenty billion dollars of food, and 50 percent of

Anna and a customer at the Gaspé Farmers Market in 2018

that could be produced locally," notes current Brickworks manager Marina Queirolo. But structural constraints abound, including government's prioritizing large-scale industrial agriculture while offering few supports to small organic farmers. The process of organic certification is an expensive and bureaucratic undertaking that many organic producers cannot afford or navigate.

Plaque at Brickworks Farmers Market in Toronto

This video serves as a catalyst for critical discussion about the history of farmers markets, and their potential and limits in the current food system. The Facilitator Guide raises questions, suggests field visits, and offers links to other videos, websites, and readings. See also the contributions of our Mexican collaborators and of antiracist food activists in Toronto, who raise critical questions about who is served in farmers markets.

This video is dedicated to the memory of Elizabeth Harris, Anna's mother, who is honored with a plaque in the Brickworks market that she founded. Dianne Kretschmar remembers Elizabeth when she says, "It's about connections. I think that's the whole secret to good health, really, to connect people with their food. Elizabeth always said that I was her farmer, not only me but all kinds of other people. When you sat down to dinner at Elizabeth's table, she knew individually the person who produced everything on the table."

Continuing the Conversation
"Why Farmers Markets?" Video

Mexican Legacies Partners

On viewing the market video, four of our Legacies collaborators compared it to their own contexts in Mexico, especially to the ancient tradition of *tianguis*, or markets, which for centuries have been major gathering places.

Valiana Aguilar: It sounds like farmers markets are new to Toronto, but in Oaxaca and the Yucatán, it's been forever . . . there have always been farmers markets.

Fulvio Gioanetto: The Paracho market near us in rural Michoacán state brings together many P'urépecha communities and so includes the kinds of products we need for traditional ceremonies, weddings, and fiestas.

María Blas: People bring what they have grown in their patios or backyards and, if they don't sell everything, they trade with each other.

Valiana Aguilar: In the rural Mixe markets in Oaxaca, they also exchange artisan work for fruits and vegetables. For example, they exchange pottery for potatoes. It's based on a personal relation with the person making them. It isn't an unequal exchange.

Lauren Baker: Well, Toronto has a long history of markets, too, but that connection with food and farmers had become lost with the rise of industrial food and supermarkets.

Urbanization in Mexico has also had an impact on market relations.

Valiana Aguilar: In Oaxaca city, the growers from Puebla state (Poblanos) control the market. Local agricultural producers wanted to sell in the urban market, but the Poblanos kept them out. They're a mafia; they have guns and can kill you; it's not a joke.

Ángel Kú: In cities today, there often aren't relations between growers and consumers like before, so this is a strong message of this video. To grow a squash, chili, or tomato is a revolutionary act. And, like Chandra said, to sit down and share food at a table is also a revolutionary act.

Continuing the Conversation
"Why Farmers Markets?" Video

Anan Lololi and Selam Teclu

Anan Lololi, Guyanese-born founder of the AfriCan Food Basket in Toronto; and Selam Teclu, Eritrean-born nutritionist, gardener, and bread maker, discuss key barriers for newcomers and people of color to participation in farmers markets—as producers or consumers.

Anan: Most of the farmers markets we have participated in are in high-end areas, where the customers have disposable incomes. When we tried to start a farmers market in Regent Park (a low-income racialized community in downtown Toronto), it didn't work, because the white farmers wouldn't go. It's a class and race thing, and they couldn't compete with the cheaper prices of No Frills and FreshCo (low-priced supermarkets).

Selam: The barriers to farmers markets begin at the application level. There are many stories where people of color (newcomers and low-income Canadians) have applied to sell at farmers markets only to be told that their products are not local enough to qualify. For example, I sell *injera* (an Eritrean bread), made from teff (an African grain). Several of the farmers markets I applied to told me I could not participate because my teff was not grown locally. The teff is grown in small-scale farms in Ethiopia, Kenya, and Ghana. Many farmers have attempted to grow teff in Ontario, but the results have been inconsistent due to our short growing season and high humidity, which result in lower fiber, protein, and inconsistent germination.

It made me think about race. Today, many people have access to land that historically was taken through European colonization. Now two hundred years later, some privileged settlers have access to that land, whereas Indigenous people or newcomers don't.

It's really a question of accessibility, whether it's the farmer or the bread maker, if a vendor can afford land, a kitchen, or transport to bring his wares to market. People of color, low-income people have to rely on community kitchens. The farmers market structure is often not very open, flexible, or equitable.

Selam in a community garden and in a collective kitchen in Nova Scotia

Deborah: Selam is an urban gardener, a nutritionist, and a facilitator of newcomer food projects.

Both Anan and Selam have suggestions for changes that could redress the class and racial barriers.

Anan: Most imports (from the Caribbean or Africa) travel by air, and that's not sustainable. With the issue of peak oil, we have to find ways to grow our traditional crops here. The government should subsidize immigrants to develop a whole new market that is more equitable, sustainable, and culturally appropriate. There are many newcomers who are hungry to farm; there could be incentives that would help them develop their own agricultural practice.

We are also introducing special cooked foods into the high-end markets; I hired a Black vegan chef who cooks dishes with quinoa, callaloo, okra, and other vegetables we grow at Black Creek Community Farm. He understands the culture of the market, is environmentally conscious, uses recycled utensils, and so forth. They love him at the market.

We need to do thorough food assessments, to look at why farmers markets are so white.

Many people look first and foremost in terms of income—poor people will go to No Frills because it has cheap food. It's culture, too—there's a clash of culture. There are no-go zones for white farmers. You have to engage people. It's about navigating in different cultures.

Selam: The steering committees or advisory boards of farmers markets need to do an assessment that asks people of color about the barriers they experience in the markets. Job descriptions for farmers markets could include issues of education, accessibility, and culture. They could offer workshops to vendors on better ways of doing things, farming or processing.

Anan (top) facilitating a food-mapping workshop and at the Sorauren Farmers Market in Toronto (bottom)

Food Justice and Urban Agriculture in Action

A Conversation between
Leticia Deawuo and *Lauren Baker* on
Black Creek Community Farm

Download the Facilitator Guide (ettl.ca/fg) for this photo essay. See hyperlinks (ettl.ca/8c) for this photo essay.

Lauren: Black Creek Community Farm (BCCF) is a seven-acre urban farm in the City of Toronto, Canada. It is located in the vibrant and dynamic Jane-Finch neighborhood on Toronto Region Conservation Authority property. As a community hub, the farm brings together a number of partners to run food and nature-based programming and grow food.

I have worked closely with BCCF since 2014 as a board member of Everdale Environmental Learning Centre and then as part of the farm's Steering Committee. Leticia Deawuo has been the director of Black Creek Community Farm since 2017. She and I sat down to talk about the farm and her work on food justice in her neighborhood and across the city of Toronto.

Leticia: I had been working on social justice and antipoverty related issues in the neighborhood when I first learned about the farm. When I was told about

Mural at entrance to Black Creek Community Farm

the farm, I couldn't picture it. Where is there eight acres of land in the Jane-Finch community?[2]

At the time I was doing a lot of community organizing work. I'm one of the founding members of Jane-Finch Action Against Poverty (JFAAP) and several other initiatives working on poverty in the neighborhood. We didn't call it food justice, but did a lot of work on Ontario Disability Support Program rates, special diet cuts, and antipoverty-related action that included housing. We did some work on vertical poverty, which is very much related to food, the cost of food, and the challenges people face in high-rise buildings. A lot of times when we talk about homelessness, it is very much associated with a downtown issue, not a community issue that includes us. We were raising awareness and bringing in new people to organize around our own community issues.

While I was on parental leave with my daughter, I was invited to come to a community consultation for the farm. I remember it well because I was given a sheet of paper with the first site plan for BCCF, and it included partner organizations including African Food Basket, Fresh City Farm, and Everdale. I remember as a resident I thought: What

is the point of a consultation? The land is already divided. I didn't understand why I was there. Were we just there to put a stamp of approval on something that was already planned? It wasn't very clear to me.

Later that year I got a letter saying that my community work was being reduced to part-time. I was very stressed—two kids, half the money, how was I going to do it? Someone sent me an e-mail asking if I was interested in a position at the farm. It was May 2013 that I became involved.

Rethinking Food Justice

Lauren: A lot of the work that you have done at the farm centers around food justice. At the farm this includes making healthy food available to local residents, children, and youth programming, antiracism workshops and training, and being involved in wider advocacy efforts to address poverty, structural racism, and oppression in the city and beyond. I think you and the Jane-Finch community members who are working on food justice have been an essential part of creating awareness and inspiring action about these issues across the city and across the food movement. What does food justice mean to you?

Leticia: As I got into the farm project, I didn't understand the term food justice. Everyone had different definitions of food justice, food sovereignty, and food security, and different ideas about what the work needed to be. Because I come from a community development background, I knew we needed community members to determine what the issues are for them and come up with the recommendations for how we move forward with the work. For me it wasn't about an outside group of people, the dominant number not from the community, determining the work.

Does everyone really want to garden, actually? What about the grocery store? How do we do the work?

I remember one evening where we had forty-four people in the room. It was very cramped, very tense, everyone using big words, big terms. The meeting was finished, and one of the moms stayed back. She said, "I need to talk to you because I've been coming to this meeting for a long time, and I'm questioning why I'm here because I don't even know what food justice is." And she said, "Well, I was at the grocery store, and they emptied out my purse onto the conveyor belt because I was accused of stealing baby food for my son. I was so humiliated in front of my child, in front of other people. Is that a food justice issue?" I said, "Of course, it is a food justice issue."

But these weren't the conversations we were having here at the meetings. For me, then, it was important to change the conversation. Instead of sitting in a room with academics, we held small community focus groups to really listen to people about what the issue was for them, how they see the challenges in their community, and what kind of actions to take.

A few important issues came up that helped me better understand food

One of many meetings with community consultations to give shape to Black Creek Community Farm

justice. Policing in grocery stores came up. None of the mainstream stuff I have read has talked about food and policing and how different communities are policed differently in grocery stores. Grocery stores in predominantly low-income communities have a different system; they have security. If you go to affluent communities, the shelves are open, they have beautiful deli sections and a bakery. Some even have restaurants within the store. But if you go to No Frills at Jane and Finch, there are security bars. When you pick up your stuff, you've got to go around to the cashier. Baby formula is locked up.

Other things, too. This is one aspect of food justice that became clear.

In our focus group research on poverty and food justice in the community, we sat down with seniors and heard that some of them have to make choices between filling their medical prescriptions, paying their rent, or getting fresh food. If you are a senior who is getting $1,100 a month and your rent is $800–$900, how much do you have left for transportation? How much do you have for food? Not that much. And then we heard that some seniors are banned from the mall where No Frills is because the No Frills uses the same security service as the mall. So, if you get caught shoplifting from the No Frills, you get banned from the mall. The problem is that the mall is also where seniors go for their programming and other services, their doctor, their dentist. So, you have the most vulnerable, seniors, who are so isolated, banned from that place where all their services are located. The fact that these corporations have the power to ban people from the mall, and the fact that there are undercover police in these grocery stores but not in every grocery store in the city, is really a serious issue in our community.

For many different people in our communities, these are everyday realities that they have to deal with. I think of this as food apartheid. One of the reasons that I like the term food apartheid over food desert is that food desert makes it seems like it just happened. Kind of like explaining climate change as a phenomenon that is just happening and not something man-made. For me, the word apartheid makes it clear that these are systemically constructed communities, in the way that food is distributed across the city and the way that people experience food—the fact that you have the Jane-Finch community with fast-food restaurants at every corner, and a community that pays more than other communities for fresh produce, a community where police are surveilling the grocery stores.

Out of those conversations and that focus group research came the report on food justice in Jane and Finch. It had a huge impact and opened up a lot of conversations, including conversations about the farm and what we are trying to do. People raised questions about how the farm is operating, how food is being distributed, where is the food being sold, and how decisions are being made. And when you talk about food justice, food security, who manages that work, who leads that work?

The community has seen a pattern over time of people parachuting into the community, of projects not hiring people from the community but getting dollars for the community on the backs of community members. These kinds of partnerships have failed several times. This is what a lot of low-income communities face. When these projects and partnerships don't prioritize hiring local people, our neighborhood doesn't reap the economic benefit that comes from hiring people who live here. A lot of residents who were engaged with the farm were worried. There were questions about who gets access to the land, who makes that decision.

To have a situation at the farm where you have predominantly Black people working in the field and other people who are white managing the work sets up a dynamic, a negative pattern. And what is the value of the work of people working the land? If we are going to talk about food justice, we need to ask who is doing that labor and acknowledge that farmers are undervalued. Those farmers happen to be Black people, and they are getting paid less. Then to have other positions led by predominantly white folks who are getting paid more, that just didn't work. We need to realize that these dynamics can be triggering and pose a huge problem. If we are doing this work to dismantle injustices across the food system, we need to make sure we aren't creating our own local food system that is just replicating those problems.

Toward Community Control

Leticia: As these issues surfaced at the farm, there was a very difficult transition process that took place. It was very challenging, with lots of emotion involved. It became very important for the community to have ownership and leadership over the farm and to be able to provide support for that. The community who became deeply engaged in the governance of the farm asked really good questions about things such as wages, about the human resources policy, about all of the important things that create solid ground and safety for people who are working on the farm. The steering committee led this process. There is still a lot of work to do related to governance, strategic planning, programming, and funding. It is all part of the process. It's a huge learning process, and it takes patience because the process takes time, and nothing happens overnight. It has been challenging, but it's also beautiful to see everybody come together in the end, and even if they don't agree on everything, they agree that community ownership of the farm is important for the future of the farm.

Lauren: The process to examine and restructure the governance of the farm was really challenging and important. It took a lot of time and commitment from yourself and the community members involved. Together, we worked on everything from HR policy, wage equity, determining what partnership meant in the context of the farm, decision making, business planning, and fundraising, and ultimately made a decision to move the project from one organization to another with the ultimate aim of creating an independent board and

nonprofit. At the center of this work is the amazing programming at the farm. Can you describe the programs at the farm?

Leticia: The programming at the farm is very strong and addresses some of the critical issues in the community on a day-to-day basis.[3]

Our community-supported agriculture program (CSA) offers sliding-scale prices and is constantly trying to improve access to healthy food. For

instance, we understand that the CSA model is not well known; it's not something that most folks are used to engaging with at the market. So, we have developed an on-site market where people can drop by Monday to Saturday and purchase whatever we have here. The sliding scale enables people who are low-income to afford some of the vegetables, but it also builds respect and dignity. The model is not one where you have to show all your paper documents

Adrianne Lickers Xavier, Indigenous studies professor, McMaster University, and Moyo Rainos Mtumba, Indigenous cultural educator, offer a workshop at the farm.

the infrastructure of the farm to make a small difference in the community.

One of the things I always say about our children's program is that we are building little environmentalists. The kids learn how to grow certain vegetables, how to take care of them naturally. They ask questions: Why do we need to grow things this way? And also, they're very likely to taste the food that they helped grow and helped cook together. That's also making a difference in the community. Now teachers and schools in the area have the farm as another space they can come to with the kids. We provide subsidies for them to be able to engage in the farm activities.

We also have the community garden plot program, where community members can get a plot of land to grow their own vegetables to supplement their food needs.

Growing a Farm: Hopeful Struggles

Lauren: What would food justice really look like for the farm and for Toronto in twenty years?

Leticia: There's still a precariousness that the farm faces. Last year was the first year we were able to make $150,000 of our own revenue; it's really great that we were able to bring in a bit of income to support the work on-site. But we face

to prove that you're really poor to be able to receive that. Instead, it builds an honest connection with people.

Our seniors' program is a free program to address seniors' isolation by building connections. We use gardening as a tool to do that. It's really important for people's mental health, especially

in a community that has a large senior population who live in poverty. Even the small thing of creating a space where seniors can come once or twice a week and just hang out, do workshops, garden, yoga, whatever it may be. This is our own way of using the space and

Foodshare staff Charlyn Ellis with two participants in a workshop, Antiracism in the Food Movement, 2016

A BCCF staff member gives a demonstration of native tree planting.

so much precariousness. So, in the next twenty years, I don't know what this farm is going to be. Politically, things are not looking that great.[4]

People are taking urban agriculture seriously. Urban ag is making a difference in our local food system; it is actually producing food. When I tell people that we grew more than twenty thousand pounds of vegetables here on this site, they're shocked, because I don't think people assume we'd actually be able to grow that much food.

I don't think people value urban farms in the same way they value other farms. So having the farm has made a huge difference in urban agriculture across the city. There are more farms popping up now. There is more interest from different groups around the world interested in the Black Creek Community Farm; they are interested in the model and want to create something like it within their own communities. I think Black Creek Farm can be a lead organization in showing the different levels of impact that urban agriculture can have:

from growing food to improving mental health. There are many different social issues that urban agriculture can tackle. But we need to do a better job at looking at that evidence base and sharing that evidence with funders and different stakeholders within this work.

I hope that in the next twenty years Black Creek Community Farm will still be here and that there will be core money that really supports the work that needs to happen here. I hope that we're growing on at least three acres of land, because last year it was less than an acre. Imagine cultivating more acres and being able to do that!

The farm is like an anchor for community transformation. It is addressing food security issues by supporting people to garden all across Jane-Finch, but it also raises the level of the conversation about food justice and food sovereignty in this neighborhood.

The impact of the farm is starting to show. We have great stories from the seniors, from the kids, from the community. Recently some of the past youth were here, talking about different ways the farm touched them. Zak'isha, who was in the youth program, has a new music video out that has to do with her journey around food and how food is important for her as a Black young woman. She's vegan now, and she talks about how the farm also influenced her and her mother around her new journey of starting a farm in Ghana. She's a hip-hop and poetry artist who's incorporating food and food justice into the conversation.

I'm hoping to tell these stories of impact, and the impact beyond the gates of the farm. How the farm is impacting people's choices or the choices of different organizations that want to do work in this area. I think there is some level of shift. One of the positive signs is that more and more people are really interested in and committed to food justice work.

The change that I'm seeing is that more and more people are becoming aware of the inequities and are looking at their own organizations and asking: How do we change this? How did it happen that we hired all white people? Was it that no Black person applied, or was it that we didn't see their strengths? How do we change that culture? What is the training that is needed? I think we've still got, oh my gosh, a long way to go. But it's still very good to see that people are actually reflecting on that, are asking the questions, and doing something about it.

Somalian-born chef and teacher Bashir Munye serves food at the BCCF farm dinner, September 2019.

BLACK CREEK COMMUNITY FARM: HEALING OUR COMMUNITY

Download the Facilitator Guide (ettl.ca/fg) for this video (ettl.ca/8d).

This video builds on the previous photo essay about Black Creek Community Farm (BCCF), Toronto's largest urban farm, which is located in the Jane-Finch or Black Creek neighborhood. The neighborhood is one of Toronto's most diverse communities and widely recognized as the most disadvantaged.

This community-produced video provides an overview of the farm and its activities, narrated by Leticia Deawuo. Before becoming the director at Black Creek Community Farm, Leticia worked in the Jane-Finch neighborhood as a community organizer. As director of the farm, Leticia works to respond to some of the structural injustices that exist in Canada, including food justice, food access, food and policing, food and community health.

Black Creek Community Farm is situated on a unique eight-acre property that includes pristine farmland, a heritage farmhouse and barn, and a surrounding forest that extends down into the Black Creek ravine. All of this is located within easy walking distance of eight schools and thousands of local residents in one of the most densely populated neighborhoods in Canada's largest city.

Black Creek Community Farm is a social enterprise and leader in Toronto's dynamic urban agriculture and community food sector. A variety of programs serve and enrich the community through these objectives:

A core focus of Black Creek Community Farm is to increase access to healthy food in the community through programming and food distribution projects. Fresh, local, and organic produce is available from June to November at accessible rates. Community programming focuses on food security, food literacy, and food skills. Thousands of children, youth, families, and seniors participate each year.

In this video, Leticia challenges us to think more broadly about farms and food justice, and the power of having diverse low-income communities controlling their own food production as a way to feed themselves, create safe spaces, and build community. The urban agriculture project addresses systemic barriers such as racism and poverty to access to healthy, culturally appropriate food, and the importance of accessible public spaces guided by community involvement and governance.

- growing a thriving farm and healthy food;
- providing hands-on training and learning experiences;
- inspiring the next generation by providing leadership in food justice; and
- supporting diverse and social ecosystems.

The farm's vision is to be an urban agriculture center that engages diverse communities through sustainable food. This vision connects to a thriving urban agriculture movement in Toronto that is linked through organizations such as the Toronto Food Policy Council and Toronto Urban Growers.

Continuing the Conversation
"Black Creek Community Farm" Video

Karen Washington

How great and refreshing it is to see Black folk expressing their desire to farm. Black Creek Community Farm should be an inspiration for those looking to farm in urban spaces. What is so unique about this farm is that they realized a need for people in marginalized communities to have access to fresh produce and decided to do something about it. It is so easy to complain about a food system that has neglected the people it is supposed to serve; after all, isn't food a human right? Yet millions of people go hungry each day. We have an extractive, exploitative food system in which food has become a commodity based on profits rather than on people—a system that produces enough food and wastes enough food, yet people in need have little to no access to it.

But Black Creek Community Farm offers an alternative: to grow food in community, food that is grown by the community and for the community, putting power and ownership back into the hands of its people. Their work is far reaching as folks from different parts on the world want to emulate not what they are growing, but how they are growing.

Let us not forget the continual struggles we have politically as we fight to have access to land, resources, healthy food, and clean water. Black Creek Community Farm is one of many farms in urban areas that relies on funding to survive. It is time for cities to put up or shut up. You can't claim you support food justice or have a food policy council without funds for urban agriculture.

Black Creek Community Farm: keep doing what you are doing. You are growing food, educating the youth, and creating a community food system that is just and equitable.

As Black folks, we have come a long way in understanding our history and our place in agriculture. Countries and empires have been built on the backs of enslaved and Indigenous Peoples. It's time for us all to go back to the land, put our hands and feet in the soil, and celebrate who we are as a people. Because as long as we are able to grow our own food, we will never be hungry again.

Karen Washington is a farmer and activist. She is co-owner/farmer at Rise & Root Farm in Chester, New York. As an activist and food advocate, in 2010, she cofounded Black Urban Growers (BUGS), an organization supporting growers in both urban and rural settings.

"Who Will Feed Us? The Farm Labour Crisis Meets the Climate Crisis"

Download the Facilitator Guide (ettl.ca/fg) for this video (ettl.ca/8e).

The year 2019 was marked by the direst prognosis about the climate crisis and by the most hopeful movement of young people taking to the streets for climate justice. The Intergovernmental Panel on Climate Change clearly named the industrial agricultural system as one of the major contributors to the crisis and a threat to biodiversity on the planet. If taken seriously by governments, this condemnation should result in policies that support small and medium producers and create more work for young people interested in sustainable farming.

This video asks the question of who will feed us in the future, and in the particular context of North America. We consider the reality that much of the food in the north (the United States and Canada) is produced by workers in the south (including Mexico).

Like many aging farmers, organic farmer Dianne Kretschmar is facing a farm labor crisis with few young people interested in putting their hands in the soil. She is hoping to pass her farming practice on to her son, Dan, who has a dream of transforming the farm into an agroecology school.

In Mexico, agroecologist Fulvio Gioanetto faces similar obstacles to interesting young people in farming, especially Indigenous youth who are often drawn into salaried work on multinational agribusinesses, working in inhumane conditions. Fulvio has been training his sons to create organic fertilizers and herbicides, to give them specialized skills through a family business that also builds a local economy.

Fulvio's daughter and son-in-law, Serena and Miguel, are interested in building their own organic farming practice in Mexico but are constrained by limited resources and an increasing threat of violence in the countryside. So, they have followed the pattern of many Mexicans who, like his parents and her grandparents, have migrated north for more than a century to work in the United States and Canada.

Ironically, while Miguel and Serena are working on Canadian farms to save money to develop their own agroecological farm in Mexico, Dan is teaching English in China to save money to start an agroecology school on his mother's

Miguel, Serena, and Lindsey on the land where they hope to start their farm

farm in Canada. They are part of a small but growing global labor force, one that is committed to a model of farming that honors the earth, promotes biodiversity, and offers dignified work, which is what the IPCC, the FAO, and other international bodies are calling for.

Many questions arise out of this video: How can the current unsustainable industrial food system be transformed? Does the context of the coronavirus pandemic open up new opportunities to promote local sustainable agriculture? What policies can support the training of young farmers in agroecological practices? What are the conditions of migrant farmworkers in all three countries? How can an exchange between organic farmers such as the Legacies collaborators cross-pollinate skills in sustainable production?

Miguel and Serena in Canada

Continuing the Conversation
"Who Will Feed Us? The Farm Labour Crisis Meets the Climate Crisis" Video

Gilberto Aboites

The idea of starting an agroecology school is great: to bring children into the countryside to see themselves as part of nature. This is the opposite of the vision of modern agriculture, where nature is only a resource to be used for human need.

The young adult children of migrants are starting to think differently. Miguel's parents left as migrants to the United States and never returned to Mexico. This loss of roots and of connection affected him deeply. He says, "I'm not going to do the same thing that my father did. I'm going to train my family members in the community in a form of production that will keep them from having to leave to make a living."

Miguel names the contradiction: although he wants to have his own organic farm in Mexico, he can earn five times more in the United States or Canada than in Mexico. Young Mexicans are also fleeing violence. In Michoacán, he's afraid of being attacked or robbed. In Canada, he feels so safe that he can even sleep in an open field. He feels the threat of violence more strongly because he has a child. He wants his daughter to grow up in a place where she feels safe.

The Canadian woman farmer (Dianne) recognizes that organic agriculture is hard work, but it's work that she does well and enjoys because it reflects her values. She understands that capitalist agriculture exploits nature, degrading the soil and environment, which also negatively impacts both farmers and their communities. Industrial agriculture is based on the idea that "more is better." If you believe that "more is better," you will seek more at the cost of everything else, which often means violating others' lives and expropriating their resources, including water, soil, seeds, technology, and culture. This idea is used to justify violence against those who follow different principles, those who might say, "I'm happy doing what I do because I'm living a life that is harmonious with my culture, tradition, and education." However, the use of power to impose a vision and way of doing things will always end in generating resistance and violence.

Ultimately, all activities require effort, and people realize their value in the world through their work. But when that work loses its intrinsic value, it's very hard to advance as a society. Basically, you have an unsustainable society.

Migrants internalize this value of work and try to create spaces where they can demonstrate their strength and dedication. The current public health crisis of COVID-19 and its resulting economic crisis have come together to reveal two things:

1. the critical role of agriculture to feed us because it's the one thing we cannot stop doing. Those who have suffered most from the crisis are the social groups that physically and emotionally are distant from their homes while producing our food; and

(continues)

2. the crisis has revalued the role of the migrant farmworkers, because they are of a demographic that for their young age should be less susceptible to the virus. But because they depend for their survival on migrant work that requires more risk, they have to accept whatever the work requires out of their own necessity and the needs of the urban population whom they feed. The countries that they have left behind have lost their strongest and most committed citizens, while the countries that receive them gain more from them than they pay them for their work.

Gilberto Aboites is director and research professor of the Socioeconomic Research Center at the Autonomous University of Coahuila in Saltillo, Mexico. His research and publications focus on poverty and marginalization, peasant rights, food security, and intellectual property rights.

A collective weeding of Dianne's field by Legacies collaborators

CHAPTER 9
TABLES

At the root of colonization was/is the stolen land and resources that continue to be at the core of the current struggles we are engaged in. Food sovereignty is strictly political to me. It's about control of land. I believe that colonial governments control us by controlling our food systems.

—Ryan, Mohawk professor, Ontario, Canada

The Haudenosaunee were absolutely critical in the forming of the countries that have become known on this continent as the United States and Canada, and therefore the influence that North America has had on the world.

—Chandra, Mohawk food leader, Six Nations, Ontario

We're also really good at roadblocks, at protests. Our people have had to defend their right to exercise their treaty rights or sovereign rights. Generations of our people have grown up trying to get the attention of Canada, of Great Britain and of the United States to realize that treaties matter, that this relationship matters. But every now and then you have to draw a line in the sand and say "we're not moving one more inch."

—Rick, Tuscarora artist, Six Nations, Ontario

The broader political tension within which we fight for healthy, sustainable, and culturally appropriate food is neoliberal capitalism and its history through European colonization and globalization, now being countered by a resurgence and reconciliation process led by Indigenous peoples defending their land and culture.

Tables can symbolize both the historical negotiations of treaties and trade agreements, for example, as well as gathering places for developing alliances between Indigenous and settler social justice movements.

Our exchange has taught many of us about buried parts of our colonial history. Not only did the colonial governments draw models of democratic governance from the Haudenosaunee.

They signed treaties that were to respect the inherent rights of the First Nations, but many broken treaties are now being challenged.

The Truth and Reconciliation Commission in Canada has unveiled and excavated the horrific impact of residential schools on Indigenous peoples, and food is an entry point into understanding that history. Not only in Canada, but in the United States and Mexico, Indigenous communities are reclaiming their worldviews, cultural practices, and spiritual relationships with food, directly challenging market-driven food systems.

In the territories of the P'urépecha Indigenous nation (in Mexico), our subsistence is based on a holistic vision of the territory and of the beings and spirits that live and interact. It is also based more on ecological exchanges (with nature) than on economic exchanges (with markets).

—María, P'urépecha healer, Michoacán, Mexico

Via Campesina, the largest coalition of eighty million peasants and Indigenous farmers around the world, has led the movement for food sovereignty. The National Farmers Union in Canada has been very engaged in this transnational movement and has facilitated exchanges among young food activists that exposed Dan to models of agroecology schools in other countries, feeding his own dream for the family farm in Ontario. The Legacies project is one small gesture within these larger networks of social and environmental justice activists.

An agroecology school could bring peoples from all over the world, with farming skills, who could help out at Grenville and build the community that we all want to see.

—Dan, young agrarian, Ontario, Canada

We're trying to connect farmers with Indigenous people and build the connection between Ontario and Mexico. We need to share knowledge and experience, to know other cultures, other experiences, and not stay inside the bubble of our own communities.

—Fulvio, Italian/Mexican, Michoacán, Mexico

 # FROM THE MUSH HOLE TO THE EVERLASTING TREE SCHOOL: COLONIAL FOOD LEGACIES AMONG THE HAUDENOSAUNEE

An Indigenous-Settler Dialogue between Chandra Maracle and Ian Mosby

Download the **Facilitator Guide** (ettl.ca/fg) for this photo essay. See **hyperlinks** (ettl.ca/9a) for this photo essay.

Deborah: The Mohawk Institute was the first residential school in Canada, founded at Six Nations in 1831. It became known as the Mush Hole, because of the bland porridge (in contrast to their more nutritious corn-based porridge) that Indigenous children were fed by the church and government

Mohawk Institute dining hall (Maracle-Hill Archives)

officials running the school. Like most settlers on Turtle Island (North America), I had only a vague notion of the reality of the residential schools in Canada and the United States. Through the Legacies project exchange, I was exposed to food stories that offered a window into that shameful part of our colonial history.

I met Legacies collaborator Chandra Maracle the same year (2015) that the Truth and Reconciliation Commission issued its report on this history with ninety-four recommendations for actions we should take, both individually and collectively. This became a part of our conversations around her kitchen table, where she described the traumatic impact of those schools on Indigenous Peoples' bodies and spirits, practices and communities. At the time, her partner, artist and historian Rick Hill, was excavating stories for a potential museum at the site of the Mush Hole, the Mohawk Institute Residential School, so we learned from his research, too.

A Community Gathering Opens the Conversation

In May 2018 Chandra organized "The Law Is in the Seed: A Community Cornvergence," held at the Six Nations Community Hall in Ohsweken, Ontario.

Framed as a "Celebration of Food, Culture and Community," it brought together more than 130 Indigenous and settler participants to share in a celebration of traditional and nutritious Haudenosaunee food, centered around corn, its history, cultural, and spiritual significance.

Cornvergence was sponsored by Chandra's organization, Kahwa'on:we, or Real People Eat Real Food. The gathering built on many years of her efforts to recover corn knowledge and healthy food practices—in her kitchen, in her community, and in other parts of Turtle Island.

But she also wanted to remind all of those attending of the devastating history of the colonial food legacies resulting from the residential schools. She invited Ian Mosby, a settler historian and food researcher at McMaster University, to reveal what was on the plates that fed the children in residential schools from 1834 until 2000, when all schools were finally closed. The intercultural conversation below was constructed from their two different perspectives, a kind of settler-Indigenous dialogue, shared at the Convergence conference as well as at other moments.

Chandra Maracle welcoming participants to Cornvergence gathering, 2018

Chandra Sets the Scene

Today we bring people together in community (ettl.ca/9a), in joy and food and conversation and love and all these things. But let's not fool ourselves. There are still some tough conversations to be had.

Going back to the table is my strategy. Residential schools had a profound effect on everything, including the food. The Mohawk Institute in Brantford, the residential school close to this territory, was called "The Mush Hole." We call it the Mush Hole because the children who went there became accustomed to the oatmeal mush served over and over.

That's its legacy.

We know that generations of children were not properly fed nourishing food. Nor were they nourished in terms

Kitchen at Mohawk Institute (Maracle-Hill Archives)

have focused on education, there has been little or no recognition that these problems may, in fact, be the legacy of colonial policies such as the residential school system.

Many former students and their families trace their contemporary unhealthy eating habits and a range of diet-related diseases directly to their own residential school experiences. Not only did residential schools forcibly strip students of their Indigenous dietary practices, resulting in generations of children alienated from their own culinary traditions during their formative years, but they supplanted them with diets that were predominantly unhealthy, nutritionally inadequate, and starch-heavy alternatives.

of love and affection. They were even abused.

Food historian Ian Mosby has become the modern whistleblower. He documented experiments conducted by the federal government on children in six residential schools across the country during the 1940s and 1950s. Ian recovered information on the nutritional neglect and experimentation on children that took place in these schools. This is part of our collective history and something that all settlers need to take some responsibility for.

The Colonial Food Legacies of Residential Schools

Ian: Although many of the efforts to combat obesity, diabetes, and other diet-related chronic diseases and risks in Indigenous communities have focused on modifying individual behavior and

Ian Mosby speaking at the Cornvergence gathering 2018

Take, for instance, the testimony of Russell Moses, who attended the Mohawk Institute as a child here in Six Nations. In response to a government inquiry, Moses said, "If I were to be honest, I must tell things as they were. And really," he added, "this is not my story, but yours, [settlers]."

The story Moses told is a harrowing one, of constant abuse and mistreatment. Food was a central part of this abuse. "We were given two slices of bread and jelly," he recounted, "oatmeal with worms and cornmeal porridge—minimal in quantity and appalling in quality. The beverage served was skim milk; we were milking 20–30 heads of purebred cattle, but we didn't once receive whole milk or butter. Lunch was no better. We received water as a beverage."

"Finally," Moses recalled, "supper consisted of two slices of bread and jam, fried potatoes (no meat), and possibly a piece of cake or an apple. The diet remained constant, and hunger was never absent."

Moses estimated that more than 90 percent of the children were suffering from some form of malnutrition. He recalled children eating from the swill barrel, picking up soggy bits of food destined for the pigs.

Survivors told the Truth and Reconciliation Commission (TRC) how they tried to overcome hunger however they could, by stealing food, eating spoiled food, or catching wild animals. The federal government was only able to conduct nutrition experiments in residential schools in the 1940s and 1950s because hunger and malnutrition were already so common in these institutions across the country.

Current health problems in Indigenous communities are the legacy of these colonial policies. Many former students and their families trace contemporary unhealthy eating habits and a range of diet-related diseases directly to residential school experiences.

What does reconciliation mean in the face of the legacy of a residential school system whose intent, according to the TRC itself, was nothing short of cultural genocide? Not only were children treated like guinea pigs in medical experiments conducted by the federal government, but the malnutrition that made these experiments possible had a profound and devastating effect on the long-term health and well-being of both survivors and their families. Hunger and malnutrition were never included as harms eligible for additional compensation under the residential school settlement.

Chandra: Ian and others have gathered many stories confirming this legacy of malnutrition. In trying to understand the impact of this history, I have found the concept of the psychology of eating developed by Marc David useful. He helped me reframe everything I've been thinking about for twenty-five years.

I now use the term "collective indigestion." There are times when we're not digesting our food properly in physical ways. Everything we take in—how we're living our lives—through our emotions, our feelings, and our thoughts—can be digested or not digested. So, when we eat foods that are not nourishing—refined wheat, refined sugar, some dairy products—our bodies aren't able to digest a lot of processed foods. When you add the emotional impact of eating these foods, we have "collective indigestion."

I'm not a proponent of a blind anti-five whites critique. This funny in-jest term known as the Five White Gifts is a play on words, as there are five things within the food system that were "given" as "gifts" from Europeans to Indigenous folks. But really, they weren't. They were foods that have been processed and industrialized and

Illustration by Justine Wong, appearing in The Walrus, *April 1, 2020*

therefore given to everybody in North America. When Indigenous people didn't have access to growing their own food, let alone buying good-quality food, some got commodity foods from the government. Those foods were often known as the five whites.

So, you have white flour, processed wheat flour. I don't like to demonize it, but almost nowhere on the planet do we actually now eat wheat in its real form. Sugar: there are many forms of sugar. But the sugar we generally think of is processed cane sugar, which is literally white. Much salt has been iodized, so all of the nutrients have been stripped out of it. Then they put iodine back in, so it sounds good when we say it's been iodized, because it sounds like it has some nutrition in it. The other ones are a little lesser known: lard, which is processed rendered pork fat; and dairy, usually in the form of milk. So, when you look at all these things, they generally look white. White people gave us these white things . . . these five white gifts.

But it's more the industrial processing and the Americanizing of these foods that makes them detrimental nutritionally. Our bodies are not able to handle some of these things. As a general rule, get rid of the five white gifts.

But if you take a deeper look, you can eat some, depending on the processing of those things.

Fry bread is the product of the five white gifts—it was originally made with processed white flour, salt, maybe sugar, baking powder—sometimes it was fried with lard. Keith Secola, a well-known native American musician, says fry bread has killed more Indians than the American government.

Suzan Harjo says "fry bread is emblematic of the long trails from home and freedom to confinement and rations. It's the connecting dots between healthy children and obesity, hypertension, diabetes, dialysis, blindness, amputations, and slow death. If fry bread were a movie, it would be hard-core porn—no redeeming qualities, zero nutrition."

The author Sherman Alexie says fry bread is the story of our survival. It relates to eating psychology—you can't vilify a food that helped people survive for generations. It became a combination of those commodity foods—those five white gifts—with which native women worked their magic.

You are literally eating the trauma of the generations when you eat fry bread. It might sustain you in the short term, but in the long run it's completely unsustainable. And it takes away from the integrity of our traditional culture. It was the survival food that has become known as *the* Native American food. But what does that mean? If anything, for Haudenosaunee people, it should be boiled cornbread. We have to acknowledge the role that fry bread played, we can thank it, and then we can move on.

The Challenge of Changing Food Practices

But it's not as simple as saying to someone, "Did you know there's no nutritional value in that?" And people will say, "Oh, really, OK," and stop eating it. Food takes its hold on you; these five white gifts become addictive, just like drugs. It's not as simple as just educating or informing somebody about this. I think eventually it will be understood, and it won't take as long as big tobacco, but it's not going to go down without a fight.

The legacy of residential schools certainly seeps into what is on people's plates now.

Many people weren't taught things that generally are passed down, generation to generation, like cooking, growing food, saving seeds. Those things often didn't happen for several generations, so there are many practical ways that the food system was

Mural by Chilean artist collective in Toronto

interrupted. Science is now understanding the value and contribution of traditional knowledge: to eat and to cook in a good mind, to eat in a way that is enjoyable.

Taking the time to slow down and think about the things we're eating . . . that's where I want to be. Looking at what happened in residential schools and in our diets over time can help us understand the issues we face today.

Recovering Haudenosaunee Food Culture

Ian: Events such as this CORNvergence gathering (ettl.ca/9a) give me hope. It celebrates Haudenosaunee agriculture and foodways, which is the most important way that communities such as Six Nations can start to undo the colonial legacy of residential schools such as the Mohawk Institute. It was the government of Canada's attempt to destroy Indigenous food cultures as well as Canada's policies denying Indigenous children sufficient healthy diets that continues to be the leading cause of many of the health issues currently affecting communities like this one. This means that events like today and efforts to reclaim and celebrate Haudenosaunee

food sovereignty and traditional diets is really one of the most important steps that can be taken to undo this harmful legacy—both of residential schools and Canadian colonial policies.

Chandra: If education and food can be used as a weapon, to take away culture, to harm people, then the opposite must be true: education and food can also be used to relearn the good way, to live a good life. The CORNvergence event is just one example. There are many others.

In 2010, I cofounded *Skaronhyase'ko:wa Tsyohterakentko:wa Tsi Yontaweya'tahkwa*, or the Everlasting Tree School on the Six Nations of the Grand River Territory.

What I most wanted to incorporate into a Waldorf-inspired Haudenosaunee school was the importance of food. I knew it was not just about nutrition nor a matter of scheduling but about seeing the cultural relevance of food in any Haudenosaunee situation. Because of the colonial legacies, most Haudenosaunee people don't know of the incredibly deep, rich, wonderful, amazing food history within the culture.

We have relationships with food going back to before the beginning of time in the Skyworld, before the creation

of the place we now call Earth. In the ethnological records from the 1600s, we see Jesuit observations of an incredibly rich agricultural tradition (ettl.ca/9a), led particularly by women and with a direct link between the landscape (hunting, fishing, gathering) and the Great Law.[1] There was a link between politics and society where food was central.

I went back through all the Haudenosaunee histories and reframed them through food. I looked at the relationships of all the players or elements in the Creation Story as family members and their role in what we now consider the scientific way of growing food—you need the sun, moon, stars, wind, and rain, all those things.

But there was so much disruption in the 1600s and 1700s that included the burning of millions of bushels of corn because of the strength of the Haudenosaunee and the centrality of food. Then in the 1800s and 1900s came the residential schools, such as the Mush Hole or Mohawk Institute. When the Truth and Reconciliation Commission began uncovering those stories, we were talking about the sexual abuse in residential schools, but we were still not talking about nutritional abuse and neglect, and how that has affected the

"Sky Woman," painting by Ernie Smith, Rochester Museum and Science Center

psychology of eating. When I discovered online the Institute for the Psychology of Eating, it all fell into place for me. Seeing the two words side by side, I thought that there's the Haudenosaunee framework.

Part of our mission at the Everlasting Tree School (ettl.ca/9a) was not just about the renewal of education and revitalization of language, but about countering the effects of residential schools, and, for me, food in particular. It's such a complicated question. We all have to be aware of our relationship with food in our lives outside the school while trying to nurture a healthy relationship with food for the children.

The first year of the school we only had twenty students and only two yurts as classrooms. It was easier for us to streamline food into the classroom. Eventually, all snacks were made at an outdoor firepit, so we stopped letting kids bring in their own snacks, which were often pop and chips. We took away all drinks except water. And then there was no problem with plastic bottles or cans.

One day a week I made a pot of food and brought it to the school for lunch. The sharing of food in an educational system, I drew directly from Waldorf practice. They sit around the table, hold

Chandra introducing Legacies collaborators and families to the Everlasting Tree School in July 2019

hands (ettl.ca/9a), and say a little verse, light a candle, and share a meal together (I was happy to welcome the Legacies partners to the school and to share a meal during our gathering in July 2019).

Little by little, I started to recruit other parents to make a pot and bring it to school. We focused on the sharing of food (ettl.ca/9a); parents came to help; we were building community. It was coming a long way just to share food.

The fourth year the school moved into a building and had more students. Parents were contributing $20 a week. We'd get together and go over the menu and the Haudenosaunee context. What should our menu look like? We decided to be wheat, sugar, and dairy free . . . because we get those outside the school.

When we come together in the collective, we can really raise the standard.

We need to better understand what people's relationship with food is like. To bring food into the school the way we do is light years ahead of what other schools are doing. It's incredible what's happening. Developing a school food system is an ongoing challenge.

Olivia, Franny, and Vyolette Maracle-Hill tasting maple sap, cornbread, and wild strawberries

Three Maracle-Hill sisters with three sisters—corn, beans, and squash

Continuing the Conversation
"From the Mush Hole to the Everlasting Tree School: Colonial Food Legacies among the Haudenosaunee" Photo Essay

Lorraine Johnson

I've always thought of food as a unifier: something that brings us together on a primal, basic level; something we all need, and something we can all understand that we all need. The foods we love because they connect us to our communities and identities, the foods we grow up eating, the foods we grow in our gardens and farms, the foods we nurture to nurture ourselves, our families and communities—I have always thought of these as positive, unifying forces.

For me, "The Mush Hole" photo essay presses into my full belly—a belly that has always been full, always been fed—reminding, teaching, showing that food is also weaponized, used as a cleaver to break bonds and sever relationships.

The violence of weaponized food is intimate, expressed in and through the body—the personal body, the ancestral body, the communal body.

For me, this photo essay also impresses, imprints, marks the full heart with hope, reminding, teaching, showing, sharing that food is also a healer, used to knit bonds back together and rebuild relationship. We eat from the land, and the land becomes us, and we become the land. Food manifests metaphor, literally embodied.

I've spent a long time thinking about land and how we might nurture healthy relationships with the land through cultivation (for example, growing native plants, growing food in cities). This photo essay helps me realize that I've been thinking of it as a trajectory instead of as a circle: land as body, body as land, and the act of eating as profound cultivation. Ancestral, in the present, for the future, in a circle to ancestors yet to come.

Lorraine Johnson is the author of City Farmer: Adventures in Urban Food Growing, along with many books about native plant gardening, such as 100 Easy-to-Grow Native Plants for Canadian Gardens, The New Ontario Naturalized Garden, and Tending the Earth. She lives in Toronto, where she is active in the community garden movement and in advocating for the legalization of backyard hens.

Continuing the Conversation
"From the Mush Hole to the Everlasting Tree School: Colonial Food Legacies among the Haudenosaunee" Photo Essay

Fulvio Gioanetto, Legacies Collaborator

The residential schools are an example of genocide. The British or Canadian system decided to eliminate First Nations with this strategy. It's brainwashing: to eliminate tradition and to put colonization inside the minds of these people. More horrible is to obligate people to a specific culture, a specific food, and to do experiments on them. It's typical of genocide.

In terms of reconciliation, of the ninety-four recommendations (made by the Truth and Reconciliation Commission), the most important is the right to the land and control of natural resources. We face the same problem in our autonomous community of Nurio in Mexico—we have control of the land; we have a flag; we have our own security force. It's better if you have natural resources within your community. But in Nurio we don't have anything.

There are 15–18 autonomous P'urépecha communities in the state of Michoacán. A Mexican Supreme Court declaration says that every community can live under traditional laws and customs. We decided not to receive any money from the state or federal government. The problem is that the majority of the people are really poor; they live on state assistance. It's very little money, but it's better than nothing. So, they want to retain a relationship with the state.

We had a similar challenge with school food such as Chandra describes with the Everlasting Tree School. In the Mexican system, the school contracts a food business to prepare and sell food, usually junk food. In Michoacán we have a state law against junk food, but it's not respected. So, María created a cooperative and asked parents to prepare traditional food and sell it inside the school. She felt that it was better and cheaper for women in the community to prepare the food. So now we have healthier traditional food within the school.

La Comida: The Core of Food Sovereignty

Gustavo Esteva, UniTierra, Oaxaca, Mexico

Download the Facilitator Guide (ettl.ca/fg) for this photo essay. See hyperlinks (ettl.ca/9b).

Deborah: Gustavo and Valiana take us to the rooftop garden of UniTierra in Oaxaca City, a place of planting and of learning; Valiana facilitates urban agriculture workshops here.[2]

For Gustavo, eating and learning always go together. *Comer y aprender.* Verbs, not nouns. Gustavo lives his life as a verb, as an active process that is always changing.[3]

At eighty-two years, Gustavo Esteva still stokes the "fire in the belly" that caused him to leave a position as an IBM executive sixty years ago and a high position in the Mexican government ten years later. At this time, Gustavo returned to Oaxaca, where his Zapotec grandmother had inspired him as a child, despite the fact that the rest of the family looked down on this "Indian" relative.

The 1980s and 1990s represented the neoliberalization of trade, epitomized by the North American Free Trade

Agreement (NAFTA) and the dramatic uprising of the Zapatistas to reclaim Indigenous territory and rights, to work outside the state and build "a world in which many worlds can be embraced."

In cofounding UniTierra, or University of the Earth, in both Oaxaca and Chiapas, Gustavo and his colleagues countered a notion of knowledge as a commodity transmitted through institutionalized education and honored the knowledges and ways of knowing of the majority Indigenous population in Oaxaca state. UniTierra is built around the verb *aprender*, or to learn, as Gustavo reminds me: "Instead of educating, we emphasize learning, both for us working here at UniTierra as well as for the communities with which we work."

I am reminded of our first intense collaboration a decade ago: along with Lauren Baker and Michael Sacco, we invited Gustavo to York University in Toronto as a guest scholar for the annual International Political Economy and Ecology Summer School. The topic of the seminar, "Food Sovereignty, Indigenous Knowledges, and Autonomous Movements," couldn't have been more prescient of the interrelated themes of the dialogue we're promoting through the Legacies Project.

As we sit down to talk about the current activities of UniTierra, Gustavo introduces me to a word or concept that encompasses the "earth to table" spread of our project: *comida*.

Gustavo: We define our priorities in verbs: to eat (*comer*), to heal (*sanar*), to settle (*habitar*), to learn (*aprender*). A central line of action is *comer*—to eat, or how to eat. We started twenty-five years ago as a center of *huertos* (gardens) and of intercultural dialogue. The question of the *comida* was born in UniTierra. Our name is University of *the Earth*. A brilliant Zapotec intellectual and composer, Jaime Martínez Luna, gave us our name. "In this university," he told us, "you must always have your feet on the earth and also take care of Mother Earth." And the whole relation with Mother Earth is centered on *la comida*.

One of our obsessions is to return eating to the center of social life. Fast food marginalizes *la comida*. It's to make food rapidly in the midst of all your activities. But in Oaxaca, everyone stops all activities at 2 p.m. to eat. The important activity then is to eat, and it's an important time for the family.

In English you don't have the word *comida*. In Spanish the technical term for food is *alimento*, not *comida*. Some people think of *comida* as just the "meal." But for us, *comida* is everything: growing food, preparing it, eating it, washing the dishes—it's all the social activities that have to do with food as really central to our lives.

Deborah: The effort to return the centrality of *comida* to daily life is challenged by a corporate global food system that has poisoned the earth and both "stuffed and starved" populations, a contradiction that Raj Patel names in a book by that title.

Gustavo: We're using the slogan, from a poem by Eduardo Galeano, "Global Fear: Those Not Afraid of Hunger, Fear Food." Of course, there's still a fear of hunger, as there are one billion people who are still going to bed hungry with empty stomachs. Hunger is here, again; it's in Oaxaca; it's in New York; it's everywhere. It's a threat again. It's shameful.

So, there's a fear of hunger, but there's also a fear of eating. Which means that our bodies are contaminated by what's in the market. The issue is very serious in Oaxaca, which has the highest incidence of diabetes in the country. Mexico is the country with the highest consumption of Coca-Cola per person: 180 liters per year. We had a president who had been the president of Coca-Cola. For these reasons, we think we need to multiply our efforts.

Selling junk food in Oaxaca City

We started a project this year, to use all forms of community media (community radio, social media, videos, Facebook, circus, theater) to share information and stories about the damage to health of fast food and *chatarra* (junk food), and to celebrate everything that can be made with maíz—all the drinks and food that can be made from corn. Our main effort is with kids and young people, and we organize many activities with them.

Deborah: Gustavo recognizes that the campaign for healthy food is part of a larger political struggle to defend maíz or corn; in fact, he has been involved in that national and global battle for a long time.

Gustavo: One of the first things that UniTierra did in Oaxaca in 2002, one year after its founding, when we discovered the contamination of our native corn by GMO corn, was to create a committee of defense of native corn with sixty other organizations. We organized actions, for example, disrupting an international meeting of NAFTA. We recognized that it was a very serious matter.

So, we launched a national campaign *"Sin maíz, no hay país,"* or "Without corn, there is no country." In Mexico City we mounted an enormous exhibit with one million visitors; it included books, videos, and music. We accomplished what we hoped for: to have many other organizations join the campaign. And they continue to be active now, fifteen years later. There's a network of groups in defense of maíz. It was very important for us to participate in a tribunal about corn denouncing the actions of Monsanto and other corporations, fully supported by the government. Vandana Shiva and many other friends joined us in this effort.

The trial, held in 2015, was built on the Permanent Peoples Tribunal created by Bertrand Russell, with headquarters in Italy. In the course of the long process in Mexico, it chose Oaxaca for a tribunal on corn, which was attended by more than eight hundred people coming from all over Mexico. The final sentence of the tribunal was a condemnation of the government and included a recommendation to expel the multinational companies responsible for the transgenic contamination of maíz from the country, including Monsanto, Novartis, DuPont, and Aventis.

Via Campesina represents the largest people's organization, with hundreds of millions of members in almost a hundred countries. They redefined food sovereignty in a way that corresponds clearly with our vision. We should define what we eat, and we should produce it. At UniTierra we are working with campesinos to recover their traditional, organic practices.

In the city of Oaxaca, we support the multiplication of gardens; we have our green rooftop garden, where we give workshops on growing food. We work mainly with women to strengthen their efforts to grow their own food at home. There are already hundreds of them in the central valleys, and this is an ongoing project. We circulate information and organize workshops both at UniTierra and in the backyards of some families. We also participate in local community fairs and events, publish materials, and organize many other activities.

Extract of Diego Rivera mural "Man at the Crossroads," Palace of Fine Arts, Mexico City

The work on *la comida* is directly connected to UniTierra's commitment to ending patriarchy and promoting autonomy.

If we do return *la comida* as a central activity, then we also return the centrality of women. Because it is women who take care of the world, take care of life, take care of the *comida*. Women are not just the cooks; they are responsible for everything that precedes the act of eating and the ceremony of *la comida*. Today, in the midst of the food crisis, small farmers, mainly women, feed 70 percent of the people on Earth, in spite of the fact that agribusiness owns and controls more than half of all the food resources on the planet. Although

Valiana facilitates a workshop on the rooftop garden of UniTierra in Oaxaca.

several men are participating in UniTierra's Milpa[4] project, all three programs under COMER (green rooftop garden, milpa, and urban gardens) are coordinated by women.

There is a consensus that we're at the end of a historical cycle and living the death of five thousand years of patriarchy. Patriarchy—the hatred of life, which is manifested in extreme violence, extreme hierarchy, extreme authoritarianism, which we see in the world today—is dying. The violence is its extreme form of defending itself.

For many it's not about recovering *comida* . . . because they never lost it. You recover what you've lost. Like recovering a territory that has been lost or taken. The best of the traditions of the Indigenous peoples is the tradition to change tradition in a traditional manner. Nobody remains what they were five hundred years ago. They've been changing all the time, but they do it in their own way.

Here's a very concrete living example: In the past ten years, 8,000 of the 12,000 communities in Oaxaca have

gathered assemblies of men and women, realizing that for centuries they hadn't had women participating in the assembly, but they now decided that women should participate. It's been part of a process we call the feminization of politics. Many women started to organize themselves and take leadership in social change.

So, women in most communities are now part of the communal assemblies and have leadership positions in the villages. At the same time, they are paying a high price—violence against them has increased a lot.

An important factor is that when many men migrated to the United States, they left everything in the hands of the women, and when they came back, the women wouldn't give them back the power. This has been a very substantial change.

Deborah: As Gustavo explained, UniTierra supported the decisions of the National Indigenous Congress (CNI) in 2018 to nominate María de Jesus Patricio, or Marichuy, as an Indigenous candidate in the presidential elections. Putting an Indigenous woman forward was the CNI's strategy to make

Women leading an assembly of the National Indigenous Congress in Tehuantepec Isthmus, Oaxaca, in 2019. Photo by Ángel Kú

Indigenous peoples and their issues visible and to create spaces around the country for Indigenous struggles for land, for identity, for their very survival.

Campaigning for Marichuy in Mexico City

Some questioned whether this strategy was congruent with the position of the CNI, of the Zapatistas, and of Uni-Tierra to not support nation-state politics or democratic elections. What they did was challenge that very system and use it for their own purposes.

Valiana, the Mayan collaborator who also works with Gustavo at UniTierra, participated in the meeting of the CNI in 2017 when the strategy to have a presidential candidate was developed. She suggested that Marichuy was chosen as a woman who represents all the ways Indigenous people, Indigenous women, and Indigenous knowledges have been marginalized. Marichuy is a gentle and

caring person who combines humility and strength. She is thus the counterpoint to the patriarchy that is in its death throes. Marichuy is part of a broader movement of Indigenous people who are reclaiming, reinventing themselves, but building on deep ancestral histories and knowledges.

For Valiana, Marichuy's candidacy was inspiring for the kind of intergenerational and intercultural exchange we are promoting with the Legacies project. Marichuy is an experienced herbalist and healer, someone who knows plants intimately and understands that all plants or food are medicine.

Thus, she embodies a broader conception of food, connected to the Earth, and a deeper understanding of food sovereignty, grounded in Indigenous knowledges about growing food and healing, both physically and spiritually, with plants. Marichuy is an advocate for *la comida.*

Gustavo Esteva is a Mexican activist, "deprofessionalized intellectual," and founder of the Universidad de la Tierra in Oaxaca, Mexico. As one of the best-known advocates of the concept of post-development, he has advised the Zapatistas as well as collaborators in the Earth to Tables Legacies project.

A ceremonial offering in Cuernavaca, Mexico, in 2015

Continuing the Conversation
"La Comida" Photo Essay

Claudia Serrato

La comida is a carrier and embodier of ancestral knowledge that can be tasted and passed down through cooking and eating. Recentering la comida as a social activity enhances these processes, which ultimately engages in the decontamination and decolonization of earthly landscapes. To do so also recenters *la mujer* and the *sabiduria de la comida* in outdoor and indoor kitchen spaces. This wisdom, grounded in traditional ecological culinary knowledge, provides opportunities to *comer y aprender* how to maintain and sustain *maneras de sanar* that create stronger relations with *la madre tierra*.

To reestablish these relationships is to honor *la comida*, or as Gustavo Esteva shared, to engage in *la ceremonia de la comida*. This ceremony is one of respect, honor, and most important, remembering food as relative, food as healer, food as knower, food as ancestor, and food as *cultura*. The dicho, "*la cultura cura*," is applicable in this sense; and if we take a deeper look, we can begin to understand that by recentering cultural heritage foods, we begin to dismantle the "taste of hierarchy" that perpetuates patriarchy, creating food systems of oppression unto the land, the body, the spirit, and the mind.

So, what does this food sovereignty work look like? How do we begin to defend *la comida*? As an Indigenous chef once told me, we need to begin by tasting and cooking our ancestral and traditional foods; in doing so, the food itself will let us know.

Claudia Serrato is a cultural and culinary anthropologist, an Indigenous plant-based chef, a womb ecologist, and a food justice activist scholar. Claudia has been writing, speaking, and cooking up decolonized flavors for more than a decade by remembering and recentering her Mesoamerican foods and foodways along with cooking traditions and nutrition.

A Three-Part Primer on Haudenosaunee History, Philosophy, and Food

Download the Facilitator Guide (ettl.ca/fg) for these videos. See the entire primer of three videos (ettl.ca/9).

The Earth to Tables Legacies project has been honored to have Rick W. Hill Sr. as an adviser. A Tuscarora of the Beaver clan, Rick is an artist, historian, writer, and curator living at Six Nations of the Grand River Territory, in so-called Ontario. He is the former special assistant to the director of the Smithsonian's National Museum of the American Indian, the museum director of the Institute of American Indian Arts in Santa Fe, New Mexico, and project coordinator for Deyohahá:ge: Indigenous Knowledge center at Six Nations, where he currently lives with his partner, Legacies collaborator Chandra Maracle, and his family.

   Rick has created three videos of his PowerPoint presentations to introduce us to the history, philosophy, and food legacies of the Haudenosaunee, also known as the Iroquois Confederacy (French) or (in English) the Six Nations (Mohawk, Oneida, Onondaga, Cayuga, Seneca, and Tuscarora). The three videos include:

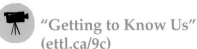 **"Getting to Know Us"** (ettl.ca/9c)

"Getting to Know Us" is based on questions from a speed-dating website. The idea is what are the usual questions one would ask if they only had a few minutes to get to know someone. Using this device of the dating game, Rick weaves his personal story with the creation story, the original instructions, the construction of the Iroquois Confederacy, the treaties that still guide us, the impacts of colonization, forms of resistance, and the food practices all shared through various forms of artistic expressions (many of his own creations).

Peace of Minds by Rick Hill

Painting by Rick Hill

Continuing the Conversation
"Getting to Know Us" Video

Patty Loew

Is there anyone who doesn't love a good story? The Haudenosaunee have a cultural treasure in Rick Hill, who is a master storyteller. Watching Hill's video reminded me of the stories my own Ojibwe uncles were forever telling my cousins and me. The stories were told so often that we knew them by heart. They became cherished memories, and with the passing of that generation, we tell them to our own children as a way to connect them to our collective past.

Native people know the power of narrative and the beauty of circular storytelling. Hill moves seamlessly between history, agriculture, spiritual beliefs, and environmental activism. Sovereignty underpins every story, from the meaning of the Two-Row Wampum and Chain of the Covenant to lacrosse and the Oka Standoff. So does gratitude and appreciation for beauty. Hill's reverence for the traditional food of the Haudenosaunee people and the reciprocal relationship he sees between humans and seeds is clear in his stories. There is kindness and humility in his voice. This is the power of Native storytelling—of the oral tradition. Could words on paper ever convey such cultural strength and texture?

I was particularly moved by the question, "What fictional place would you most like to go to? 'The SkyWorld,'" Hill tells us and adds that he hopes it is *not* fictional. This—the oldest of his stories—gives us insights into Haudenosaunee values and how his people see themselves connected to all life. The oldest story affixes to the future—the ability of the Haudenosaunee to adapt to new ways. In closing, he tells us he hopes that we will leave enriched. We absolutely do.

Patty Loew, PhD, is director of the Center for Native American and Indigenous Research at Northwestern University and a professor in the Medill School of Journalism. A citizen of Mashkiiziibii (Bad River Band of Lake Superior Ojibwe), Loew is a former broadcast journalist in public and commercial television and the author of four books.

 "Living with Your Mother: The Great Dish" (ettl.ca/9d)

Through beautiful paintings, wampum belts, wooden and ceramic vessels, cradleboards, and clothing, we learn more about the creation story, the original instructions, the Thanksgiving Address of greetings and thanks for all living things, and the ceremonies that honor these relationships.

The Great Dish with One Spoon Treaty offers a poignant lesson for all of us facing a global environmental crisis:

- take only what you need,
- share or leave something for others, and
- keep the dish clean.

With climate change, our ceremonies have to be strong enough to help us survive this change. Rather than look at the earth as a commodity, we have to realize the Earth is alive; she has expectations of us, and we have a responsibility to her.

Continuing the Conversation
"Living with Your Mother" Video

Timothy B. Leduc

"Renewing Settler Responsibilities on the Dish"

The Earth is alive, we are part of this Earth, and our human responsibilities arise from nurturing our deep roots in this life source. These are the central messages that stir in my heart and mind as I listen to Rick Hill talk about the Dish with One Spoon as an "earthen jar" that, in his Haudenosaunee stories, is the body of our Mother. It is from Her being that the sustenance of the medicinal plants, Three Sisters, beaver, and so much more arises, and with them our human responsibility to embody what he refers to as our original instructions. These call us to express Thanksgiving for all that makes life good on this dish—from the sustenance of the land, waters, and sky to the celestial and spirit beings that energize life in this great mystery of the Creator.

When I hear this teaching, I feel my settler ancestry being called to deepen my learning by finding a cultural way into what is being asked of us today as a climate of change swirls around us. Following the matrilineal protocols of these lands, I root myself in the French Canadien being of my mother and our ancestral relations to the 1701 Montreal Tree of Peace that was suffused in wampum belt teachings, including the Dish with One Spoon. I can almost hear the French governor Callière lifting up our responsibilities as he talks about how this "big dish" represents all the common lands we will share through "a *misouaine* [spoon] to eat the meat and drink the broth all

together." A *misouaine*, rather than a knife, represents our intention to be careful with all our relations so as to share all that is given by lands that are beyond human ownership.

Some surely sensed the sharp words of disrespect carried by French officials like the Jesuit missionaries who were translators for the hopeful tree planting. As Father Charlevoix wrote, "This ceremony, as serious as it was for the Savages, was for the French a kind of comedy, which they enjoyed very much."[*1] The Jesuits saw the "wild" nature around Montreal as outside divine grace, and Indigenous Peoples as *sauvages* who were similarly uncultivated. With this view and the Doctrine of Discovery that gave Europeans the right to control "discovered" lands, an unraveling of our shared responsibilities was enacted through religious missions that converted peoples away from an "evil" world and economic missions that appropriated our Mother's abundance into the unsustainable wealth of colonial nations and corporations. The intersectional intensity of this violence is today represented in the coinciding calls for change by survivors of residential schools, families of murdered and missing Indigenous women and girls, and the climatic turbulence of our Mother.

Agreeing to care for the Dish goes far beyond the dominant political, economic, and cultural sense of treaties in the settler mind. It is, at root, a spiritual contract between human nations, the beings of creation, and the land's spirit. In trying

(continues)

to reconnect with it, I am, we are agreeing to find ways of embodying an expression of gratitude for all our relations. Contrasting the colonial assumptions of unending economic growth and geographically fixed borders, the Dish reminds us that multiple nations can coexist on common lands in ways that are culturally and ecologically unique yet mutually beneficial. But to do so, settlers need to do the hard work of relearning how to embody those original life-affirming values of sharing, respect, and peace from Indigenous teachings such as those of Rick Hill. It is in fostering these roots that we may renew ways for sustaining the diversity of life in our Mother.

Tim Leduc is author of the book A Canadian Climate of Mind: Passages from Fur to Energy and Beyond *(2016), which looks at the colonial roots of today's climate change–energy issues. He is faculty in land-based social work at Wilfrid Laurier University and has also published* Climate, Culture, Change: Inuit and Western Dialogues with a Warming North.

*Gilles Havard, *The Great Peace of Montreal of 1701: French-Native Diplomacy in the Seventeenth Century* (Montreal: MQUP, 2001), 137–47.

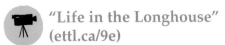 **"Life in the Longhouse"**
(ettl.ca/9e)

Rick Hill speaking to Legacies group in Six Nations Longhouse

The Haudenosaunee are "people of the longhouse," a way of living under one roof, a metaphor for life. Rick suggests the longhouse reflects the characteristics of the culture: its clan-based system, matrilineal descent, cooperation, respectfulness, and peacefulness.

Haudenosaunee villages remained sustainable by moving every few years in an economy based on hunting, gathering, and cultivating through mound agriculture (exemplified by the three sisters). Rick shows us evidence of a tremendous biodiversity of corn, of beans, of squash, a diversity that has been lost in the industrial food system and in our diets.

This video offers very practical information about the planting, harvesting, and cooking of traditional Haudenosaunee food. We also see the centrality of gathering nutritious foods such as mushrooms, berries, nuts (and their oils).

Ultimately, these tasks were shared, so that different families would bring different skills and foods to a cooperative living within the longhouse. Rick concludes that this should not be seen as a thing of the past, but rather as a way of life in the future.

Continuing the Conversation
"Life in the Longhouse" Video

Kiera (Kaia'tanó:ron) Brant-Birioukov

"Our First Teacher: Kanenhstóhare (Corn Soup)"

When it comes to education, the most important principle I stress with my students who are studying to become teachers is that land is our first teacher. Everything we need to know is in the land. In turn, we have a responsibility to honor the life that sustains us, such as our mothers and the foods that provide nourishment.

In Haudenosaunee society, our worldview is derived from the natural world around us. One of the most sacred properties in the natural world is corn—the eldest of the Three Sisters (corn, beans, squash). Corn is a central teacher for both traditional and contemporary Haudenosaunee identities. Growing up in my ancestral community of Tyendinaga Mohawk Territory, I grew up learning from and alongside the land with my father and grandfather, who were avid gardeners. My first teacher was corn—she taught me patience, hard work, sacrifice, and reciprocity.

Food, as it is for many cultures around the world, is also an important Haudenosaunee symbol of bringing community together. Hence, the process of making lyed corn soup, *kanenhstóhare*, embodies the sacred, symbiotic relationship between corn-as-teacher and corn-as-sustenance. It is what nourishes our bodies and our spirits.

When we make *kanenhstóhare*, we recognize the time it takes to patiently grow the corn, harvest the crop, braid the corn so it can be hung to dry, and finally transform the dried corn into lyed corn (also called *hominy*) through a process called "lying." When done correctly, the corrosive lye transforms the corn into a nutritious and delicious ingredient that has sustained Haudenosaunee peoples for generations. The heart of "good" corn soup is in this lying process—trusting the transformation that unfolds without guarantees. Lying corn is dangerous but necessary; just like education. Discomfort is necessitated if meaningful growth is sought. When we lean into discomfort, we lean into an education system that can be transformative.

Our language learners best embody the possibilities of *kanenhstóhare* as an educational framework. Indigenous language learners make immense sacrifices as they study to revitalize their ancestral languages. Just like the vigorous boil with lye when making corn soup, our language learners are confronted with discomfort, disconcertment, and disorientation. The demands of (re)learning our languages pose not only linguistic challenges that all second language learners face, but they are also faced with shifting ontological perspectives.

(continues)

Relearning our ancestral languages invites opportunities to reconsider our relationships with the land, our communities, and ourselves. But this transformative way of seeing the world requires a trust of faith in the disorienting processes of transformation.

Corn continues to be a teacher—and the teachings of corn are rearticulated every time I have a bowl (or two) of corn soup.

Kiera (Kaia'tanó:ron) Brant-Birioukov (Wolf Clan) is a Haudenosaunee educator, academic, and lifelong student. She completed a PhD in education at the University of British Columbia in 2021 and joined the Faculty of Education at York University. From Tyendinaga Mohawk Territory, Kiera is committed to theorizing the possibilities of land-based pedagogies based on Haudenosaunee teachings. When not writing, she can most likely be found in the garden. She lives in Toronto or in her great-grandfather's cabin in Tyendinaga with her husband, Anton, and cat, Hemingway.

 # Cooking and Eating Together: From the Kitchen Table to the Community Meal

> Download the Facilitator Guide (ettl.ca/fg) for this photo essay. For the essay here, see hyperlinks (ettl.ca/9f).

Deborah: I grew up in the 1950s in a rural farming community in the United States, where we sat down to dinner as a family. As a community, we often gathered in the Grange Hall or the church basement for potluck suppers. Everyone would bring a home-cooked dish, often made of fresh vegetables from their gardens, farm-raised animals, fruit from their orchards, or berries gathered in the woods abutting their fields.

A new food guide issued by the Canadian government in 2019 proclaimed, "Healthy eating is more than the foods you eat. It is also about where, when, why and how you eat." It suggested involving others in planning and cooking meals, integrating cultural and food traditions into healthier eating, and eating meals with others.

Stories about sharing food together abound in the Earth to Tables Legacies project. The project is framed by the complementary passions of Dianne, a settler farmer who focuses on growing food; and Chandra, an Indigenous community food leader, who focuses on the kitchen table as a site of deep cultural

meaning, sharing good food, nurturing healthy bodies and good minds, and building community. From the start of our exchange, Chandra has been emphasizing the collective impacts resulting from the loss of this practice (ettl.ca/9f) and inviting us back to the table.

Chandra: Sometimes food itself and the eating of food gets lost in the context of the larger discussion of the food system. We forget that at the end of the day, it comes down to what's on your table, what's on your plate, and what's going to go inside your belly. And that we are eating it with people we like, with our family, or with whomever we're calling our family at that point.

The wicked question is: What did you feed your kids today, and what did you talk about?

Family and food around the table taps into childhood memories, and a lot of people don't have those childhood memories anymore. Food pushes people's buttons, because it is life itself. It can stir up a lot of things for people. As you go further back into your family and collective cultural history, there are other issues. Particularly if you are in the Americas, there is the precolonial and colonial legacy that includes food.

Before and after European Colonization

The beauty of living in a communal longhouse style precontact was that you knew where your next meal was coming from, because they had a lot of food stored. That's why the community and culture were able to thrive, and they had the time to be artists and deep thinkers. When you have that level of food security, you can get on with your life.

It's different when you are hunting and gathering every single meal. That's a really big difference in how Haudenosaunee people were living at the time of European arrival. They had a thriving culture because of food, because of the diversity of food available and their

Friends and Legacies partners at Chandra's table in 2016

storage practice. This allowed them to stay in one place. And they were also able to have this deep political philosophy based on the good mind.

But how do you feed a good mind? With good food! I'd love to see that

happen again. But it happens rarely these days; it's rare that I go to a function and am happy with what my kids are eating.

After four hundred years of contact, the issues are around not being able to

Legacies collaborators visit a traditional longhouse at Six Nations.

grow food. It's trying to convince people why they should grow food or go to the local health food store and buy good food instead of going to Tim Horton's or McDonald's. There's a big gap between Indigenous thought and philosophy, on the one hand, and Indigenous people and how they eat, on the other.

We're seeing the history of residential schools brought to life and understand how they separated people from the land and fed them bad food. If education and food can be used as a weapon, to take away culture, to harm, then the opposite must be true: education and food can also be used to relearn the good way, to live a good life.

I'm trying to take a practical, realistic approach. We have big social gatherings in this community where food is present all the time. I'm trying to make sure that every time we gather, we are cooking food that is a little bit better. The way I can do that is to be the go-between for what people such as Dianne do—growing food—and what people eat.

Creating Mindful Eaters

I try to get my family to do some mindful eating, so we've had many different rituals at our table. And one that our six-year-old came up with is that **we all hold pinkies (ettl.ca/9f)**, and we take a nice deep breath together and we'll just say: "*Nya:wen tsi enskatne tentewa'ts-ka:hon*" (or "We are thankful that we are eating this food together"). And that's both with our family and when others are here at the table with us.

My interest in eating psychology led me to the realization that when you slow down before you eat, it helps the nervous system to slow down so that you digest food better. So that's what I'm trying to teach my girls. It's not just hovering around the table, scarfing it down, and running away. Eating together is something we do every day, at least once a day, if not more. It's really important to me.

Deborah: At the potluck dinners in my rural community in the 1950s, there was always a wonderful array of food spread out buffet style. We would line up to fill our plates with contributions from many different families.

Whereas restaurant and take-out meals have come to dominate urban eating experiences, the potluck tradition is practiced by small pockets of people, whether food-conscious young people or members of the dwindling number of farming communities. The tradition is well and alive, for example, in rural Quebec.

Community Potluck Suppers in Rural Quebec

Legacies collaborators Anna and Adam live in the small coastal community of New Carlisle in the Gaspé region of Quebec. They have organized community meals with other vendors in their farmers market. In 2016, more than twenty-five people gathered at the Community Centre (ettl.ca/9f) for a Thanksgiving dinner. The turkeys raised by Anna and Adam were central to the menu, and their preparation was a collective effort.

Anna was influenced by her mother, Elizabeth Harris, famous for

Chandra introduces their family ritual before a meal with Legacies collaborators in 2016.

the community meals that she organized in their downtown Toronto neighborhood where Anna grew up.

Communal Cooking and Eating in a Mexican P'urépecha Community

Deborah: Every time we visit Legacies collaborators Fulvio and María in the autonomous Indigenous community of Nurio in Michoacán, Mexico, we experience the tradition of the fiesta and feast, and in particular, the collective cooking and communal eating that accompany

John assists his daughter Anna and her partner, Adam, in preparing a Thanksgiving turkey.

A communal meal organized by Elizabeth Harris in Riverdale Farm Park, Toronto, in 2009

couple of pickup trucks to the brim with bags of fruit (oranges, bananas), baskets of bread, and pastries to be delivered to the bride's family.

My family served each relative as they arrived, gathering outside the house, waiting to go in a parade to the bride's house. They also brought wine to offer to the bride's extended family. When they finished eating in the groom's house, the women danced in the streets (ettl.ca/9f) with a band, while the men walked behind. They were followed by the trucks filled with fruit and bread, which then got deposited into the kitchen of the bride's house.

The offering of bread comes out of the Catholic tradition. With the bread, you are thanking the whole community for receiving the new bride or groom into the family. It's a commitment from

any special event. In early 2019, we witnessed the importance of food in one of a series of pre-wedding events, celebrating their son Jorge and his bride, Belen. Jorge's sister Serena explained to us the different food traditions in the *"agradecimiento"* or "thank-you" ceremony.

Serena: The *agradecimiento* ceremony is held after the bride has lived for a few months with the groom's family and proven herself compatible and capable

of managing a household. Jorge's mother was joined by other women to cook an enormous pot of *morisqueta* (rice with meat and tomato sauce), which she served to all her relatives (more than one hundred) as they were gathering outside her house, accompanied by a brass band.

The previous day, my parents had gone to town to buy the food they will present to Belen's family. They filled a the community that they will support the couple and that they will never go hungry.

At the bride's house, women have gathered in the kitchen to cook chicken mole for the feast. Every woman contributes some particular skill. They work collectively to make these large meals. It's a social experience for them, in the kitchen. They fill containers with the cooked food for all of those who helped to take home to their houses.

In front of the bride's house, all the groom's relatives eat at long tables. The bride's family sits along the wall or inside the house. There might be as many as three hundred people.

It's a big investment for both families. There are many fiestas like this every year—maybe thirty. In all the fiestas, they share large meals with everyone. They have lots of food for three days.

Potluck Dinner of Urban Gardeners in Guadalajara, Mexico

Fernando: In talking with Chandra at her table (in 2016), I understood something that is really important that I hadn't realized. What she's doing is really important for farmers who are trying to do things in the right way. Because, finally, who has the last word is the

consumer. If all the consumers agree how and what they want to eat, that will force the food system to change.

That kind of inspires me. Because I'm doing urban agriculture in Guadalajara, I thought that maybe the best way to promote agriculture for people in the cities is to share the food with them (ettl.ca/9f). We need to try to stop the rhythm of life for a few minutes and show them how they can cook more nutritious vegetables and share what they've grown.

Eating food is part of farming for me. From Chandra, I realized that that's my passion; that's why I like farming. But it's not something that I had focused on. I want to get the food finally to a plate that I can share with people I love, in a moment that I can enjoy with music, good wine, good friends, and great food. That's the whole meaning for me. I'm looking forward to making some changes in the way I'm doing things right now.

Chandra showing Dianne how to process corn and create cornbread in 2017

Dianne connects with the soil, and works outside. Chandra is inside, at the kitchen table. They're the two ends of the process. Chandra would not be able to do what she does if there were not farmers such as Dianne. And Dianne would not be able to sell anything, to be farming, if there were not conscious people such as Chandra who really appreciate what she does. That's what I'm trying to bind together—both parts.

So, I organized a communal meal in our garden with the students who had taken my classes on growing food in their own backyards.

Cooking in the Earth in the Yucatán, Mexico

Deborah: For ten days in January 2020, John and I shared daily life with Ángel and Valiana, Legacies collaborators, in Valiana's hometown of Sinanché, an hour from Yucatán's capital, Merida, and fifteen minutes from the Gulf of Mexico. We were honored that they spent a day preparing tamales for us that are typically cooked in the ground for the Day of the Dead celebrations in October/November.

Valiana: Our culture is very rooted in *la comida* (food); it is the center of our lives; it is who we are. *La comida is not just something you eat; it carries the memories of our abuelos/ as (elders) (ettl.ca/9f)*. Each time we hold the corn dough and make a tamale, we are reminded of our ancestors.

Ángel: This form of cooking in the earth is a legacy our ancestors left us (ettl.ca/9f). Today we prepared Pip (buried food); it's what we offer the dead November 1. The tamales we wrap in banana leaves represent the people who are no longer here. What's inside represents the blood, the meat, the bones. To bury the food is an act of returning to who we are; we are of the land, and one day we will return to the land.

Valiana: We really like to cook together with others. It's the spirit of the space that we connect not only with the planting and harvesting of food, but

Community dinner hosted by Fernando with Cosecha en Casa participants

also with the art of cooking and the art of eating together.

Ángel: We call those who are already there to come again to eat with us at our table. We offer the food to the dead first, so they can eat before us. It's a sacred moment.

Valiana: La comida is an act of resistance. What we did today confronted a system that says to cook in this way and to eat this food is backward, is the way of poor Indians. But no, our *comida* is very rich. To make these tamales reconnects us with our past and our ancestors. To bury the food, to cook in the Earth is to connect again with the Earth.

Cooking Together at Our Legacies Gathering

When Chandra hosted a gathering of Legacies collaborators at Six Nations in Ontario in July 2019, she created an opportunity for us to cook together in a communal kitchen, learning how to make cornbread from Bonnie Sky. This was not only a fun activity that stimulated informal conversations, but one that gave all of us a sensory and visceral understanding of this staple food for Haudenosaunee cuisine.

There are many different kitchens and tables in the diverse cultural context of the Legacies Exchange. Each of the stories above speaks to the importance of commensality, or gathering around the table to share a meal, and to reclaim cooking as a cultural practice. And more than that, to the importance and power of building community through food.

Legacies collaborators learn to make cornbread at Six Nations.

Continuing the Conversation
"Cooking and Eating Together" Photo Essay

Joshna Maharaj

This collection of stories is like a road map, or a collection of signs, all pointing toward the need to make food and our relationship with it a more important part of our lives. The contexts, people, and times are different, but the thread through all of it is the deep value of connecting to good food and sharing it with others.

Something that really resonated with me was in the piece about cooking in the Yucatán in Mexico. One of the women in the group said, "Each time we hold the corn dough and make a tamale, we are reminded of our ancestors." I love this idea of lineage, and that food is what enables connection to the ancestors. I was instantly reminded of the spluttery excitement of green chilies and cumin seeds blistering in hot oil as the base of so many of the dishes made in my Indian family's kitchen. As a child, it was the promising sound and smell of something delicious being cooked.

As an adult who now cooks like this in my own home, and in professional kitchens, every time I drop spices and chilies into hot oil, I feel that spluttering invoking every other dish or pot of curry I've made this way. I do it (mostly) the way my mom did it, which was (mostly) the way my grandmother and great grandmother did it. And somehow, as I'm standing over that oil, blistering chilies and roasting spices, they are all there with me. It's wonderful that simple things such as turning on the stove, or adding water to masa to make dough, are what open the door to welcome in our ancestors.

After reading this piece and sitting with some of the stories, I was grateful for the beautiful reminder about how food and our relationship with it is about so much more than putting calories in the tank. In my work in public institutions, this is something I'm constantly talking about. Once you shift your perspective and understand that our relationship about food is about our connection to the goodness and nourishment from the Earth, the way you grow, cook, and serve food will change in a significant way. I want to change the attitude behind the meals served in hospitals, schools, and prisons. I want to open up the connection available through good food for everyone, particularly those who are healing, learning, and rebuilding.

What I love so much about this photo essay is the resounding invitation back to the table. I, too, have been thinking

(continues)

about what Chandra describes as "the collective impacts resulting from the loss of this practice" during the pandemic. Yes, many people ate more family meals at the table than ever before in their lives, but many other people ate more meals alone than ever before as well. One of the most fundamental questions of this moment, as vaccines are giving us all hope that the end is near, is what has happened while we were all away from the table, away from each other. And how will we learn to be together again? I'm not entirely sure how this will happen, but I am 100 percent positive that more time around a tableful of good food with good people is the right way to start.

I want to invite you into a conversation about the table as a colonial imposition. In so many cultures around the world, people cook and sit to share food on the ground, with no table in sight. In fact, here in North America, there are many cultural images of the hostility of the table, where Indigenous people were forced to sit to participate in a thanksgiving meal that was not quite as full of gratitude as it should have been. I'm starting to realize that spinning dreams around the table might not be as full of good feelings for everyone.

Joshna Maharaj is a chef, author, and activist with big ideas for helping people make deeper connections with their food. Joshna recently published her first book, Take Back the Tray: Revolutionizing Food in Hospitals, Schools, and Other Institutions. *She cohosts the* HotPlate *podcast and hosts* Kitchen Helpdesk, *a weekly call-in show on CBC radio. Joshna is a two-time TEDx speaker and was recently named a fellow at Trinity College at the University of Toronto.*

ACKNOWLEDGMENTS
Greetings and Gratitude

This book opened with "Greetings and Gratitude," inspired by the Haudenosaunee Thanksgiving Address that starts any event or day by thanking all of the beings, both other-than-human and human, that sustain our lives.

We are closing the book with "Greetings and Gratitude" as well, thanking again the plants and animals, sun and wind, the insects and birds, all living within the stories represented here.

In this acknowledgments section, we want to thank in particular the many people who have collaborated with the Legacies project over seven years to bring these stories to life.

Storytellers

The Legacies project involved thirteen people, young food activists and elders, rural and urban, settler and Indigenous, Mexican and Canadian, whose experience and wisdom are the heart of this book: Valiana Aguilar, Maria Blas, Leticia Deawuo, Ryan DeCaire, Fernando Garcia, Fulvio Giaonetto, Rick Hill, Dan Kretschmar, Dianne Kretschmar, Ángel Kú, Chandra Maracle, Anna Murtaugh, and Adam Royal. See their bios in chapter 5 and full profiles online.

As their stories were embedded in communities, their families, friends, and coworkers also appear in the videos and photo essays: Solin Alejo, Christian Besnier, Nicole Bilodeau, Bryan Gioanetto Blas, Jorge Gioanetto Blas, Serena Janicua Hoscua Gioanetto Blas, Abena Boahemaa, Isidro Alejo Cacari, Miguel Quetzecua Torres Correo, Lindsey Magdalena Quetzecua Gioanetto, the late Elizabeth Harris, Santiago Cacari Leon, Marc-André Longpré, Aly Othmer, Keira Maracle, Olivia Maracle-Hill, Franny Maracle-Hill, Vyolette Maracle-Hill, John Murtaugh, Marina Queirolo, Erin Rhodes, Doña Yolanda Rivera, Don Toño Rivera, Amelia Murtaugh-Royal, Katherine Murtaugh-Royal, Theo Murtaugh-Royal, Julie Schell, Hilda Villaseñor, Diego Garcia Villaseñor, Kevin White, and Peter Wiley.

In the early years, we also learned a lot from Haudenosaunee food activists Kitty and Adrienne Lickers, who coordinated the Our Sustenance Program at Six Nations; and the late elder Iowne Anderson, who was an inspiring organic gardener.

To broaden the perspectives of our small group, we invited activists and experts in the themes that emerged to offer commentaries. These are the voices who "continue the conversation," and their bios can be found with their commentaries: Gilberto Aboites, Amber Meadow Adams, Molly Anderson, Kiera Brant-Birioukov, Harriet Friedmann, Lorraine Johnson, Tim Leduc, Patty Loew, Anan Lololi, Joshna Maharaj, Fred Metallic, Monique Mojica, Claudia Serrato, Laura Solis, Selam Teclu, Samantha Trumbull, Penny Van Esterik, Karen Washington, and Dr. Lorna Wanosts'a7 Williams.

From the start of the project in 2015, we called upon people who could give us guidance as we tried to cocreate a genuine exchange. Secwepemc food leader Dawn Morrison accompanied us through the first year and taught our team a lot about decolonizing research and relationships. Her deep understanding of the impact of colonization in so-called Canada and her commitment to Indigenous food sovereignty influenced our thinking profoundly. Documentary filmmaker Min Sook Lee offered critical advice about the collaborative production process and proposed the form of short videos that we adopted. Tuscarora historian and artist Rick Hill advised us about the approach, content, and form throughout the last three years of the project, and generously offered his own knowledge and art as part of the educational package.

Greetings and Gratitude to these storytellers, commentators, advisers, partners, and children—who continue to teach us in so many ways.

Researchers

Our research was primarily participatory and arts-based (see pages 51–52), resulting in the photo essays and videos. Archival and Web-based research was coordinated by Deborah Barndt, reflected in the resources named in the Facilitator Guides and bibliography. Production team members—Lauren Baker, Alexandra Gelis, and John Murtaugh—did further research while Mexican friends Antonieta Barrón and Serena

Gioanetto fed us information about migration and labor.

Our SSHRC funding allowed us to hire student research assistants. Alexandra Gelis was supported by a PhD research assistantship for her work as codirector of the project. In 2015, Amandeep Kaur Panaq helped with the initial stages of the project; Sheema Sheenoy joined in 2016–2017, taking on various roles from assisting sound on video shoots to preparing indices and transcriptions of interviews. RAY research assistant Codrina Ibanescu coordinated testing of the material with university classes in 2018–2019; Tzazná Miranda Leal was an invaluable assistant in 2017–2019, setting up accounting procedures, translating Spanish subtitles, organizing the logistics for our July 2019 gathering, and shaping the migration mapping with original food icons.

Greetings and Gratitude to these young team members for their energy, skill, creativity, and commitment.

Book Producers

We have been fortunate to have a twenty-year relationship with Rowman & Littlefield, which originally published Deborah's book, *Tangled Routes: Women, Work and Globalization on the Tomato Trail*, as well as Lauren's book *Corn*

Meets Maize: Food Movements and Markets in Mexico. Our original editor, Susan McEachern, former vice president and senior acquisitions editor, championed this new project from the beginning. Her interest in the food theme (as a gardener and beekeeper) and in multimedia book hybrids paved the way for this experimental educational package to come to life. When Susan retired in 2021, Katelyn Turner took the reins to coordinate the project. Jehanne Schweitzer ably guided the production process, with the support of designer Rosanne Schloss. The index was prepared by Jennifer Rushing-Schurr.

Greetings and Gratitude to the editorial, design, and production teams at Rowman & Littlefield.

The book outline was conceived by coeditors Deborah Barndt and Lauren Baker. Deborah, along with Lauren, wrote many chapters and edited photo essays, with ongoing feedback from codirector Alexandra Gelis. Creative writing consultant Laurel Waterman offered invaluable advice on the narrative forms, templates, and select essays. John Murtaugh read the manuscript and offered editorial suggestions. Deborah's writing group (Mary Corkery, Barbara Rahder, and Barb Thomas) read earlier drafts of video scripts, photo essays, and Facilitator Guides, offering useful suggestions at critical points in the project's development.

When we were ready to submit the book to the publisher, we were blessed with a volunteer, Rosie Shephard, who spent three months transforming our drafts into the required manuscript form. Her skill, efficiency, and attention to detail were a godsend for the project.

Greetings and Gratitude to all who helped shape the raw material into a book form.

Video Production Teams

Cameras have been our main accomplices, as images—both still and moving—are central to the Legacies project. The production of ten videos and eleven photo essays has tapped the skill and creativity of dozens of people. Codirectors Alexandra Gelis and Deborah Barndt coordinated the shooting, compiling, and editing of most videos. Alexandra was the principal videographer, with additional footage from Deborah Barndt, Jorge Lozano, John Murtaugh, and Juan Pablo Pinto.

We are grateful to filmmaker Ilana Linden, who planted the seed for this project as a film, even though it went in a different direction than she had hoped.

For specific productions, we called upon the filmmaking and editing skills of Aram Collier, Alyssa (Megan) General, Gary Joseph, Esery Mondesir, Andrew Osei, and Shane Powless. Many others assisted the production process: sound assistants included Joshua Barndt, Raquel Bolaños, Amélie Lambert Bouchard, John Murtaugh, and Seema Shenoy. In the early years, the first video was produced by Sylvie Van Brabant and edited by Louise Dugal, assisted by Francis Bernier and Vincent Laroche-Gagnon. Over the five years, editing studios were generously offered by Jorge Lozano Studios, Toronto; Rapide Blanc, Montreal; and Red Door Productions, Six Nations. Archival footage was provided by CTV News Toronto archives, Shutterstock, and Anne Lewis Productions. Deborah Barndt was producer of the majority of the videos; Lauren Baker coproduced, with Leticia Deawuo, the Black Creek Community Farm video.

Two community-based productions drew on the original music of their communities: Zak'isha Brown on the Black Creek Community Farm video and Malia Bomberry, Kyleeya Johnson, and Kiera Maracle from Six Nations on the Thanksgiving Address video. Original scores were produced by Lalo Lorza-Baker, Jackeline Rago, Nano Valverde, and Juan Dino Toledo. We drew on the recorded music of others: Claude Arsenault, Eve Goldberg, Genticorum, and Orquesta Tatá Vasco, and So Long Seven.

Narration for two of the videos was written and read by Deborah Barndt. Leticia Deawuo narrated the Black Creek Community Farm video. Rick Hill provided the narration for the three videos that comprise the Haudenosaunee Primer. The translation of subtitles was taken on as a class project by the York University Glendon College School of Translation. In 2017–2018, Professor Martin Boyd supervised these students: Beatriz Funes, Catherine Gryfe-Seeley, Maria Gutierrez Ramirez, Maria Heron, Nicoleta Nagy; in 2018–2019, Professor María Constanza Guzmán supervised the work of Analía Molina, Beatrice Nkundwa, Farhana Ahmed, Jacqueline O'Neill Huerta, James Phan, Mariana Zir, Ferreira Santos, Virginia Maldonado Barrios, and Wendy Barillas. Other subtitles were translated by Deborah Barndt, Alexandra Gelis, and Tzazná Miranda Leal. The task of integrating the subtitles into the videos was accomplished by Alexandra Gelis.

Overall production was coordinated at different points by Deborah Barndt, Lauren Baker, and Alexandra Gelis.

Greetings and Gratitude to the dozens of people who generously offered their vision, skills, and hard work to the final video productions.

Photo Essay Production

The photo essays were largely drawn from transcriptions of video footage, so we thank the storytellers for sharing their stories, the videographers for capturing them, and the transcribers for creating indexes that became the skeletons for photo essays. Alex was the primary videographer while Deborah was the primary transcriber, and photographer, often supplemented by the cameras of Alexandra Gelis and John Murtaugh. In fact, many still photos are screenshots from videos shot by Alexandra. Other images for specific purposes were offered by Miguel Quetzecua Torres Correo, Bryan Gioanetto, Serena Janicua Hoscua Gioanetto Blas, Rick Hill, Cristina Lombana, and the Maracle-Hill Archive.

Contributions from visual artists enriched the images in the Thanksgiving Address video and essay (Rick Hill), The Mush Hole photo essay (Justine Wong), Language and Food (Cindy Martin). The artwork of Joseph Brant, Suzanne Brant, John Fadden, Rick Hill, Stan Hill, and Ernie Smith were integral to the

videos in the Haudenosaunee Primer. The food icons in chapter 6 were created by Tzazná Miranda Leal. Helios Design created more icons and the drawing for introduction to the "Conversations" section, part IV. Alexandra Gelis designed the logo for both the website and the intro to all videos.

Deborah, along with Lauren, crafted and edited the photo essays. They also created the Facilitator Guides, which are critical to the collective use of the material.

Greetings and Gratitude to the storytellers and the photographers, artists, writers, and editors who crafted the oral stories with images into photo essays.

Website Producers

Codirector Alexandra Gelis created the first website as a live research space, which was programmed by Jésus Flores. She uploaded productions as they were completed, allowing us to share the material with interested people and groups. When we chose to produce a multimedia package rather than one feature-length documentary, we dreamed of an interactive website that would engage viewers critically with the issues raised by the videos and photo essays. Helios Design Labs understood the deeper purpose of our project and its

unique pedagogy. The knowledge, skill, and creativity of Heather Grieve, Mike Mali, and Alex Whittholz are evident in the beautiful website that resulted. Their collaborative way of working made the process a cocreation between two committed teams.

Greetings and Gratitude to Helios Design Labs for producing a dynamic interactive website that carries our project into the broader world.

Gathering Organizers

Our three gatherings were vital to building our relationships, and were made possible by many people, who offered space, transport, child care, and food.

June 2016—Sparrow Lake: John Murtaugh offered the family cottage and transport, local food activist Alison Young catered two of our meals, and a customer from a local market offered a special treat of Einkorn bread to the group.

November 2016—Native Canadian Centre, Toronto: For a daylong meeting, the NCC kitchen provided traditional Indigenous food, Seema Shenoy organized logistics while Megan General and Karolina Kisiel took care of our children. The following day, Jon Johnson of the Centre's First Story Toronto took us on an Indigenous food tour along the Humber River.

July 2019—Six Nations of the Grand River Territory: The final two-day gathering was cocreated by many hands. Our hosts, Chandra Maracle and Rick Hill, generously curated a two-day immersion in their community. Their daughters Olivia, Franny, and Vyolette Maracle-Hill provided child care. Legacies RA Tzazná Miranda Leal arranged all logistics, travel, accommodations, and materials. Lisa Johnson welcomed us warmly to the Bears Inn.

Spanish-English interpretation was provided by Raquel Bolaños and Julieta Maria. Chandra and Rick invited us into the Everlasting Tree School, Kerdo Deer gave us a storied tour of the Kayanese Greenhouse, Callie Hill introduced us to the Our Sustenance Greenhouse, Terri-Lynn Bryant shared the innovative Earthship, and Cristall Bomberry offered a presentation on community health issues. Gary Joseph hosted our session at Red Door Productions, where we reviewed our videos.

Good food, prepared by Nince Wahsontiio Hill and Chandra Maracle, was central to our experience. Bonnie Sky involved all of us in a cornbread workshop. Our final dinner at the Maracle-Hill home featured venison and

a dance performance by Keira Maracle Henderson, Olivia Maracle-Hill, Franny Maracle-Hill, and Malia Bomberry.

During the week that our Mexican collaborators were in Canada, they were able to visit ChocoSol Traders, Nish Dish Restaurant, Black Creek Community Farm (thanks to Leticia Deawuo and Melissa Vargas) and FoodShare (thanks to Charlyn Ellis and Bibiana Virguez).

Greeting and Gratitude to all of these who nurtured us in so many ways as we gathered to share our stories, deepen our connections, and shape our project.

Testers and Users

From the start, we have been seeking feedback from many potential users, both in educational institutions and community organizations. In 2018–2019, we began testing the videos and photo essays as well as Facilitator Guides with university classes. Andreas Moraes used select videos with her Food Systems class at Ryerson University and Sylvia Vasquez screened several videos with her York University course "Food Land and Culture." Codrina Ibanescu coordinated feedback from students in the Faculty of Environmental Studies. Over

the years, select videos were screened at academic conferences of the Canadian Food Studies Association; Agricultural, Food, and Human Values, Food Secure Canada Assembly, and Environmental Studies Association of Canada.

In 2019 and again in 2021, Lauren Baker designed her University of Toronto, New College Equity Studies course "Theory and Praxis in Food Security" around the whole package engaging students in presenting, engaging, and adding to the material. Three public events brought in collaborators Chandra Maracle and Leticia Deawuo to broaden the conversation to address biodiversity, food sovereignty, antiracism, and reconciliation. Special thanks to students Krystal Bernardo, Kyra Bingham, Joanna Blenke, Fatema Diwan, Simona Frias, Megan Grella, Yalda Mousavi, Nikki Pagaling, Isabella Ruzicka, Ariane Wichert for offering their critical perspectives on the material. In early 2021, the class participated in our interactive global webinar and produced new Facilitator Guides and social media campaigns for the website. Thanks to students Hannah Benyamin, Brooke Burlock, Sarah Folk, Kai Halligan, Alaina Hamid, Vibhuti Kacholia, Julia Rapai, Ruth Rodrigues, Mollie Sheptenko, Hana Tagaki, and Maria Takacs.

In 2018 Alexandra Gelis offered a workshop on the multimedia package for a teacher training program of Eco-Source titled "Food Systems and Gardening for the Curriculum." Deborah Barndt tested two videos and two photo essays with seventy teachers attending a Change Your World conference at York in 2019. She also facilitated a three-part film series on food justice and food sovereignty for the Parkdale Free School in Toronto.

As we began to promote the site with users in late 2020, we had the generous and skill support of a social media team—Tim Murtaugh, Wafaa El-Osta, and Seema Shenoy—who initiated our Facebook and Instagram pages. Raquel Bolaños produced a beautiful poster for our global online launch.

In late 2020 and early 2021, two students of York University's Public Anthropology practicum, Colleen Boggs and Diego Lopez, became part of the team, joined later by Maria Cappelletti in late 2021. In the spring of 2021, we added two University of Toronto students, Hannah Benyamin and Hana Tagaki, as additional research and development assistants. This team of five has helped organize webinars, added resources to the guides, edited videos of users, created campaigns on Legacies social media and helped us envision the future of the project.

Two teachers, Nathan Tidridge and Kiera Brant-Birioukov, created short videos sharing the ways they have used the multimedia packages with their classes and teachers in training. Kiera, Mohawk scholar teaching in York University's Faculty of Education, joined the Legacies team in late 2021, along with her partner Anton Birioukov. They brought new energy to the project, Anton helping us to clarify our vision for the future and Kiera involving her students in an arts-based response to the photo essay "Language and Food," through beadwork.

Greetings and Gratitude to all the teachers, students, and community activists who offered us valuable feedback and have helped to promote the website for educational purposes.

Financial Supporters

We could not have brought the collaborators together, visited them in action, filmed and photographed their activities. or transformed their stories into a book and multimedia website without financial support. Deborah Barndt secured three grants from the Social Science and Humanities Research Council, two Connections Grants (2016, 2018), and one Exchange Knowledge Mobilization Grant (2019). Her home Faculty of Environmental Studies at York University offered support in the form of small research grants, travel grants, and a Dean's contribution for the 2019 gathering. Lauren Baker secured funding from New College at the University of Toronto for production of a video on Black Creek Community Farm and for two public events on local food justice and global food sovereignty initiatives. From 2020 on, funding for the final production came from the Legacies Project Fund and personal donors.

Greetings and Gratitude to the funders who made our gatherings and productions possible.

Notes

Introduction

1. Thomas King, *The Truth About Stories: A Native Narrative* (Minneapolis: University of Minnesota Press, 2003), 29.
2. Deborah Barndt, *Naming the Moment: Political Analysis for Action* (Toronto: Jesuit Centre for Social Faith and Justice, 1991).
3. Lisa Richardson and Allison Crawford, "COVID-19 and the Decolonization of Indigenous Public Health," *Canadian Medical Association Journal* 192, no. 38 (September 2020): E1098–100, https://doi.org/10.1503/cmaj.200852.
4. High-Level Panel of Experts on Food Security and Nutrition, "Interim Issues Paper on the Impact of COVID-19 on Food Security and Nutrition (FSN)," Committee on World Food Security, last modified March 24, 2020, http://www.fao.org/fileadmin/templates/cfs/Docs1920/Chair/HLPE_English.pdf.
5. International Panel of Experts on Sustainable Food Systems (IPES-Food), "COVID-19 and the Crisis in Food Systems: Symptoms, Causes, and Potential Solutions," last modified April 2020, http://www.ipes-food.org/pages/covid19.
6. Michael Enright and Gisèle Yasmeen, "The Pandemic Has Laid Bare Structural Inequalities in Our Food Systems, Advocate Says," *CBC Radio*, May 15, 2020, https://www.cbc.ca/radio/sunday/the-sunday-edition-for-may-17-2020-1.5564926/the-pandemic-has-laid-bare-structural-inequalities-in-our-food-systems-advocate-says-1.5564966.
7. Michael Fakhri, "The U.S. Food System Creates Hunger and Debt—But There Is Another Way," *The Guardian*, April 14, 2021, https://www.theguardian.com/environment/commentisfree/2021/apr/14/the-us-food-system-creates-hunger-and-debt-but-there-is-another-way.
8. Arundhati Roy, "The Pandemic Is a Portal," *Financial Times*, April 3, 2020, https://www.ft.com/content/10d8f5e8-74eb-11ea-95fe-fcd274e920ca.
9. Daphne Ewing-Chow, "COVID-19 Has Given Consumers Five Reasons to Eat Local," *Forbes*, July 30, 2020, https://www.forbes.com/sites/daphneewingchow/2020/07/30/covid-19-has-given-consumers-five-new-reasons-to-eat-local/?sh=13cdc2703ccc.
10. Sara Jabakhanji, "Meet Some of Toronto's Food Justice Advocates Championing Black Food Sovereignty," *CBC News*, January 2, 2021, https://www.cbc.ca/news/canada/toronto/black-food-sovereignty-toronto-food-advocates-1.5857154.
11. Fernando Reimers et al., "Supporting the Continuation of Teaching and Learning during the COVID-19 Pandemic: Annotated Resources for Online Learning," Organisation for Economic Co-operation and Development, last modified 2020, https://www.oecd.org/education/Supporting-the-continuation-of-teaching-and-learning-during-the-COVID-19-pandemic.pdf.
12. King, *The Truth About Stories*, 2.
13. King, *The Truth About Stories*, 10.

Chapter 2: Navigating Dynamic Tensions on Common Waters

1. We use the term "settler" while problematizing its meaning. Commentator Amber Meadow Adams reflected: "I don't see much that's unsettled about ten or fifteen millennia of continuous occupation (by Indigenous peoples). Even as a term of détente, the concept of a Euro-Canadian *settler* still suggests its obverse: the threadbare trope of the savage nomad that is still, as recently

as last year, being offered by the governments of Canada and Ontario as sufficient reason to refuse to return land it took unlawfully from Indigenous nations, or even offer them fair compensation for this theft. Climate refugees, transported convicts, trafficking victims, economic migrants—all of these terms describe methods by which Europeans (and Africans, and others) arrived in North America, and none of them describe people in a settled state."

2. Gina Starblanket and Heidi Kiiwetinepinesiik Stark, "Towards a Relational Paradigm—Four Points for Consideration: Knowledge, Gender, Land and Modernity," in Michael Asch, John Burrows, and James Tully, eds., *Resurgence and Reconciliation: Indigenous-Settler Relations and Earth Teachings* (Toronto: University of Toronto Press, 2018), 181.

3. James Tully, "Reconciliation Here on Earth," in Michael Asch, John Burrows, and James Tully, eds., *Resurgence and Reconciliation: Indigenous-Settler Relations and Earth Teachings* (Toronto: University of Toronto Press, 2018), 85.

4. Tully, "Reconciliation Here on Earth," 108.

5. Leanne Simpson, "Pedagogy as Land," quoted in Starblanket and Kiiwetinepinesiik Stark, "Towards a Relational Paradigm," in Michael Asch, John Burrows, and James Tully, eds., *Resurgence and Reconciliation: Indigenous-Settler Relations and Earth Teachings* (Toronto: University of Toronto Press, 201, 183.

6. Lynn Margulis, quoted in Tully, "Reconciliation Here on Earth," 98.

7. Robin Wall Kimmerer, *Braiding Sweetgrass: Indigenous Wisdom, Scientific Knowledge, and the Teaching of Plants* (Minneapolis: Milkweed Editions, 2014), 42.

8. Kimmerer, *Braiding Sweetgrass*, 100.

9. Kimmerer, *Braiding Sweetgrass*, 10.

10. Tully, "Reconciliation Here on Earth," 114–15.

11. "Bless This Land," from *An American Sunrise: Poems* by Joy Harjo. Copyright 2019 by Joy Harjo. Used by permission of W. W. Norton and Company.

12. P. Freire, *Pedagogy of the Oppressed* (New York: Herder and Herder, 1972).

13. S. Díaz et al., eds., Summary for Policymakers of the Global Assessment Report on Biodiversity and Ecosystem Services of the Intergovernmental Science-Policy Platform on Biodiversity and Ecosystem Services (IPBES secretariat, Bonn, Germany, 2019), 17.

14. Just Transition Alliance, http://jtalliance.org/.

15. Climate Justice Alliance, https://climatejusticealliance.org/just-transition/.

16. National Black Food and Justice Alliance, https://www.blackfoodjustice.org/; Soul Fire Farm, http://www.soulfirefarm.org/. See also Leah Penniman, *Farming While Black: Soul Fire's Practical Guide to Liberation on the Land* (Hartford, VT: Chelsea Green, 2018).

17. National Farmers Union in Canada, https://www.nfu.ca/; National Family Farm Coalition in the United States, https://nffc.net/; Via Campesina, https://viacampesina.org/en/.

18. https://migrantworkersalliance.org/ in Canada; https://ciw-online.org/—Coalition of Immokalee Workers in the United States.

19. http://foodchainworkers.org/.

20. "Unravelling the Food–Health Nexus: Addressing Practices, Political Economy, and Power Relations to Build Healthier Food Systems," Global Alliance for the Future of Food and IPES-Food, 2017.

21. https://climatejusticealliance.org/just-transition/.

22. Statistics of disproportionate number of racialized people who have died from COVID-19.

23. Vandana Shiva, "The Emancipation of Seed, Water and Women," https://forthewild.world/listen/vandana-shiva-on-the-emancipation-of-seed-water-and-women-118, May 8, 2019.

24, The notion of nature as resource was reinforced by key Enlightenment thinkers, such as Francis Bacon, who proposed that humans could dominate and tame wild nature; and Descartes, who reinforced that idea through dualisms such as the separation of the mind and the body.

25. Nancy Turner and Pamela Spalding, "Learning from the Earth, Learning from Each Other: Ethnoecology, Responsibility and

Reciprocity," in *Resurgence and Reconciliation: Indigenous-Settler Relationships and Earth Teachings*, Michael Asch, John Burrows, and James Tully, eds. (Toronto: University of Toronto Press, 2018), 270.

26. Tully, "Reconciliation Here on Earth," 110.
27. The Oka Crisis of 1990 grew out of a conflict between the town of Oka, Quebec, approving an extension of a golf course on the territory of the Mohawk people. *Kanehsatake: 270 Years of Resistance* (Montreal: National Film Board of Canada, 1993).
28. Murray Sinclair and TRC members, Final Report, TRC (Winnipeg: Truth and Reconciliation Commission of Canada, 2015), quoted in Turner and Spalding, "Learning from the Earth," 265.
29. Tully, "Reconciliation Here on Earth," 83.
30. Timothy A. Wise, *Eating Tomorrow: Agribusiness, Family Farmers, and the Battle for the Future of Food* (New York/London: New Press, 2019), 224.

Chapter 3: Pollinating Relationships

We reflect critically on our collaborative methodology in a recent article by Alexandra Gelis and Deborah Barndt, "A Field Report on the Earth to Tables Legacies Multimedia Educational Package," Food Pedagogies Issue, *Canadian Food Studies* 8, no. 4: 120–134.

1. As the initiator and coordinator of this exchange, I have written this reflection on our methodology. So, while I have shared it with production team members and other collaborators for comments, it represents primarily my perspective on our process. At some points I use the personal pronoun "I" when it makes sense.
2. From Secwepemc Dawn Morrison, an Indigenous adviser for the project during its first year, we learned the term "so-called Canada" as a way to critically acknowledge the colonial construction of the Canadian state.
3. See the video "The Alchemy of Agroecology" (page 130) and the photo essay "Medicinal Plants" (page 96).
4. The gender-neutral short term for Latin Americans is Latinxs.

5. See "Language and Food" photo essay (page 91).
6. See "Why Farmers Markets?" video (page 154).
7. Ruth Koleszar-Green, "What Is a Guest? What Is a Settler?," *Cultural and Pedagogical Inquiry* 2, no. 10 (2018): 166–77.
8. Links to Rick's videos, "The Thanksgiving Address" video, the Mush Hole photo essay, and "Cooking and Eating Together" photo essay.
9. https://firststoryblog.wordpress.com/aboutfirststory/.
10. Though July 2019 was the last time we were all together in person, we have continued to connect in 2020–2022, with Zoom conversations stimulated by the crises and opportunities presented by the coronavirus pandemic.
11. See photo essay "Cooking and Eating Together" on page 206.
12. Both Lauren and Deborah have had long-standing relationships with Black Creek Community Farm, and when we realized that we lacked stories from urban contexts in Canada, we decided to add Leticia Deawuo as a Legacies collaborator and to feature the farm as an example of food justice in North America.
13. The letters LGBTTIQQ2S refer to lesbian, gay, bisexual, transgender, transexual, queer or questioning, two spirited.
14. I was involved in the early formation of an international network of participatory research in the 1970s, and previous transnational research projects in the 1990s and 2000s were arts-based and community-engaged, feeding intercultural education and often collective action. *VIVA! Community Arts and Popular Education in the Americas (Albany: SUNY Press, 2011).*
15. See Deborah Barndt and Laura Reinsborough, "Decolonizing Research, Education, and Art in the VIVA Project," in *Alliances: Re/Envisioning Indigenous-non-Indigenous relations* (Toronto: University of Toronto Press, 2010).
16. Linda Tuhiwai Smith, *Decolonizing Methodologies: Research and Indigenous Peoples, 2nd ed.* (Dunedin, NZ: Otago University Press, 2012); Margaret Kovach, "Emerging from the Margins: Indigenous Methodologies," in L. Brown and S. Strega, eds., *Research as Resistance: Critical, Indigenous and Anti-Oppressive Approach* (Toronto: Canadian Scholars' Press/Women's Press,

2005), 19–36; Shawn Wilson, *Research Is Ceremony: Indigenous Research Method* (Halifax: Fernwood Publishing, 2009).

17. Verna Kirkness and Ray Barnhardt, 1991.
18. Deborah McGregor, Jean-Paul Restoule, and Rochelle Johnston, eds., *Indigenous Research: Theories, Practices, and Relationships* (Toronto: Canadian Scholars, 2018).
19. In between these dates, the production and editorial team made visits to all the sites: Mexico (Guadalajara, Michoacán, Oaxaca): February 2015, December 2016, February 2018, 2019, and 2020. Quebec: November 2016, August 2018, November 2019)
    Six Nations: at least eight times between September 2015 and November 2019
    Muskoka: 15–20 times between September 2015 and January 2020
    Black Creek Community Farm: various times over the same period
20. McGregor, Restoule, and Johnston, eds., *Indigenous Research*, 15.
21. McGregor, Restoule, and Johnston, eds., *Indigenous Research*, 7.
22. Susan Finley, "Arts-Based Research," in A. Cole and G. Knowles, eds., *Handbook of the Arts in Qualitative Research* (Los Angeles: Sage, 2008).
23. Gina Starblanket and Heide Kiiwetinepinesiik Stark, "Towards a Relational Paradigm: Four Points for Consideration, Knowledge, Gender, Land and Modernity," in Michael Asch, John Borrows, and James Tully, *Resurgence and Reconciliation: Indigenous-Settler Relations and Earth Teachings* (Toronto: University of Toronto Press, 2018), 198.

Chapter 5: Stories of the Storytellers

1. "Time Consciousness of Guatemalan Indigenous Peasants" (master's thesis, Michigan State University, 1968).
2. *Education and Social Change: A Photographic Study of Peru* (Whitby: Kendall-Hunt, 1978).
3. Deborah Barndt (with Christine McKenzie), "Whose Nicaragua? Popular Communications across Eras, Regions, and Generations,"

in Deborah Barndt, *Wild Fire: Art as Activism* (Toronto: Sumach Press, 2006), 46–57.
4. *Tangled Routes: Women, Work, and Globalization the Tomato Trail*, 2nd ed. (Lanham, MD: Rowman & Littlefield, 2002).
5. Deborah Barndt (with Laura Reinsborough), "Decolonizing Art, Education and Research in the VIVA! Project," in L. Davis, *Alliances: Re/Envisioning Relationships between Aboriginal and Non-Aboriginal Peoples* (Toronto: University of Toronto Press, 2010).
6. "OKA Is All of Us," photo exhibit, Toronto, 1990.
7. "Revisiting the Boats and Canoes: Popular Education around the 500 Years," *Convergence 25, no. 1 (1992): 50–60.*
8. "The Native Right to Self-Government," *The Moment* (Winter 1987).
9. At the time of this writing, a growing alliance of Indigenous and non-Indigenous activists have blockaded major transport lines, in solidarity with the Wet'suwet'en defending their land against the CoastLink pipeline.
10. I documented my growing interest in Toronto's biological and cultural diversity in a report titled "Seeds of our City: Case Studies from 8 Diverse Gardens in Toronto."
11. See "The Mush Hole" photo essay and "The Thanksgiving Address" video.
12. Ruth Koleszar-Green, "What Is a Guest? What Is a Settler?," *Cultural and Pedagogical Inquiry 2, no. 10 (2018): 174–75.*

Chapter 6: Ways of Knowing

1. We form a part of the Mayan peoples of the Yucatán Peninsula, of the community of Sinanché and Ticul, respectively. Our way of experiencing the world is rooted in the Mayan way of thinking/ feeling, which our elders have shared with us and has been the legacy that they wish to leave for us.
2. Drink made of non-nixtamalized corn, water, and honey.
3. Alux is a type of dwarf that lives in and cares for the wilderness, that the elders set in the wilderness to take care of the fields. Every once in a while, they have to be fed the sakab, which is their food.

4. Type of communal land ownership focused on agriculture.
5. The Mayan Train is a proposed train through the Yucatán Peninsula, the largest infrastructure project of President López Obrador's National Development Plan, with multiple ecological and social impacts; https://towardfreedom.org/story/the-tren-maya-and-the-remaking-of-mexicos-south-border/.

Chapter 7: Earth

1. Hilda and Serena are family members of Legacies Project collaborators. To learn about Chandra, Anna, and Maria, see bios in the Storytellers section.

Chapter 8: Justice

1. Semillas Globales is a pseudonym.
2. For more information about the Jane-Finch community, please see Jane-Finch.com and this report on Fighting for Food Justice in the Black Creek Community (ettl.ca/8c) created by the Black Creek Food Justice Network.

3. More information about Black Creek Community Farm programs can be found on the Farm's website.
4. At the time of publication, Ontario's Conservative government was making cuts to social services.

Chapter 9: Tables

1. The Great Law of Peace, or Kaianere'kó:wa, conceived precontact by Dekanawidah or the Peacemaker and his spokesman, Hiawatha. Represented in a wampum belt, it laid out the principles upon which the Haudenosaunee or Iroquois Confederacy was founded.
2 Valiana worked with UniTierra for five years; in late 2019, she and her partner, Ángel, moved back to the Yucatán to create their own project. See details at the end of the photo essay "Mutual Nurturing."
3. To compare Gustavo's notion of verbs with Ryan DeCaire's emphasis on Mohawk as a verb-based language, see the photo essay "Language and Food: A Worldview of Verbs."
4. See Valiana's explanation of the *milpa* in the photo essay "Mutual Nurturing: Reweaving Community with Our Elders" in chapter 6.

BIBLIOGRAPHY

Below are some select books and articles, in addition to those provided in the footnotes throughout the book, that informed our thinking and writing. The Facilitator Guides for all of the videos and photo essays include these as well as additional relevant books and articles, websites and videos that speak to the specific theme. We encourage you to review the online resources and organizations links in the guides.

Food Sovereignty/Agroecology

Altieri, Miguel. "Agroecology: The Science of Natural Resource Management for Poor Farmers in Marginal Environments." *Agriculture, Ecosystems, and Environment* 93, nos. 1–3 (December 2002): 1–24.

Altieri, Miguel, Clara Nicholls, and Fernando Funes. "The Scaling Up of Agroecology: Spreading the Hope for Food Sovereignty and Resiliency." Sociedad Científica Latinoamericana de Agroecología, 2012. https://www.weltagrarbericht.de /fileadmin/files/weltagrarbericht/The_scaling_up_of _agroecology_Rio.pdf.

Baker, Lauren. *Corn Meets Maize: Food Movements and Markets in Mexico.* Lanham, MD: Rowman & Littlefield, 2013.

Barndt, Deborah. *Tangled Routes: Women, Work, and Globalization the Tomato Trail*, 2nd ed. Lanham, MD: Rowman & Littlefield, 2002.

De Schutter, Olivier. "Report of the Special Rapporteur on the Right to Food." January 24, 2014. http://www.srfood.org/images /stories/pdf/officialreports/20140310_finalreport_en.pdf.

Desmarais, Annette Aurélie, ed. *Frontline Farmers: How the National Farmers Union Resists Agribusiness and Creates Our New Food Future.* Halifax: Fernwood, 2019.

ETC Group. "VIDEO: Who Will Feed Us? The Peasant Food Web vs the Industrial Food Chain." February 18, 2019. http:// www.etcgroup.org/content/new-video-who-will-feed-us -peasant-food-web-vs-industrial-food-chain.

Farmers' Markets of Nova Scotia. "A Short Guide to Food and Farming Terms." February 24, 2016. https://farmersmarkets novascotia.ca/2016/02/25/a-short-guide-to-food-and -farming-terms/.

Food and Agriculture Organization of the United Nations. "Agroecology Knowledge Hub." http://www.fao.org /agroecology/home/en/ (accessed June 24, 2020).

The Food and Land Use Coalition. "Growing Better: Ten Critical Transitions to Transform Food and Land Use." September 2019. https://www.foodandlandusecoalition.org/global-report/.

Food Tank. "24 Groups Leading the Charge in Cultivating Urban Farming." *EcoWatch*, April 26, 2016. https://www.ecowatch .com/24-groups-leading-the-charge-in-cultivating-urban -farming-1891123567.html.

Fortier, Jean-Martin. *The Market Gardener: A Successful Grower's Handbook for Small-Scale Organic Farming.* Gabriola, BC: New Society Publishers, 2014.

Friedmann, Harriet. "Scaling Up: Bringing Public Institutions and Food Service Institutions into the Project for a Local, Sustainable Food System in Ontario." *Agriculture and Human Values* 24, no. 3 (September 2007): 389–98.

Gemmill-Herren, Barbara, Lauren E. Baker, Paula A. Daniels, eds. True Cost Accounting for Food: Balancing the Scale. London: Routledge, 2021.

Global Alliance for the Future of Food. "Beacons of Hope: Trans- forming Food Systems." https://foodsystemstransformations .org/ (accessed June 24, 2020).

Johnson, Lorraine. *City Farmer: Adventures in Urban Food Growing.* Vancouver: Greystone Books, 2010.

Koc, Mustafa, Jennifer Sumner, and Anthony Winson, eds. *Critical Perspectives in Food Studies*, 2nd ed. Don Mills, ON: Oxford University Press, 2016.

La Via Campesina. "United Nations Declaration on the Rights of Peasants and Other People Working in Rural Areas: Download." December 28, 2018. https://viacampesina.org/en/united -nations-declaration-on-the-rights-of-peasants-and-other -people-working-in-rural-areas/.

Leiner, Katherine. *Growing Roots: The New Generation of Sustainable Farmers, Cooks, and Food Activists.* Durango, CO: Sunrise Lane Productions, 2010.

maitreuweb. "Declaration of Nyéléni: Sélingué, Mali." La Via Campesina. February 27, 2007. https://nyeleni.org/spip .php?article290.

Pacor, Antonio, Bettina Gozzano, and Focuspuller. "La Via Campesina in Movement . . . Food Sovereignty now!" La Via Campesina. August 9, 2011. Video, 20:03. https://vimeo .com/27473286.

Roberts, Wayne. *The No-Nonsense Guide to World Food,* 2nd ed. Toronto and London: New Internationalist Press, 2014.

Shukla, P. R., et al., eds. "Technical Summary, 2019." In *Climate Change and Land: An IPCC Special Report on Climate Change, Desertification, Land Degradation, Sustainable Land Management, Food Security, and Greenhouse Gas Fluxes in Terrestrial Ecosystems,* edited by P. R. Shukla, et al. IPCC.

Streckenbach, Rosch, Marcus Illgenstein, and Maik Lochmann. "Let's Talk About Soil—English." Institute for Advanced Sustainability Studies. November 15, 2012. Video, 5:24. https://vimeo.com/53618201.

Wilson, Charles, and Will Allen. *The Good Food Revolution: Growing Healthy Food, People and Communities.* New York: Gotham Books, 2013.

Wise, Timothy A. *Eating Tomorrow: Agribusiness, Family Farmers, and the Battle for the Future of Food.* New York/London: New Press, 2019.

Wittman, Hannah, Annette Desmarais, and Nettie Weibe, eds. *Food Sovereignty in Canada: Creating Just and Sustainable Food Systems.* Black Point, NS: Fernwood, 2011.

Food Justice and Antiracism in the Food Movement

Agyeman, Julian, and Alison Hope Alkon, eds. *Cultivating Food Justice: Race, Class, and Sustainability.* Cambridge, MA: MIT Press, 2011.

Black Creek Food Justice Network. "Fighting for Food Justice in the Black Creek Community: Report, Analyses and Steps Forward." 2016. http://tfpc.to/wordpress/wp-content/uploads/2016/07 /FullReport_small.pdf.

Cadiot, Jonathan, and Arthur Rifflet, dirs. "Sin Maíz No Hay País: Las Semillas de la Dignidad." Culture Unplugged. 2008. Video, 39:16. https://www.cultureunplugged.com/documentary/ watch-online/festival/play/5911/Sin-Ma--z-No-Hay-Pa--s--Las -Semillas-de-la-Dignidad (accessed April 11, 2020).

Field, Tory, and Beverly Bell. *Harvesting Justice: Transforming Food, Land, and Agricultural Systems in the Americas.* New Orleans, LA: Other Worlds, 2013.

Julier, Alice P. *Eating Together: Food, Friendship and Inequality.* Urbana: University of Illinois Press, 2013.

Lessa, Iara, and Cecilia Rocha. "Nourishing Belonging: Food in the Lives of New Immigrants in T.O.," in *The Edible City: Toronto's Food from Farm to Fork*, edited by Christina Palassio and Alana Wilcox, 148–53. Toronto: Coach House Books, 2009.

Penniman, Leah. *Farming While Black: Soul Fire's Practical Guide to Liberation on the Land.* White River Junction, VT: Chelsea Green Publishing, 2018.

Ramsaroop, Chris, and Katie Wolk. "Can We Achieve Racial Equality in the Food Security Movement," in Christina Palassio and Alana Wilcox, eds., *The Edible City: Toronto's Food from Farm to Fork*, 252–63. Toronto: Coach House Books, 2009.

Indigenous History, Cosmologies, Struggles, and Food Perspectives

Akwesasne Notes, ed. *Basic Call to Consciousness.* Summertown, TN: Native Voices, 2005.

Asch, Michael, John Borrows, and James Tully, eds. *Resurgence and Reconciliation: Indigenous-Settler Relations and Earth Teachings.* Toronto: University of Toronto Press, 2018.

Carlson-Manathara, Elizabeth, with Gladys Rowe. Living in Indigenous Sovereignty. Halifax/Winnipeg: Fernwood Publishing, 2021.

Cornelius, Carol. *Iroquois Corn in a Culture-Based Curriculum: A Framework for Respectfully Teaching about Cultures.* Albany: State University of New York Press, 1999.

Davis, Lynne, ed. *Alliances: Re/Envisioning Indigenous-non-Indigenous Relationships.* Toronto: University of Toronto Press, 2010.

George-Kanentiio, Doug. *Iroquois Culture & Commentary.* Santa Fe, NM: Clear Light Publishers, 2000.

Global Forest Coalition. "The Rights of Indigenous Peoples Are Key to Saving Our Global Ecosystems." *IC*, September 4, 2018. https://intercontinentalcry.org/the-rights-of-indigenous -peoples-are-key-to-saving-our-global-ecosystems/.

Hill, Susan M. *The Clay We Are Made Of: Haudenosaunee Land Tenure on the Grand River.* Winnipeg: University of Manitoba Press, 2017.

Koleszar-Green, Ruth. "What Is a Guest? What Is a Settler?" *Cultural and Pedagogical Inquiry* 2, no. 10 (2018): 166–77.

Leduc, Timothy B. *A Canadian Climate of Mind: Passages from Fur to Energy and Beyond.* Montreal and Kingston: McGill-Queen's University Press, 2016.

McGregor, Deborah, Jean-Paul Restoule, and Rochelle Johnston, eds. *Indigenous Research: Theories, Practices, and Relationships.* Toronto: Canadian Scholars, 2018.

Mihesuah, Devon A., and Elizabeth Hoover. *Indigenous Food Sovereignty in the United States: Restoring Cultural Knowledge, Protecting Environments, and Regaining Health.* Norman: University of Oklahoma Press, 2019.

Mintz, Corey. "The History of Food in Canada Is the History of Colonialism." *The Walrus,* last modified March 27, 2020. https:// thewalrus.ca/the-history-of-food-in-canada-is-the-history-of -colonialism/?fbclid=IwAR2ycY65v0Z6F5xZPtOJV82SWU08 odgwMSq7xJIZ1R6wTvr5YSXEs-Tu6gI.

Monture, Rick. *We Share Our Matters: Two Centuries of Writing and Resistance at Six Nations of the Grand River.* Winnipeg: University of Manitoba Press, 2014.

Morrison, D. "Indigenous Food Sovereignty: A Model for Social Learning," in *Food Sovereignty in Canada: Creating Just and Sustainable Food Systems*, edited by Hannah Wittman, Annette Aurélie Desmarais, and Nettie Wiebe, 97–113. Black Point, NS: Fernwood, 2011.

Nadeau, Denise M. *Unsettling Spirit: A Journey into Decolonization.* Montreal and Kingston: McGill-Queens University Press, 2020.

Native Languages of the Americas website. "Native Languages of the Americas: Amerindian Language Families." Last modified 2014. http://www.native-languages.org/linguistics.htm.

Settee, Priscilla, and Shailesh Shukla. Indigenous Food Systems: Concepts, Cases, and Conversations. Toronto/Vancouver: Canadian Scholars, 2020.

Smith, Linda Tuhiwai. *Decolonizing Methodologies: Research and Indigenous Peoples.* London: Zed Books, 1999.

Truth and Reconciliation Commission of Canada. *A Knock on the Door: The Essential History of Residential Schools.* Winnipeg: University of Manitoba Press in Collaboration with the National Centre for Truth and Reconciliation, 2016.

——— . "Truth and Reconciliation Commission of Canada: Calls to Action." 2015. http://trc.ca/assets/pdf/Calls_to_Action _English2.pdf.

Animal-Human Relations

Arnaquq-Baril, Alethea, dir. "Angry Inuk: The Anti-Sealing Industry Has Had Dire Impacts on Canada's Inuit families—CBC Docs POV." CBC Docs. January 12, 2018. Video, 44:18. https://www .youtube.com/watch?v=85Ns94DWAQ8.

Bost, Jay. "The Ethicist Contest Winner: Give Thanks for Meat." *New York Times Magazine,* May 3, 2012. https://www.nytimes. com/2012/05/06/magazine/the-ethicist-contest-winner-give -thanks-for-meat.html.

Foer, Jonathon Safran. *We Are the Weather: Saving the Planet Begins at Breakfast.* New York: Farrar, Straus & Giroux, 2019.

Food and Agriculture Organization of the United Nations. "Livestock and Agroecology." 2018. http://www.fao.org/3 /I8926EN/i8926en.pdf.

Hawkin, Paul. "Eating Plant-Based Diets Can Play a Huge Role in Limiting the Effects of Climate Change." Bioneers. https:// bioneers.org/eating-plant-based-diets-can-play-huge-role -limiting-effects-climate-change-ze0z1709/ (accessed June 24, 2020).

Henderson, Fergus. *The Whole Beast: Nose to Tail Cooking.* New York: HarperCollins, 2004.

King, Samantha, R. Scott Carey, Isabel Macquarrie, Victoria N. Millious, and Elaine M. Power. *Messy Eating: Conversations on Animals as Food.* New York: Fordham University Press, 2019.

Morell, Virginia. *Animal Wise: The Thoughts and Emotions of Our Fellow Creatures.* New York: Crown, 2013.

Pollan, Michael. *The Omnivore's Dilemma: A Natural History of Four Meals.* New York: Penguin, 2006.

Russell, Joshua. "'Everything Has to Die One Day:' Children's Explorations of the Meanings of Death in Human-Animal-Nature Relationships." *Environmental Education Research* 23, no. 1 (February 2016): 75–90.

Index

and farmers markets, 154–57; and languages, 44; and migration stories, 79–80; and project, 43; so-called, term, 227n2

Canadian Association of Food Studies, 55

Canadian Organic Growers, 53

capitalism, 37–40, 105, 177

Carcari, María Blas, 62*f*, 63, 97*f*; and borders, 43; and Earth, 130; and farmers markets, 157; food icon of, 76; and food sovereignty, 32; and migration, 78; and mother's milk, 122–24, 122*f*; and ways of knowing, 96–105

Cartesian dualism, 28, 226n24

cattle, 133–34

ceremonies. *See* rituals

cheese, 136

chia, 99

chickens, 135

chinampas, 129

ChocoSol, 53

climate issues: and farm labour crisis, 173–74; justice strike, Toronto, 28*f*, 31*f*, 35*f*, 37*f*; Leduc on, 203; Rick on, 202; ways of knowing and, 29

closed loop agriculture, 133

coconut, 71

collaborators, 6, 11*f*, 44*f*, 54*f*, 62*f*, 187*f*; and communal meals, 206–16, 206*f*, 216*f*; food icons of, 73–76

collective indigestion, term, 181–82

colonization, 37–40, 117, 177; and community meals, 207–10; and food legacies, 178–90; Maharaj on, 218; and Mayan, 106; and migration stories, 80; Williams on, 95. *See also* industrial food system

colostrum, 126

comida: Gustavo on, 192–98; Serrato on, 199; term, 40, 193; Valiana on, 212

commodification: of animals, 142; of Earth, 202; of food, x

commons, enclosure of, 38

communication, generations and, 43

community: and Black Creek Farm, 163*f*, 164–65, 168; Gustavo on, 192–98; urban agriculture and, 146–48

community-engaged research, 49

community meals, 206–16, 207*f*, 209*f*–11*f*, 213*f*, 215*f*; Chandra on, 186–88; Maharaj on, 217–18

community-supported agriculture (CSA), 165–66

consumer, and food system change, 211

contraception, 104–5, 126

COP 15, 38

corn, 43, 46, 74–75, 90*f*, 92*f*–93*f*, 100*f*, 189*f*, 195*f*; Brant-Birioukov on, 204–5; Fulvio on, 99; gratitude to, 21; Gustavo on, 194; Mayan and, 106–7; Ryan on, 93–94; storage of, 46, 88–91, 207; Valiana on, 111–12

cornbread, 46*f*, 118, 183, 188*f*, 216*f*

Corn Mother, 112*f*, 116

corn tortillas, 124

corporations: Fernando on, 144–50; Gustavo on, 194–95; and Indigenous people, 39; Letitia on, 164; Trumbull on, 153. *See also* industrial food system

Corredor, 72–73

Cosecha en Casa, 64, 144, 145*f*, 146–47

COVID-19, 1, 4, 37, 40, 175–76, 218

Creator, gratitude to, 22

culture, language and, 94

David, Marc, 181

Day of the Dead, 99, 112, 212, 214

Deawuo, Leticia, 62*f*, 63–64; and equity, 35–36; and farmers markets, 154; food icon of, 75; and food justice, 160–70; and food sovereignty, 33; and generations, 42; and migration, 79; and organizations, 53

DeCaire, Ryan, 62*f*, 63, 77*f*, 84*f*, 90*f*–91*f*; food icon of, 76; and food sovereignty, 33; and generations, 43; and migration, 78; and *Ohen:ton Karihwatehkwen*, 15, 17–20; and ways of knowing, 88–91

Delgamuukw decision, 39

dialogue, 2, 4, 29, 42, 45; facilitating, 57–59

diet-related diseases: colonial food legacies and, 180; in Mexico, 193

doctrine of discovery, 38, 203–4

eagles, 21

Earth, 117–42; Adam and Anna on, 133–40; cooking in, 212–14, 214*f*; Dianne on, 127–28; Fulvio on, 130–31; gratitude to, 20; Kimmerer on, x; Leduc on, 203–4; María on, 98; Rick on, 87, 128, 202; term, 4; UniTierra and, 193

Earth to Tables, term, xi

Earth to Tables Legacies project, 4–6; context of, 27–40; evolution of, 6; global launches of, 4, 5*f*

eating: fear of, 193–94; mindful, 208–9; psychology of, 181, 186, 208. *See also* community meals

Echerendi, 98

Ecological Farmers of Ontario, 53

education, 2–4; Brant-Birioukov on, 205; Chandra on, 184; Gustavo on, 192; Indigenous, 49; Valiana on, 108. *See also* learning

eggs, 135

elders: Black Creek Community Farm and, 166; food justice and, 163–64; Gelis and, 73; Mayan and, 106–15; Rick and, 64; Valiana and, 212

Ellis, Charlyn, 167*f*

enclosure of commons, 38

environment: Ryan on, 88; Van Esterik on, 125. *See also* climate issues

environmental justice movement, 37

equity, tensions on, 35–37

Esteva, Gustavo, 43, 109–10, 110*f*; on food sovereignty, 192–98

Eurocentric ways of knowing, 28–31

Everlasting Tree School, 46, 65, 178–89, 187*f*

farmers. *See* labourers

farmers markets, 154–56, 154*f*–55*f*; Lololi and Teclu on, 158–59; Mexican Legacies Partners on, 157

Farm to Table, term, xi

fast food, Gustavo on, 193–94

Felipe, 122*f*

Fenton, William, 104

fish, 20, 71

Five White Gifts, 181–82, 182*f*, 184

flour, 182, 182*f*

Floyd, George, 37, 40

food icons, 73–76

food justice, 35, 143–76; Fernando on, 144–52; future of, 166–67; Kimmerer on, xii; Leticia and Lauren on, 160–71; opportunity for, 1–2; term, 162–63; Trumbull on, 153

Food Secure Canada, 35, 53

FoodShare Toronto, 71

food sovereignty, 31–35, 143; Friedmann on, 132; Gustavo on, 192–98; Kimmerer on, xi; mother's milk and, 119–20; Serrato on, 199; term, 32

food systems. *See* Indigenous food system; industrial food system

forests, 21

Forum on Food Sovereignty, 34–35

Friedmann, Harriet, 132

fry bread, 117, 182–83

funding issues, 49; Washington on, 172

future of food: Aboites on, 175–76; Barndt on, 69; climate change and, 173; food justice and, 166–67

Gaia hypothesis, 29

Galeano, Eduardo, 193

Garcia, Fernando, 62*f*, 64, 144*f*–45*f*, 148*f*; and agriculture in Mexico, 144–52; and borders, 43; and community meals, 211–12; and Earth, 127–28, 127*f*; food icon of, 75; and food sovereignty, 32; and migration, 79

Garcia Villaseñor, Diego, 121*f*–22*f*, 147–48, 149*f*

gardens: chinampas, 129; community, 166; Fernando on, 148–49; Gustavo on, 193; malocca, 147*f*; UniTierra and, 192, 192*f*

Gaspé Farmers Market, 155*f*

Gelis, Alexandra, 43, 46*f*, 53*f*, 66, 69, 71–73; food icon of, 74; and food sovereignty, 33; and migration, 79–80

generations: Gelis on, 73; pollinating, 42–43

gift giving, 50

Gioanetto, Fulvio, 62*f*, 64, 97*f*–98*f*, 131*f*, 152*f*; and borders, 43; and Earth, 130–31; and farmers markets, 157; and farm labour crisis, 174; and Fernando,

Trumbull, Samantha, 153

Truth and Reconciliation Commission, 2, 39, 69, 177, 181

Tully, James, 28–29

turkeys, 136, 209, 210*f*

Turtle Island, 43, 47*f*

Two-Row Wampum, 27, 27*f*, 45

Tyendinaga, 78

Tyonnkehhwen, term, 29, 92–93

uncertainty, moment and, 1

United States, construction of, Haudenosaunee and, 85–87

UniTierra, 43, 53, 196*f*; Gustavo on, 192–98; Valiana on, 108–10

urban agriculture: and community meals, 211–12; Fernando on, 146–48; Leticia and Lauren on, 160–71; Nicole on, 109–10; Trumbull on, 153; Washington on, 172

Urban Harvest, 70–71

urbanization, in Mexico, 157

Van Brabant, Sylvie, 69

Van Esterik, Penny, 125

verbs: Gustavo on, 192; Ryan on, 91–94

Via Campesina, 34, 53, 64, 178, 195

Villaseñor, Hilda, 118–24, 121*f*–22*f*, 149*f*

vision, 41

Wahta, 78

Waldorf schools, 186–88

wampum pbelt, 87*f*

Washington, George, 86

Washington, Karen, 172

water, gratitude to, 20

ways of knowing, 51, 83–115; Chandra on, 29–31; Dianne on, 31; Friedmann on, 132; tensions on, 28–31

weaving: Mojica on, 116; Valiana on, 106

weeds: Adam on, 134; Friedmann on, 132; Fulvio on, 130

Wemigwans, Jennifer, 52

wheat, 182

Williams, Lorna Wanosts'a, 95

winds, gratitude to, 21

Wise, Timothy, 39

women, 1; Adams on, 104–5; and food justice, 36; and food sovereignty, 33; Gustavo on, 195–98, 197*f*; Leticia and, 64; María on, 99, 101*f*; and mother's milk, 118–24; Serrato on, 199; Valiana on, 108–9

Xate, 102, 102*f*

Xavier, Adrianne Lickers, 166*f*

York University, Toronto, 7, 43, 147*f*, 193

Young Agrarians, 53

youth: Aboites on, 175–76; Black Creek Community Farm and, 168; in collaboration, 42–43; and farm labour crisis, 173–74; Fulvio and María on, 103; Gelis on, 73; Haudenosaunee and, 104–5; Valiana on, 106, 108, 113; and videos, 52

Zak'isha, 168

Zapatistas, 67–68, 110, 192, 198